INSCRUTABLE HOUSES

INSCRUTABLE HOUSES

Metaphors of the Body in the Poems of Elizabeth Bishop

Anne Colwell

The University of Alabama Press

Tuscaloosa and London

∞

Excerpts from "The Fish" by Marianne Moore reprinted with the
permission of Simon & Schuster and with the permission of Faber &
Faber Ltd. from THE COLLECTED POEMS OF MARIANNE
MOORE. Copyright © 1935 by Marianne Moore, Renewed 1963 by
Marianne Moore and T. S. Eliot.

The paper on which this book is printed meets the minimum
requirements of American National Standard for Information
Science-Permanence of Paper for Printed Library Materials,
ANSI Z39.48-1984.

Library of Congress Cataloging-in-Publication Data

Colwell, Anne, 1964—
    Inscrutable houses : metaphors of the body in the poems of
Elizabeth Bishop / Anne Colwell.
        p.   cm.
    Includes bibliographical references and index.
    ISBN 0-8173-0808-3 (hard: alk. paper)
    ISBN 0-8173-0890-3 (pbk.: alk. paper)
      1. Bishop, Elizabeth, 1911–1979—Criticism and interpretation.
    2. Women and literature—United States—History—20th century.
    3. Body, Human, in literature.   4. Metaphor.   I. Title.
    PS3503.I785Z6   1997
    811'.54—dc21   96-39167

British Library Cataloguing-in-Publication Data available

CONTENTS

Acknowledgments   *vii*

Introduction   *1*

1. *North & South:* Finding a Language for
   How We Know   *18*

2. *A Cold Spring:* The Moving Self in the Moving World   *71*

3. *Questions of Travel:* The Poetics of Evasion   *123*

4. *Geography III:* The Art of Losing   *170*

Afterword   *231*

Notes   *233*

Works Cited   *237*

Index   *243*

ACKNOWLEDGMENTS

I MUST FIRST thank the people who have read and reread this manuscript and who have given me their invaluable advice, criticism, and insight: Gibbons Ruark, Jeanne Murray Walker, Steve Helmling, Ron Martin, and Elaine Terranova. W. D. and Kathy Snodgrass, Fleda Jackson, and especially Gibbons Ruark, my friends and teachers, have shown me the joy of the word and taught me how to listen. The Women's Studies Program of the University of Delaware provided me the travel grant without which I never could have had access to Bishop's manuscript collection. The librarians both at Vassar Library and in the University of Delaware Special Collections were a great help. I owe particular thanks to Nancy MacKechnie, at Vassar, and Rachel Johnson Melvin, at the University of Delaware. The University of Delaware awarded me a Competitive Fellowship, which gave me the time and resources to complete this book. I would especially like to thank James Keegan and my family: my parents, Thomas and Maryanne Colwell, my brothers, Thomas and James Colwell, and particularly my sister, Jeanne Colwell.

I also thank those who gave permission to quote from their works:

Excerpts from "The Fish" by Marianne Moore reprinted with the permission of Simon & Schuster and with the permission of Faber & Faber Ltd. from THE COLLECTED POEMS OF MARIANNE MOORE. Copyright © 1935 by Marianne Moore, Renewed 1963 by Marianne Moore and T. S. Eliot.

Elizabeth Bishop Collection, Special Collections of the Vassar College Libraries, Poughkeepsie, New York.

John Malcolm Brinnin Papers, MS 103, Series F, Special Collections of the University of Delaware Library, Newark, Delaware.

Gibbons Ruark, Lecture Notes, Spring 1991.

INSCRUTABLE HOUSES

INTRODUCTION

IN INTERVIEWS AND letters, Elizabeth Bishop espoused a rather strict "sit down and force yourself to work" theory of the creative process, a theory she almost universally contradicted in the way she produced her own poems. For example, in an interview with Ashley Brown she said, "Ideally, I suppose any writer prefers a hotel room completely shut away from distractions" (1966, 12); however, Bishop always lived in and traveled to distractingly beautiful places. Everywhere she worked—her apartment in Rio de Janeiro overlooking the beach, her study above the waterfall in Petrópolis, her mountain house in Ouro Prêto, her Lewis Wharf condo above Boston Harbor—had a magnificent view. Her letters speak repeatedly of the good of sitting quietly in one's room, staying still. She often expressed a desire to "stay in one place and work for a change" (Brinnin Papers). This letter is followed a few months later by a postcard from Greece.

Of course, Bishop worked extremely hard at writing poetry, but her hard work, as her manuscripts show, often consisted of drafting a poem nineteen or twenty times and then leaving it with perhaps one blank space for months, even years, until she found the right word or phrase. Perhaps her compositional process comes about because of what James Merrill calls Bishop's "instinctive, modest, lifelong impersonations of an ordinary woman," her love of travel, music, company, and dinners to cook, nightclubs, her willingness to "jot a phrase or two inside a nightclub matchbook before returning to the dance floor" (1983, 259). Her compositional process also demonstrates a deep faith in her ability to grow and change, a faith Robert Lowell describes in his late sonnet dedicated to Bishop wherein he compares her compositional process to an inchworm

1

clinging to the end of a leaf, hoping "to reach something" (1976, 44). Bishop's search, to "reach something," was both intellectual, a search that one could conduct sitting at a desk, and also real, physical, a search of the senses and the sensuous life.

A 1948 letter to Lowell in which Bishop explained why she was turning down a poetry reading to travel captures much of the ambivalence that surrounds Bishop's relationship to the sensuous, "bodily" life as opposed to the solitary life of the imagination, and the paradoxical desire both to connect with the contingent world and to remain within the isolated self:

> Seldon Rodman has written and wants me to come to Haiti—I would board with Margaret Sanger! He has a jeep and knows all the little villages where the painters and poets live and I know it would be beautiful, but—you can imagine why I hesitate. I suppose it is too good an opportunity to pass up and . . . I seem to be talking to you like Dorothy Dix but that is because you apparently are able to do the right thing for yourself and your work and don't seem tempted by the distractions of travelling—that rarely offers much at all in respect to work. I guess I have liked to travel as much as I have because I have always felt isolated and have known so few of my "contemporaries" and nothing of "intellectual" life in New York or anywhere. Actually it may be all to the good. (Giroux 1994, 154)

The world of sensuous experience and the heightened sensitivity Bishop acquired by traveling and living in different countries produced a great deal "in respect to work." However, her ambivalences about travel and work, body and imagination, are not an indication of her failure to know herself or to believe in her creative processes, but rather an indication of the paradox and ambiguity that come out of her life and inform all of her work. Bishop continually fought with the imagined split between the internal and the external worlds, a paradox mirrored in the split between the world of human commerce and the world of the imagination, between the self and the other, and, perhaps most importantly, between the visible body and the invisible life force within it. Thus, the paradox of embodiment, both in bodily and poetic form, arises directly from the paradoxes that animate Bishop's creative process. Robert Dale

Parker provides a thorough discussion of Bishop's relationship to the imagination and the imagined world, seeing Bishop as a poet who must rely on "ever-renewing sight instead of trusted faith" (1988, 32). Also, C. K. Doreski cites the "complex interplay between knowledge and language" and a differentiation between "gaze of plain sight and the interiority of vision" (1993, 5) as forces in tension at the heart of Bishop's poems.

The paradoxical relationship of the human body to the self that inhabits it and to the world around it emerges again and again as a theme in Bishop's poems. Her poems often re-create that relationship in the conflict between poetic form and theme or content. Metaphors of the body, and the tension of opposition with which Bishop surrounds them, create much of the energy and the rich and frightening ambiguity of her work. Many of the poems explore what it means to inhabit a body: "Why," she says in "In the Waiting Room," "should I be my aunt, / or me, or anyone":

> What similarities—
> boots, hands, the family voice
> I felt in my throat, or even
> the *National Geographic*
> and those awful hanging breasts—
> held us all together
> or made us all just one? (*Poems*, 161)[1]

Bishop's poems explore the paradox of this bodily existence that both isolates us and joins us; they depict the body as both the imperfect vehicle, the reason for distortion, the limit of the otherwise boundless imagination, and yet the only means of connecting with other people and the external world.

Bishop's expressions of ambivalence about the body could be productively approached by many theoretical and philosophical roads. Certainly, feminist critics exploring the dynamics of language and power have attempted to articulate the significance of the woman's body as a cultural space. Teresa de Lauretis notes that "if Nietzsche and Derrida can occupy and speak from the position of woman, it is because that position is vacant, and what is more, cannot be claimed by women" (1989, 240). This sensation of separateness rending the woman from her body, the enforced schizophrenia that de Lauretis sees in diverse signifying systems—from contemporary scientists' discussions of knowing to Lévi-Strauss's recordings of Cuna childbirth rituals—may play a part in Bishop's ability to shift between subjective and objective perspectives as she explores the meaning of bodiliness.

Bishop's struggles with and within the tensions of this separateness call attention to metaphors of the body and point up the ambiguous possibility that cultural suppression, the violent splitting of woman from her physical self, her most basic identity, can become artistic power. As Amy Kaminsky explains, "Insofar as the culture's dominant discourse is taken on as one's own, it gives shape—meaning—to women's bodies both as external and self-generating constraint. This is the skin that the writer sheds" (1993, 101). And it is the constant work of shedding and growth that animates both the body and the work. Bishop's personal struggles with bodiliness, both in terms of her struggle with a social order that repressed her sexual choices and in terms of her struggles with asthma, alcoholism, and recurrent illness, may have made her even more sensitive to the weight of meaning the physical body must bear in a culture in which no agreed-upon metaphysical realm exists. In her own words, what we have in this world is bodiliness, simply "all the untidy activity . . . awful but cheerful" (*Poems*, 61).

Approaching the significance of the body through a study of the erotic, Peter Brooks suggests that this doubleness is neither new to our time nor gender specific: "In imaginative literature the body has always been an object of fascination, at once the distinct other of the signifying project . . . and in some sense its vehicle" (1993, 1). Literature has always derived power from the tension of our paradoxical feelings about our bodies. They are self and not-self; they straddle the line between the natural world with which we are in constant contact and an invisible world we seem to intuit within or beyond us. The body, then, is the source of all metaphor, as all language is metaphor, the substitution of the word for the thing itself. Roland Barthes (1974) argues that the symbolic field and the body must converge at some point, and Bishop's use of metaphors of the body often deliberately complicates this convergence, both welcoming, even rushing it, and simultaneously refusing it, calling attention to the constructedness of the device and the qualified nature of the likening.

Although we could point out similar themes in any number of modern poets, particularly women poets, Bishop's work is unique in her refusal to attempt to answer this paradox of embodiment, or even to narrow the field of questioning. The poems in each of her four books range on a continuum from complete pessimism about the body, concentrating on how it stifles the imagination, distorts comprehension, dies, and causes all loss, to complete optimism, concentrating on how the body transforms and reveals reality, how it facilitates connection, love, and knowledge. However, most of her poems balance somewhere in the middle of that continuum, hold in tense opposition at least two sides of her profound ambivalence about embodiment. These poems—"The Fish," "The Shampoo," "Questions of Travel," and "One Art," for example—refuse to resolve into a decision, or even into one question, but instead gain power by force of opposition, acquire ambiguity and resonance through their ever-multiplying questions.

Ambivalence about human embodiment in the flesh translates, in Bishop's work, into ambivalence about creating the figure of the poem, that is, embodying invisible thought in visible form, with its concurrent possibilities for connection and understanding, and also for misperception and loss. One of the most striking features of Bishop's ambivalence about the body is the way it translates into tone. Randall Jarrell comments on the vivid physicality, the apparent certainty of Bishop's description: "All of her poems have written underneath, *I have seen it*" (1983, 181). In fact, in many instances she cultivates not just the techniques of physically accurate description but an almost schoolmarmish tone of authoritative certainty: "Finish your breakfast. The tender is coming," or "Now can you see the Monument?" or "We must admire her perfect aim." As these examples illustrate, this tone of certainty usually involves the action of the senses, exhorts the reader to pay attention, to notice or experience something. However, that teacherish tone of authoritative certainty never appears in her poems without being undercut by a deeper ambivalence, a threatening or mystifying uncertainty, which does not cancel the certain tone but complicates and opposes it. As Gibbons Ruark notes, if all of her poems have written underneath, "I have seen it," underneath that is written, "and I can't be sure what it was" (1991).

This deep uncertainty comes through in Bishop's self-conscious evasiveness of statement, a tone that seems unique to her voice. When she appears to be on the verge of an answer, or even of isolating a single question, she artfully complicates the picture with an unexpected word, a change of perspective, or, especially in her last two books, a parenthetical rephrasing and rethinking of what had almost settled the problem. This is apparent in the final, italicized stanzas of "The Armadillo" and "Questions of Travel," the change in perspective in "Large Bad Picture," "The Monument," and "Poem," and the parenthetical rephrasings in "One Art" and "Brazil, January 1, 1502," all of which I discuss in detail in later chapters. In all these poems, evasiveness and ambivalence are not mere poetic "tricks"; they come from Bishop's emotion and experience, from her grappling with the paradoxes she finds at the center of her own life, a life marked very early by traumatic loss and strange, fleeting happiness.

Out of the Village: A Biographical Sketch

In a letter to Anne Stevenson, the author of the first book-length critical study of Bishop's work, Bishop wrote, "Although I think I have a prize 'unhappy childhood,' almost good enough for the textbooks—please don't think I dote on it" (Kalstone 1989, 25). In both poetry and prose, Bishop's reminiscences of her childhood avoid doting on the unhappy outline, bleak as it sometimes was, and instead fill in that framework with rich detail—colors, the sound of the blacksmith's hammer, the primer class chalkboard, the *National Geographic*—connections that make the losses seem, as we will see, both more painful and more bearable. However, the unhappy outlines of Bishop's childhood are indeed "good enough for the textbooks," and knowing them helps illuminate many of Bishop's lifelong struggles and passionate obsessions.

Elizabeth Bishop's parents, William Thomas Bishop and Gertrude Bulmer Bishop, came from rather disparate circumstances. The Bulmer (or Boomer—both spellings were still in use in the early 1900s) family, simple Nova Scotia farm people, lived without electricity or indoor plumbing. The Bishop family, on the other hand, owned a prosperous construction company in Boston. However, both families had roots in Nova Scotia—John Wilson Bishop, Elizabeth's paternal grandfather, originally came from Prince Edward Island. Her parents' marriage seems to have been a happy one. William worked as a principal executive in his father's construction firm, the J. W. Bishop Company, contractors famous for erecting grand and stately buildings at West Point, Harvard, and Princeton (*Prose*, x). William and Gertrude Bishop were living in Boston when, a little more than two years after their marriage, Gertrude became pregnant with Elizabeth. Elizabeth Bishop was born on February 8, 1911.

Just eight months after Elizabeth's birth, William Bishop died of Bright's disease. He was only thirty-nine. In the years that followed, Gertrude Bishop suffered a series of mental breakdowns. Her family blamed these on the shock of her husband's untimely death, but as an adult Elizabeth came to believe that her mother had experienced mental distress previous to William's death, distress that this new grief and the prospect of raising a child alone exacerbated.[2] For a while Gertrude Bishop attempted to care for the young Elizabeth on her own. Then, when Elizabeth was a toddler, they both returned to the Bulmers' farm in Great Village, Nova Scotia, where Elizabeth could be cared for while Gertrude worked toward recovery.

Bishop's prose masterpiece, "In the Village," chronicles the failure of this attempt at recovery and the devastating effects her mother's breakdown had on the young Elizabeth. Until Bishop was five, her maternal grandmother and aunts cared for her while her mother was hospitalized, at first in McLean's Sanatorium outside Boston. Then, after the decisive breakdown on the farm in Great Village, Gertrude Bishop entered a mental hospital outside Dartmouth, Nova Scotia, where she spent the remaining eighteen years of her life. Gertrude Bishop died in 1934, the same year Elizabeth graduated from Vassar and met Marianne Moore. Bishop's 1964 letter to Anne Stevenson reveals the mixed resignation and regret Bishop felt when she recalled the loss of her mother:

> She did receive the very best treatment available at that time, I feel sure. . . . The Bishop family spared no expense. . . . That generation took insanity very differently than we do now, you know. . . . The tragic thing was that she returned to N.S. [Nova Scotia] when she did, before the final breakdown. At that time women became U.S. citizens when they married U.S. citizens—so when she became a widow, she lost her citizenship. Afterwards, the U.S. would not let her back in, sick, and that is why she had to be put in the hospital at Dartmouth, Nova Scotia (across the harbor from Halifax). My Bishop grandfather tried for a long time to get her back to the U.S. One always thinks that things might be better now, she might have been cured, etc. . . . Well—there we are. Times have changed. I have several friends who are, have been, will be, etc. insane; they discuss it all very freely and I've visited asylums many times since. But in 1916 things were different. After a couple of years, unless you cured yourself, all hope was abandoned. (Kalstone 1989, 25)

The Bulmer family loved and cared for Elizabeth, and she loved them. Even as a young child, the external details of life in Great Village fascinated Bishop and earned her constant, careful attention. Bishop's letters to her Aunt Grace (Vassar Boxes 18 and 19), exchanging recipes and family chat, attest to the lifelong affection that had its foundation in these early years. The memoir "Primer Class" and her prose piece "In the Village" capture the confusion of joy and sadness in Bishop's years on the Bulmer farm. She adored farm life and the village and people around her, but she simultaneously lived in fear that all she loved would vanish. In "Primer Class," Bishop recalls that, until she was teased out of it, she used to make sure before she went off to school in the morning to "ask Grandmother . . . to promise me not to die before I came home" (*Prose*, 6).

Bishop's poems and prose concerning her childhood experiences show a felt necessity to piece together reality from whatever clues were available. The young Elizabeth surely needed to interpret correctly the physical signs of truth in what must have been an atmosphere of protective secrecy erected by those who loved her. Both published and unpublished accounts of her childhood are marked by a profusion of half-heard, whispered conversations, unexplained tears, and strange, sudden disappearances of beloved people. The death of Bishop's cousin Frank, recounted in the poem "First Death in Nova Scotia," and the death of her playmate and next-door neighbor Gwendolyn Patroquin, described in the short story "Gwendolyn," added to the losses Bishop experienced in very early childhood.

Undoubtedly, though, the most traumatic loss came when she was six and her Bishop grandparents arrived to "rescue" their only son's daughter from a life of poverty on the Nova Scotia farm. In "The Country Mouse," Bishop recounts her sudden and over-whelming feeling of displacement: "I had been brought back un-consulted and against my wishes to the house my father had been born in, to be saved from a life of poverty and provincialism, bare feet, suet puddings, unsanitary school slates, perhaps even from the inverted r's of my mother's family. With this surprising extra set of grandparents, until a few weeks ago no more than names, a new life was about to begin" (*Prose*, 17). The new life did not present itself hopefully; Bishop recalls "The house was gloomy, there was no de-nying it, and everyone seemed nervous and unsettled" (17). In this new rigid atmosphere of humorlessness and stuffy good breeding, Bishop felt herself on the same terms as Beppo, the family's Boston bull terrier. Though her grandparents certainly believed they were acting correctly and generously in taking Elizabeth, the ordeal proved too much for the child. Within a few months of her arrival in Worcester, she contracted crippling asthma, eczema, bronchitis, and St. Vitus's dance. These nervous ailments resurfaced from time to time, especially during periods of emotional stress, in Bishop's adult years. Combined with her constant battle with alcoholism, these diseases would often make her work difficult in later years.

Shortly after the move to Worcester, young Elizabeth's health grew so bad that her grandparents admitted that the experiment had failed. They arranged for her to move in with Maude Shepherdson, her mother's eldest sister, who lived on the top floor of a South Boston tenement. By this time, Elizabeth had grown so weak that her grandparents' chauffeur carried her up the steps. After the move, however, Elizabeth began slowly to recover, and Maude arranged for her to spend summers in Great Village. Her sicknesses constantly interrupted her schooling, and Bishop spent a great deal of time in bed, left to her own devices and imagination for entertainment— "wheezing and reading," as she later put it (Kalstone 1989, 27). At eight years of age, Elizabeth Bishop began to write poems.

In the tenement Bishop found something of the camaraderie and unselfconsciousness she had known in Nova Scotia. She particularly liked the Irish immigrant family who lived below her, and an unpublished story called "Mrs. Sullivan Downstairs" (Vassar Box 27) describes the family's lively kitchen, smelling of urine and cabbage, and the "nice mournful songs in Celtic" that Mrs. Sullivan was fond of singing.

Bishop loved all kinds of music: Mrs. Sullivan's songs, hymns of all varieties, classical music, rock, the bossa nova. She played the clavichord and at Vassar studied to become a conductor until the prospect of repeated public recitals dissuaded her. Though she would have called herself an unbeliever, hymns remained her favorite songs. She explained in an interview, "Where I lived in Canada, people used to sing hymns in the evening. They liked to play the piano and organ, and they'd sing and sing. My grandfather went to two churches—one Presbyterian, one Baptist—one in the morning and one in the afternoon. So I'm full of hymns" (*Prose,* xiii). Frani Muser, a lifelong friend of Bishop's from the Walnut Hill boarding school days, remembers Bishop and her love for music of all kinds:

> When I arrived at the Walnut Hill School in Natick in 1927, I met a most remarkable girl. She looked remarkable, with tightly curly hair that stood straight up. . . . She had read more widely and deeply than we had. But she carried her learning lightly. She was very funny. She had a big repertory of stories she could tell, not read, and of wonderful songs she could sing, like ballads and sea chanteys. And if some school occasion called for a new song, or a skit, it would appear overnight like magic in her hands. Her name was Elizabeth Bishop. We called her "Bishop," spoke of her as "the Bishop," and we all knew with no doubt whatsoever that she was a genius. (*Prose,* xiii)

Although most critics of Bishop's poems discuss her "eye," the tendency of her descriptions to imitate the exactness of painting, Bishop's love of music also deeply influenced her poetry, and in my discussions of individual poems I have concentrated on Bishop's ingenious musical composition within the verbal medium.

Bishop enjoyed the intellectual companionship and stimulation she found at Walnut Hill and grew stronger during her summers spent in Great Village and at Camp Chequesset, or, as she called it, the Nautical School for Girls, at Wellfleet. After Walnut Hill, Bishop went on to Vassar, where she continued to distinguish herself intellectually and socially for her wit and charm and remarkable ability to come up with just the right song or the funniest story. At Vassar, Bishop, along with Mary McCarthy and several other women, edited *Con Spirito*, an underground literary magazine that accepted more irreverent and unusual work than the sanctioned press. Mary McCarthy remembers Bishop's poem about living next to the toilet that began, "Ladies and gents, ladies and gents, flushing away your excrements" (*Voices and Visions*).

In her senior year at Vassar, Bishop met Marianne Moore, who almost immediately became an important influence and point of departure for Bishop's life and work. After leaving Vassar, Bishop moved to New York and took her first job with a shady correspondence school called the U.S.A. School of Writing, where, under the pseudonym Mr. Margolies, she read piles of "primitive" writing and sent back what "correction" and encouragement she could. In her detailed and humorous account of her first job, the memoir "The U.S.A. School of Writing," she confessed, "For a long time afterwards I used to feel that the neurotically 'kind' facet of my personality was Mr. Margolies" (*Prose*, 36).

After New York, Bishop lived in Key West, traveled across Europe, and lived in Paris, London, Cape Cod, Brazil (for fifteen years), San Francisco, Mexico, Boston, and Worcester. But in 1979, when Elizabeth Spires asked about her travels, she said, "I really haven't traveled that much" (1979, 8). Yet she also said, in her acceptance speech for the Neustadt International Prize, that all of her life she had behaved like the subject of her poem "The Sandpiper," "just running along the edges of different countries 'looking for something' " (*Prose*, viii). Bishop's poems chronicle that search and the conflicting, paradoxical feelings surrounding it. Her poems conduct a search that never ends in one answer and never simplifies into one line of questioning but rather explores the paradoxes that derive from bodily existence, paradoxes that cannot be resolved, and that come naturally from Bishop's experiences.

To illuminate the connection between Bishop's experience and achievement, I begin each chapter with a detailed discussion of the biographical circumstances surrounding the publication of each of her four books. I discuss her friendships with Moore, Jarrell, and Lowell and examine briefly the circumstances and influence of her years in Brazil. For much of the information, both in this introductory biographical sketch and in the chapter introductions, I am indebted to David Kalstone's *Becoming a Poet: Elizabeth Bishop with Marianne Moore and Robert Lowell,* an insightful evaluation of Bishop's life and work, to Candace MacMahon's *Elizabeth Bishop: A Bibliography,* and to Robert Giroux's edition of Bishop's *Complete Prose.* While revising the manuscript, I read Victoria Harrison's *Elizabeth Bishop's Poetics of Intimacy,* another book I found enormously helpful and perceptive, and Brett Millier's *Elizabeth Bishop: Life and the Memory of It,* to which I am also indebted. In the last stages of my revision, Robert Giroux published *Elizabeth Bishop: One Art,* a book I have found both helpful and enjoyable.

The Critical Reception

It has become axiomatic in Bishop criticism to say that she is "a writer's writer" or, as John Ashbery says, "a poet's poet," and this is so if that statement is taken to mean that Bishop's work has been appreciated by and has influenced other talented writers, including Robert Lowell, Randall Jarrell, Lloyd Schwartz, Alice Fulton, Elizabeth Spires, and Gibbons Ruark, to name a handful. If, however, calling Bishop "a writer's writer" means she is a poet whose craftsmanship and technique find an audience in other writers but whose appeal to the general public is limited, I believe the term is misapplied. Bishop's absolutely lucid surfaces that cover elusive depths have appeal for a wide audience, one as diverse perhaps as that for Robert Frost's poems.[3] However, the critical history of Bishop's work is marked by a tendency to try to narrow her appeal, to find a category into which her poems fit neatly. Yet her career, like each of her poems, refuses to be easily resolved. The desire on the part of many critics to categorize Bishop's work narrowly, either according to her contemporaries or according to some linear structure imposed on her poems from without, has made it difficult to get a true sense of her work from reading the bulk of Bishop criticism. As Denis Donoghue writes, "The received sense of Bishop's work, so far as I can judge it, makes her poetry sound far more domestic than it is" (1984, 246). By "domestic" Donoghue refers, I believe, to a critical tendency to see in Bishop's work a nice, non-threatening picture of a manageable world. Interestingly, this is the same tendency to domesticate with which many critics approached Frost's poems, classifying him as a charming nature poet.

Some critics of Bishop's work, particularly the earliest ones, domesticated her achievement by comparing her poems with those of her friends and her contemporaries or near contemporaries, by saying, in praise, that she "assumed the mantle of Marianne Moore" (Gould 1984, 51), or, in reprobation, that her poems are "Audenary and Wallace Stevens-ish" (Williams 1983, 185). These comparisons almost always obscure the individuality of both Bishop's achievement and the achievements of the poets with whom she is compared. Although I think a qualified comparison of Bishop's work with Moore's could teach quite a bit (I have undertaken such a comparison in a limited way in the opening of chapter 1), we gain little by seeing Bishop as merely assuming Moore's mantle. In their correspondence, both Moore and Bishop refer to these comparisons as blurring the individuality and difficulty of their work, as any such comparison, unqualified and unanalyzed, illuminates neither the author nor the author's contemporaries.

More recently, however, such critics as Joanne Diehl, Robert Dale Parker, and Robert Pinsky have explored Bishop's relationship to her poetic predecessors. Diehl expands on a remark that Bishop made in a letter to Anne Stevenson, "Cal [Lowell] and I in very different ways are both descendants from the Transcendentalists" (Diehl 1985, 123). Discussing the application of the Emersonian

Sublime to gender issues in Bishop's poetry, Diehl fruitfully explores how Bishop deals with or avoids dealing with the problem of gender. Parker, in contrast, compares Walt Whitman and Bishop as two poets who experience the anxiety of influence. He notes that both are constantly concerned with boundaries, with drawing or eliminating the line between foreign and familiar (1988, 74). Similarly, Pinsky (1983) sees Bishop's work in relation to Wordsworth's and compares Bishop's use of concrete detail and landscapes with the nature images of the romantics. These studies and others like them prove helpful because they uncover sides of Bishop's work that may otherwise be overlooked; they facilitate a new perspective. However, influence studies can also become a way to banish the central and unique ambiguity in Bishop's poems.

Some critics have domesticated Bishop's elusiveness by dividing her work into stages that are not organic to her career but derived from the critic's own thesis. Although much can be learned from many of these studies, the overall picture they present of Bishop's career seems skewed. For example, Thomas Travisano looks for "coherent and consistent" development in Bishop's three stages, which he identifies as (1) prison, "the exploration of sealed imaginary worlds"; (2) travel, the use of "actual places and people"; and (3) history, poems that explore "the challenge of public and private history" (1988, 3). According to Travisano's scheme, the prison stage comprises only the very first and earliest poems of *North & South;* the travel stage ranges across what he calls the middle of her career, which is actually the latter half of *North & South* and all of *A Cold Spring* and *Questions of Travel;* and the history stage is represented by *Geography III.* Robert Dale Parker's (1988) division of Bishop's career is similar to Travisano's. Parker calls his three stages (1) poems of wish, (2) poems of where, and (3) poems of retrospect.

These divisions domesticate Bishop's poems because they do not allow for the elusiveness, the ambiguity, of each work. The divisions seem lopsided and externally imposed rather than arising organically from Bishop's work. This is, in part, why I have chosen to use Bishop's books themselves as the organizing principle. Bishop spent at least a decade working on each of her four books; her untiring revision of her collections deserves note and weight in constructing any argument about her career. Millier's (1993) biography details Bishop's constant and often apparently nitpicking battles with publishers, conflicts reflecting her desire to construct a book consistent in tone, for which she must always finish just a few more poems. Bishop's four books span her adult lifetime and facilitate a discussion of her career and her development that hangs naturally on the work she herself produced. More importantly for my purposes, Bishop's books, like the poems themselves, become yet another concrete form in which Bishop must embody invisible thought, another level of the metaphor of the body. In a letter to Houghton Mifflin's Ferris Greenslet of November 20, 1945, Bishop writes: "It will be possible for me, won't it, to have some choice about the 'physical embodiment' of the book that you mention?" (Giroux 1994, 128). Moreover, Bishop was one of relatively few of her women contemporaries whose books were published in a form that had the author's approval; for example, Anne Sexton constantly revised after publication, whereas Ted Hughes changed or deleted poems from Sylvia Plath's collections.

Any comparison of Bishop with her women contemporaries leads to what has become a central issue in Bishop criticism. Bishop's feminist convictions or perceived lack thereof remains one of the most debated topics surrounding her work and her career. Many of her earliest critics emphasized and perhaps overpraised what they called Bishop's "modesty," her use of detail; some approved of her working, as Helen McNeil notes, "in the typically feminine art of the miniature" (1987, 397). Roy Harvey Pearce, for example, applauds Bishop's work, saying she is "modest and she is dignified" (Ostriker 1986, 3), and Anne Stevenson uses the adjectives "elegant," "generous," "modest," and "dignified" (1966, 121, 126). While these readings may be skewed in their tendency to concentrate on the lucid surface and miss the frightening depths, they seem to me no more insulting than they would be if applied to Robert Frost's or Richard Wilbur's poetry. However, this reading of Bishop's poems becomes a kind of "straw woman" against which critics like Alicia Ostriker could juxtapose more overtly political poets like Anne Sexton, Sylvia Plath, or Adrienne Rich. However, in her interview with Elizabeth Spires, Bishop noted that she considered herself "a strong feminist" and that she hated being played off against writers like Adrienne Rich and Erica Jong (1979, 8). Much of the debate over her relative feminism derives not from Bishop's work but from her refusal to publish in all-women anthologies or women-only magazines. She asserts, in both letters and interviews, that the gender of the poet should remain forever secondary to the quality of the poem. Andrew Motion's argument that "the insights and arguments that Bishop ranges against maleness are coherent but lack imaginative convictions" (1985, 310) suggests that all fine poems written by women must necessarily take up some argument with maleness. The lack he sees is not the fault of the poems but of a reader looking for the politically acceptable language of the ongoing argument rather than the perceptive rendering of individual experience.

Beneath the issue of feminism lies the larger issue of Bishop's reticence, her refusal to align herself and announce her convictions about art, lifestyles, sexuality, or politics. Critics have consistently denounced her on this ground, as is seen in Jerome Mazzaro's complaint that Bishop practices too much restraint (1980, 193) and Andrew Motion's suggestion that her images "dazzle" and therefore obscure other concerns and qualities (1985, 301). However, some more recent studies, especially Denis Donoghue's (1984) chapter on Bishop in *Connoisseurs of Chaos* and Wyatt Prunty's (1990) chapter on Bishop and Mona Van Duyn in *Fallen from the Symboled World*, have undertaken an exploration of the strangeness and ambiguity in Bishop's work. Donoghue's study concentrates on the importance of presence and absence and the tension between *in* and *out* in Bishop's poems. Prunty looks at Bishop's odd, "askew" images and compares them with the work of other women writers, especially Mona Van Duyn, to suggest the similarity in both poets' relationships to the inconstant and often terrifying world of concrete objects and other people. Bonnie Costello, in *Elizabeth Bishop: Questions of Mastery*, looks at issues of control and dominance—"artistic, personal, and cultural"—in Bishop's poetry and explores "more inclusively what it means to be a visual poet" (1991, 2, 5). C. K. Doreski, in *Elizabeth Bishop: The Restraints of Language*, discusses

Bishop's restraint as a refusal to either "resolve or deconstruct binary opposition" (1993, 3), an argument that provides interesting readings of some of Bishop's most elusive poems.

Several gender theorists have recently reexamined Bishop's work. Lois Cucullu argues that Bishop's poems repeatedly question the use of language as a gendered coding system (1988, 264). Victoria Harrison, in her book *Elizabeth Bishop's Poetics of Intimacy* (1993), perceptively uses Bishop's drafts, letters, and journals to show connections between the author struggling and surviving in a society that constantly threatens her and the poet writing and trying to forge connections with others in that society.

Although any number of critical theories could inform a reading of Bishop's struggle with the paradox of embodiment—among them Derridean deconstructionism, Spivak's cultural criticism, and gender theories of gender space—Bishop's poems tend to resist the language of such interrogation. Concentration on Bishop's uniqueness, and the uniqueness of each of her poems, both as compared with those of other poets and as compared with each other, yields the most insight into her work. Therefore, by examining the way Bishop uses metaphors of the body within her poems and the way she uses the poetic form itself as a metaphor for the body, I have suggested a way to locate some of the ambiguity and evasiveness that are so thoroughly characteristic of her voice and her poems. At the center of Elizabeth Bishop's poems I find a sensibility deeply divided about human embodiment, both literally, in the flesh, and figuratively, in the poem. That conflict translates into the energy, the balance, and the beauty of her poems.

1

NORTH & SOUTH
Finding a Language for How We Know

ELIZABETH BISHOP DID not possess a lifelong ambition to become a poet. In fact, while she was studying at Vassar she majored in conducting, an expression of her deep love for music. Bishop also painted, especially watercolors, and told Elizabeth Spires in an interview for the *Vassar Quarterly* that she had often thought she would rather have been a painter (1979, 7). Her first published work outside of school and college publications was a short story, "Then Came the Poor" (1934); her contributor's note mentioned only that she was working on a novel.[1] In her more despairing moments, Bishop had long toyed with the idea of returning to Vassar, taking premedical courses, and becoming a physician, an idea she was dissuaded from by Marianne Moore (Kalstone 1989, 43). At the beginning of her career, Bishop was often extremely shy and reticent about her poetry, as she continued to be almost all her life about reading her poetry in public. In a note included with some of the first poems she submitted for publication to the *Westminster Magazine* after graduating from Vassar, Bishop self-effacingly offers just a few verses that "I do just for fun . . . the only ones I have any success with" (Kalstone 1989, 40). An untiring and passionate student of poetry, especially that of Hopkins, Herbert, Donne, Stevens, Auden, and Moore, Bishop seemed to feel, at least in her twenties, in awe of the art itself and tentative about presenting her own work. More than just a matter of years, though, I believe her early reticence about publication came naturally from her struggle with embodying thought and feeling in poetic form. Bishop sought, especially in the poems of *North & South,* a method of expressing the ways that the body knows, a task she knew to be both mammoth and circular.

Bishop's friendship with Marianne Moore proved to be, in many ways, the impetus for overcoming these feelings of shyness and the intellectual reticence that kept her from publishing. Bishop met Moore while a senior at Vassar through the auspices of the Vassar librarian and longtime friend of Marianne and Mrs. Moore, Fanny Borden. Fanny Borden cuts an impressive figure, as Kalstone points out, a pleasingly eccentric, strangely appropriate liaison for the two women (1989, 6). Tall and very thin, she never spoke above a whisper, rode a chainless bicycle, and was related to the notorious Lizzie Borden. She also owned the only copy of Moore's *Observations* available on Vassar's campus, a copy she loaned to Bishop when Bishop inquired about why the book was not in the library. Fanny Borden arranged a meeting of the two poets outside the third floor reading room of the New York Public Library. Bishop arrived early, as she told Elizabeth Spires years later, and was alarmed to find "a tall, eagle-nosed, be-turbaned lady, distinguished-looking but proud and forbidding" (1979, 8). Fortunately, this formidable woman wasn't Moore at all. As Bishop wrote in her memoir of Moore, the poet was forty-seven, had red hair tinged with white, braided and wound in a crown, pale blue eyes, a small, pointed face, and a "delicately pugnacious-looking jaw" that made her resemble a "female Mickey Rooney" (*Prose*, 133).

This meeting was to mark the beginning of a most extraordinary literary and personal relationship.[2] Moore and her mother offered Bishop encouragement and support, both by example (Bishop suggests in her memoir that she never left their Manhattan apartment without feeling that she would certainly try harder, work more, and never publish until she had done her best with each poem) and by direct suggestion and "correction" of her stories and poems. Moore not only encouraged Bishop to submit her poems to Moore's favorite editors (especially to Morton Zabel at *Poetry*), but for a while, in 1936, Moore mailed Bishop's work herself. In 1935, Moore had presented Bishop in an anthology called *Trial Balances,* in which established poets introduced younger poets of promise; here Louise Bogan presented Theodore Roethke, and Stephen Vincent Benét presented Muriel Rukeyeser.

Though Moore consistently understood what Bishop sought to accomplish in her poetry, she was not consistently in favor of that accomplishment. One area in which Moore and Bishop differed most concerned what Moore would have called questions of delicacy—questions, most often, of bodies and the modesty or breach of modesty involved in focusing on the human body. On the surface, this difference seems an ordinary, even nonliterary, clash of the generations; Moore's deleting the word "watercloset" from Bishop's "Roosters," for example, seems the indication of the modesty of an age that had passed even in Moore's girlhood. However, that incident is a small indicator of a chasm that divided, not Moore and Bishop, but Moore's and Bishop's poetry, their distinct treatment of the individual and the individual body. John Ashbery's contention that the two poets "couldn't be more different" (1983, 201) reflects an essential and sometimes overlooked divergence in their perspectives, styles, and goals, a divergence that directly involves their apprehension of the singular living body.

Comparing, for example, Bishop's poem "The Fish" and Moore's poem of the same title, the reader finds that Bishop's work concerns a particular fish, the body of one fish, while Moore's work concerns all fish, fish as phenomenon. Bishop insistently refers to her fish as "he": "He didn't fight. / He hadn't fought at all. / He hung a grunting weight" (*Poems*, 42), and this personification, this identification of the speaker with the fish, is crucial to the speaker's progressive realization that she must let the fish go—from her boat, from her scrutiny, and from her poem. Bishop's fish is an individual, with a will and with a body. And the imagining of the individual body, as I will demonstrate in my discussion of the poem later in this chapter, is the central paradox on which the poem hangs. Moore's fish, in contrast to Bishop's, is a species—"The Fish / wade" (1986, 32)—or an "it" that the poem holds at a distance until the very last line, when Moore suggests a powerful and abstract correlation between the human and the animal:

Repeated
      evidence has proved that it can live
on what can not revive
      its youth. The sea grows old in it. (1986, 33)

Bishop is preoccupied with the body, Moore with bodies. When, in the early forties, Bishop began to move further and further from what she called Moore's "protective apron" (though never away from Moore's friendship), it was, at least in part, because of their fundamental differences of opinion over the importance of the body.

In December of 1944, Moore offered to recommend Bishop's manuscript, one that Bishop had been trying for more than five years to publish, for the Houghton Mifflin Award, a prestigious poetry prize. Bishop's application manifests that same overly modest, self-effacing tone she often used in talking about her own work, explaining that she wanted "to finish six or seven poems of what I hope may be a serious nature and more appropriate and intense form than those enclosed" (Kalstone 1989, 99). Moore, however, wrote with earnest praise for Bishop's work, and the manuscript that would become *North & South* was chosen over eight hundred other entries. Bishop won one thousand dollars and, finally, the publication of her first book. *North & South* contained thirty poems and introduced a poet widely and deeply read, especially in the poetry of the metaphysical and seventeenth-century religious poets, a poet with her own powerful voice and individual creative obsessions.

In her review of *North & South*, Moore wrote, "At last we have a prize book that has no creditable mannerisms. At last we have someone who knows, who is not didactic" (1983, 179). Moore's emphasis on Bishop's lack of didacticism, Bishop's uncanny ability to express both knowledge and uncertainty simultaneously, proves not only insightful as it concerns *North & South* but prophetic of the concerns and challenges Bishop would struggle with throughout her career. The creative tension, the paradox of *North & South*, comes from Bishop's search for a language to express and explore how the individual, within the confines of an individual body, can connect with the contingent world of other people and things. *North & South* struggles to find a language for the instability of knowing, even though the language itself is born of uncertainty and the necessity to negotiate a reality between isolated individuals.

I discuss the poems of *North & South* in three basic categories: I begin with Bishop's experiments in personification, surprisingly perhaps the least successful of Bishop's attempts to explore the problem of human perception; then I discuss poems that concern the "clean cage" of human perception, or the way the body invisibly distorts the reality it mediates; and finally I look at the poems of internalization, those that suggest an escape from the isolation of the body through attention to and connection with the contingent world.

Experiments in Personification

The power of personification, like any figure of speech, resides in the fresh look at reality it can afford; by endowing an animal, a thing, or an abstraction with human qualities, a writer reveals something about him- or herself, about human nature, and perhaps also about the thing personified. However, in *North & South*, Bishop's experiments with personification, particularly personification that she extends to conceit, as in "The Colder the Air," "From the Country to the City," and "Cirque d'Hiver," express the frightening and inescapable nature of both the device and the human perspective that has created the device. Her use of conceit reveals the influence of Eliot and the modernists and her own reading of the metaphysicals, especially Herbert and Donne. However, in these poems Bishop demonstrates that personification is not just interesting but inescapable; we can conceive of nothing beyond human terms of conception, can conceive of nothing without a body, and yet that personification is wholly unsatisfactory because, conceived of in human terms, the only terms available, reality eludes us. In a number of poems in *North & South*, Bishop rests the meaning of the poem almost completely on the device of a personified conceit.

"The Colder the Air," for example, embodies the invisible force of winter, the cold, in the guise of a human huntress. Cold seems especially elusive; it is not an object or an idea, but a force whose effects, whose "vast properties," like the moon's in "The Man-Moth," we feel acutely, yet whose substance we cannot see. This is a particularly dark poem, one that suggests, if obliquely, that the whole enterprise of looking and writing may be worthless. While the personification works by developing correlations—the sure aim, the weapon, the target—the power of the conceit finally derives from its own failure, from the differences between the cold and the huntress, the tension between cold's association with death and the quick humanity, the vitality, of the huntress. In "The Colder the Air," the personified figure simultaneously establishes and undermines itself. The abcbca rhyme echoes this circularity, turning back on its own beginning in each stanza. The rhyme and meter make the cycle seem easy and light, and yet also somehow insidious and inescapable. The first stanza establishes the sense that the personification is both forced and forced upon us:

> We must admire her perfect aim,
> this huntress of the winter air
> whose level weapon needs no sight,
> if it were not that everywhere
> her game is sure, her shot is right.
> The least of us could do the same. (*Poems*, 6)

Though we are bound to admire any huntress whose "level weapon needs no sight," we are aware at the same time that without "sight," without perception, the possibility of misperception disappears. The joy of hitting the mark diminishes almost entirely when "her game is sure." The circumstances of cold's accomplishment, completely unlike the huntress's circumstances, make it both miraculous, for her shot can be nothing but right, and meaningless, since under the same conditions, "The least of us could do the same."

In the second stanza, Bishop explores the miraculousness of the cold's achievement in implied comparison with the difficulties that the huntress, being human, must face:

> The chalky birds or boats stand still,
> reducing her conditions of chance;
> air's gallery marks identically
> the narrow gallery of her glance.
> The target-center in her eye
> is equally her aim and will.

Like Donne or Herbert, Bishop pushes the figure to its limit, drawing it out into conceit until everything in the landscape is defined by the figure; the air is a "gallery," birds and boats her prey, the "target-center" her eye. However, pushed this far, without any shift in metaphor or viewpoint, the device does what Donne and Herbert almost never let it do; it paradoxically shows that cold is more unlike than like the huntress. It introduces a chasm of meaning that, in Derridean terms, will cause the poem to deconstruct.

The final stanza subtly dismantles the device the first two stanzas established and enlarged on:

> Time's in her pocket, ticking loud
> on one stalled second. She'll consult
> not time nor circumstance. She calls
> on atmosphere for her result.
> (It is this clock that later falls
> in wheels and chimes of leaf and cloud.)

The cold is not prey to perception, chance, or death, all of the traps set for the human huntress. Though the suggestion of death remains ("Time's in her pocket, ticking loud"), the next words revoke death's power—"on one stalled second." The cold finally moves beyond the figure, or the body, the poem has fashioned for it. Paradoxically, although the cold can accomplish much more than the huntress because it does not fall prey to any of the forces humans fall prey to, the cold, in human terms, achieves less because it risks nothing.

This consideration of risk and achievement comments directly on the task of the image maker, the poet. The tone of "The Colder the Air" is itself cold—distanced, exact, and almost emotionless. Bishop seems to imitate the sure action of the cold itself, which can certainly capture without risk any prey it seeks. However, for Bishop, the prey is the cold itself—a knowledge of the cold, the ability to capture the cold in the device she has created—and this prey has escaped. The device itself collapses under the weight of the comparison, and both poet and reader are left holding the empty figure, like someone looking into a cup with a hole in the bottom through which the contents have just spilled out. What the human figure sought to contain has escaped our understanding again. This complex and philosophical attempt to understand human ways of knowing, and its inevitable circularity and beautiful, troubling inadequacy, may account for some of Bishop's shyness about her poetry.

In Bishop's poems, personification fails to convey accurate vision without distorting emotion, and this failure comments both on the

difficulty of perceiving the contingent world through human senses
and on Bishop's ambivalent feelings about poetic device and form.
Traditionally, as in much of Herbert and Donne, personification
opens out the meaning of the poem and reveals the emotions of
the speaker. Like Robert Frost, James Wright, Philip Larkin, and
any number of modern poets, Bishop seems to feel anxious about
this intrusion, this projecting human meaning onto the nonhuman
world. Her early experiments with personification suggest that a
writer is both powerless to refuse human perspective, the confines of the single body, and powerless to gain, through its figures,
the knowledge she seeks. Thus, the writer's relationship with the
figure seems ambivalent; it can shield her from the risk of knowledge—keep her, like the cold, from all misperception—but the
figure can also separate the writer from real and frightening connection, from accurate knowledge that requires the risk of human
perception.

In "From the Country to the City," Bishop again chooses a subject for personification that, like the force of the cold, seems noto-
riously elusive. She personifies space, specifically the stretch of space
"From the Country to the City," as a clown or harlequin:

> The long, long legs,
> league-boots of land, that carry the city nowhere,
>   nowhere; the lines
> that we drive on (satin-stripes on harlequin's
>   trousers, tights);
> his tough trunk dressed in tatters, scribbled over with
>   nonsensical signs; (*Poems*, 13)

"The long, long legs, / league-boots of land, that carry the city nowhere" figure the space closest to the country as the lower part of a
gigantic body. The highway's line, refashioned, becomes "the satin-
stripes on harlequin's / trousers, tights." The city, presumably the
city at night, becomes the head and heart. The comparison, like
the comparison between the huntress and the cold in "The Colder
the Air," pushes further and further toward reason's limits. The
"nonsensical signs" scribbled over the harlequin's trunk suggest the
fate of the comparison pushed to its limit, the collapse of meaning.

That limit is reached, oddly, at what is usually the center of meaning, the head:

> his shadowy, tall dunce-cap; and, best of all his
>   shows and sights,
> his brain appears throned in "fantastic triumph,"
>   and shines through his hat
> with jeweled works at work at intermeshing crowns,
>   lamé with lights.

Reading the poem involves a kind of mental gymnastics, connecting visual fact with the element of the poetic device—the hat, the brain—that figures this fact. The mental participation needed to work out the figure progressively overwhelms the figure's meaning.

As in "The Colder the Air," the interdependence of the device and the thing described, the justness of the figure that the beginning of the poem works to establish, is undermined as the poem moves along. The surreal city-as-brain overwhelms the space-as-body stretching away toward the country in the same way that the space and our imagining of the city begin to overwhelm the figure the poet has created to capture them:

> As we approach, wickedest clown, your heart and head,
>   we can see that
> glittering arrangement of your brain consists, now,
>   of mermaid-like,
> seated, ravishing sirens, each waving her hand-mirror;
>   and we start at
> series of slight disturbances up in the telephone wires
>   on the turnpike.

The city-as-brain turns back on itself, striking a tuning fork against the mirror frames of the "ravishing sirens, each waving her hand-mirror," the sirens who are themselves part of the city/brain. The mirror is the image of this reflexivity, the city's turning back on itself, just as the figure in the poem turns back on itself. However, the city/brain also exhibits another motion, also sends itself, its dreams, outward, "out countrywards." Through this double motion, the head and heart overwhelm the body, a kind of attack that Bishop imagines as sound vibrations visible in short lines that fly outward, sounds and lines reminiscent of the sounds and visible lines of poems:

> Flocks of short, shining wires seem to be flying sidewise.
>   Are they birds?
> They flash again. No. They are vibrations of the tuning-fork
>   you hold and strike
> against the mirror-frames, then draw for miles, your dreams,
>   out countrywards.
> We bring a message from the long black length of body:
>   "Subside," it begs and begs.

As in "The Colder the Air," the first-person "we" forces the reader to participate; we become part of the neural pathway by which the body communicates and the city overwhelms: "We bring a message from the long black length of body." The reader, and the poet, too, seem to have been caught in the circular motion of the poem, to have been used to bring a message, like a poem.

If in "The Colder the Air" meaning leaked out of the figure, in "From the Country to the City" the figure circles back on itself and consumes the meaning, just as the city/brain overwhelms the country/body. This duality suggests many themes that Bishop would constantly return to: the relationship between the life of the body and the life of the mind, the conflicts between expectation and reality and between perception and fact. Again, though, the point of the figure becomes its failure to capture and hold—to resolve—any question that it raises, the inability of our human tendency toward personification to expose reality.

In its circularity, "From the Country to the City" bears a resemblance to "Cirque d'Hiver." Though the latter is more whimsical and humorous, begins as straight description, and moves only gradually toward personification, this movement toward endowing a lifeless music box with humanity and what the movement betrays in its attempt to construct relationship and meaning seems the point of the poem. The first two stanzas describe the circus horse carrying the tiny pink dancer on his back:

> Across the floor flits the mechanical toy,
> fit for a king of several centuries back.

A little circus horse with real white hair.
His eyes are glossy black.
He bears a little dancer on his back.

She stands upon her toes and turns and turns.
A slanting spray of artificial roses
is stitched across her skirt and tinsel bodice.
Above her head she poses
another spray of artificial roses. (*Poems,* 31)

Although the verbs could suggest personification—"He bears," "She stands," "she poses"—in the first two stanzas the figure remains suggestion. The simple sentences, end-stopped lines, and "poses/roses" rhyme make the tone singsong, like a child's rhyme.

In the third and fourth stanzas, however, the poet turns her attention from the apparently cliché ballerina to the more interesting and strange horse; she connects the tiny toy to the larger world of art and moves toward constructing a relationship, a human figure, that goes beyond a childlike appreciation, that seems meant, in a lighthearted but serious way, to facilitate adult understanding and access:

His mane and tail are straight from Chirico.
He has a formal, melancholy soul.
He feels her pink toes dangle toward his back
along the little pole
that pierces both her body and her soul

and goes through his, and reappears below,
under his belly, as a big tin key.
He canters three steps, then he makes a bow,
canters again, bows on one knee,
canters, then clicks and stops, and looks at me.

In these stanzas, the body and soul are paradoxically separated and inseparable, completely joined by the little pole and separated in motion and meaning, like the horse and the dancer. This paradox suggests levels of difficulty in creating a figure, in embodying the invisible in the visible. Personification fails, in part, because we cannot successfully divide visible from invisible. The split between body and soul defines a construction of human perception as much in doubt as any other human perception. Therefore, the cyclic, clever motion of the horse—"He canters three steps, then he makes a bow, / canters again, bows on one knee"—parallels the cyclic and clever motion of the figure that, despite its promise of meaning, brings us back full circle. Bishop suggests both the figure's failure and its joy and beauty in the way the verse parallels the motion of the toy horse in the final stanza of the poem:

> The dancer, by this time, has turned her back.
> He is the more intelligent by far.
> Facing each other rather desperately—
> his eye is like a star—
> we stare and say, "Well, we have come this far."

The personification brings the reader and the speaker full circle, both looking "rather desperately" at an "eye . . . like a star," an intelligence that promises meaning. We are both disappointed. Both the figure and the form of the poem mirror the motion of the mechanical horse; the quatrain plus one with an abcbb rhyme scheme allows each stanza to end with a couplet that is a kind of finishing bow. However, the end of the poem refuses to resolve any of the myriad questions that the resigned and weary, or hopeful, phrase, "Well, we have come this far," elicits. Instead, Bishop allows the figure itself and the speaker's personification to stand without comment.

However, in another poem, "Quai d'Orléans," Bishop comments directly on the relationship between device and reality, between what we are and know and what we see. The tone of the poem is powerfully informed by the grief and pain Bishop experienced in the aftermath of a car accident in which her friend, Margaret Miller, to whom the poem is dedicated, lost her arm. Bishop, Miller, and Louise Crane, the friend with whom Bishop lived during her years in Key West, had been driving through France during a vacation in Europe. The car overturned, and, though Bishop and Crane suffered only minor injuries, Miller, a painter, was badly hurt and lost her right arm. Although Bishop never directly mentions the incident, the poem's attempt to sort out what we can keep and what we must lose centers on the vulnerability of the human body and human perception, the body as the medium of loss. This poem does not experiment with personification in the same way that the more whimsical "Cirque d'Hiver" or "From the Country to the City" do, but it uncovers something of Bishop's thought about the necessity, the beauty, and the failure of all figures of speech, of all embodiment, and to reveal her insight into human loss:

Each barge on the river easily tows
a mighty wake,
a giant oak-leaf of gray lights
on duller gray;
and behind it real leaves are floating by,
down to the sea.
Mercury-veins on the giant leaves,
the ripples, make
for the sides of the quai, to extinguish themselves
against the walls
as softly as falling-stars come to their ends
at a point in the sky.
And throngs of small leaves, real leaves, trailing them,
go drifting by
to disappear as modestly, down the sea's
dissolving halls. (*Poems*, 28)

Here, Bishop juxtaposes the figure of the leaf that the mind creates with real leaves that float and throng and reveal the calculated, human quality of the figure. The images in these opening lines all surround loss: the ripples extinguish themselves, the stars come to their ends, the leaves disappear "down the sea's / dissolving halls."

However, in the lines that follow, Bishop suggests that the source of the loss is not a predetermined pattern or the evil in natural law, but her own perspective. The speaker and another, presumably Margaret Miller, "stand as still as stones," both seemingly stilled, trapped in their perception. In sharp contrast to the "nervous" moving water and light, the two women seem, like stones, to be washed over by the motion around them. The poem ends with a complicated, circular, evasive comment on human perspective:

We stand still as stones to watch
    the leaves and ripples
while light and nervous water hold
    their interview.
"If what we see could forget us half as easily,"
    I want to tell you,
"as it does itself—but for life we'll not be rid
    of the leaves' fossils."

The final lines of "Quai d'Orléans" suggest that we cannot forget ourselves long enough to see clearly, but they do not say that. Instead, these lines project our failure back onto the landscape, reinforcing that failure: "If what we see could forget us," if it could stop reflecting what we put there. The noun "leaves" suggests also the verb "to leave" and adds another dimension, as the vision obstructed by human perspective parallels the speech obstructed by human emotion: "I want to tell you" implies "but I do not tell you." Thus, this poem comments indirectly on the way any imposition of human perspective both promises to facilitate and also promises to limit understanding—what we see cannot forget us. The obstruction underlies the structure and content of poems such as "The Colder the Air," "From the Country to the City," and "Cirque d'Hiver," Bishop's experiments with personification.

All of these poetic experiments, these attempts at enlarging and undermining the form of personification, represent "dramatic explorations of the psychology of perception" (Travisano 1988, 90); however, they are often missing the sense of the speaker that Bishop achieves in other poems. Their drama is lessened somewhat, and their speaker obscured, by Bishop's reliance on a single, circular device to carry the entire meaning of the poem. These experiments are not as compelling as other poems that rely less on versification for meaning; once Bishop has established the concept of simultaneously creating and undermining the figure, any number of personified subjects could make a poem. Perhaps this is why she chooses only the most elusive and complicated subjects to treat, like the force of cold, or geographic space. What is missing from these poems becomes clearer when I compare them with poems such as "The

Map" and "The Imaginary Iceberg," which use and undermine personification but do not rely on this tactic as the central conceit, the locus of meaning. "The Map," "The Imaginary Iceberg," "The Gentleman of Shalott," and "Large Bad Picture" all explore the boundaries of human perception, the human body, in much the same way as Bishop's personified conceits. However, rather than concentrating on the fixed form that loops back, like the infinity symbol, to the same place, these poems progress through time and thought, are truly dramatic; they represent the movement of thought and emotion that Bishop admired in Hopkins and Herbert, what M. W. Croll called "the mind in action rather than in repose" (1966, 210). Moving beyond the strict conceit allows Bishop to escape the relatively fatalistic vision of the figure of personification and to explore the terrible power of human perception to both distort and imaginatively transform.

The "Clean Cage" of Human Perception

"The Map," the first poem in *North & South*, introduces the problem of human perception, the difficulty of endeavoring to know, in terms of defining topography, of understanding the physical contours of the land that supports us. Bishop uses metaphors of the human body to express the tension between self-actualization and self-destruction that she finds in the act of mapping, an attempt at accurate perception. The poem's first stanza describes land, using verbs and adjectives that quietly, unintrusively, personify land and suggest the pervasiveness of the human form, the body, in any human vision of form:

> Land lies in water; it is shadowed green.
> Shadows, or are they shallows, at its edges
> showing the line of long sea-weeded ledges
> where weeds hang to simple blue from green.
> Or does the land lean down to lift the sea from under,
> drawing it unperturbed around itself?
> Along the tan sandy shelf
> is the land tugging at the sea from under? (*Poems*, 3)

Bishop's initial observation that "land lies in water" reveals the problematic relationship between what we know or believe and what we sense, between maps and real geography, between what looks true and what is true; it is the problem that haunts human attempts at perception. This reminds me of a well-known visual trick: draw two equal lines, then add arrows that point outward to one line and arrows that point inward to the other; the intellect says the lines are still equal, but the senses report that they must be different sizes. Similarly, on a map, the land resembles a body stretched out on the water that upholds it. The two-dimensional map, our artifact, our attempt to control through understanding and representing, actually misrepresents the reality of the land. Yet, more terrifying than the failure of the artifact, "Land lies in water," like the visual trick I mentioned above, points to the failure of our senses. The play of refracted light causes land looked at through water to "lie," to have an appearance other than its reality. What we see, what we hear, smell, taste, and touch—and what we create—cannot accurately reproduce what is. However, Bishop is not so wedded to what is that this failure becomes pathos; instead, she finds in our human plight a strange kind of humor. The tone of the poem is light, playful.

Frankenburg, praising "The Map," asserts that Bishop's is "a clearly delineated world" and that her poem, like a good map, possesses "precision, compression" (1949, 331, 333). Nothing could be further from the truth. Over and over in "The Map," Bishop rephrases her original assertions because they fail to delineate what she sees and what she knows. Frankenburg himself quotes the second line of the poem, "Shadows, or are they shallows, at its edges," without recognizing that Bishop's attempt at "precision" here and throughout the poem fails, must fail, because human perception is filtered through human senses that are flawed, both by natural imperfection and by the imposition of perspective and imagination, the subjective point of view, the imposition that creates meaning in objective reality. And that meaning is exciting, transforming, "as when emotion too far exceeds its cause." The way Bishop employs and calls attention to personification in "The Map" reveals her struggle to see both accurately and meaningfully.

The description of the land leaning down "to lift the sea from under, / drawing it unperturbed around itself" and the land "tugging at the sea from under" embodies the inexplicable motions of the sea in the comprehensible human figure of a person drawing up a blanket. The repetition of soft "l," "n," and "s" sounds reinforces both the sound of the water and the world of the sleeper. However, because Bishop phrases these lines as questions, they seem paradoxically to create the figure and, by calling the reader's attention to it, destroy the figure's effect. Of course, the answer to her question "Is the land tugging at the sea from under?" is no. The land and sea are not human, have no will, are not, finally, any figure we can create to understand them. These opening questions seem playful, seem to be said with a wink. If, as Bonnie Costello argues, the questioning tone is more contrived than the strategies in Bishop's later work, looks like mere cleverness in contrast to the serious questions of "Questions of Travel," for example (1983, 132), the tone is nevertheless integral to Bishop's concept of perception and her use of metaphors of the body in "The Map."

The effect of the opening questions echoes the effect of the poem's structure. Just as the questions simultaneously establish and undermine personification, the structure of the poem—an eleven-line, unrhymed stanza caught between two eight-line rhymed stanzas—establishes a form in the first and last stanzas that the middle stanza undercuts or escapes.[3] The poem's structure juxtaposes opposites, says yes and no at the same time, like the personifications phrased as questions. Moreover, even in the first and last stanzas the rigid, formal pattern seems to break down, to be pushed, like the experiments with personification, so far in one direction that the pattern circles back. In every case, the first and final lines of the abba quatrain rhyme exactly, repeating the same word. While this repetition enriches and deepens the resonance of the repeated words, there is a curious way in which it hides the structure, the music (Ruark 1991). Rhyming words are drawn together as much by their differences as by their similarities; somehow "edges" and "ledges" call attention to rhyme, while "green" and "green" do not. The rigidity of the repetition ironically overreaches its purpose, "as when emotion too far exceeds its cause," and illustrates the tension between freedom and enclosure that pervades the poem.

The dialectic between freedom and enclosure, between meaning and meaninglessness, relates to and returns to the figure of the human body. In the second stanza, visual appreciation of the map tempts the speaker to impose imagination more overtly, to desire a tactile relationship, and this imposition signals the break from the more structured stanza form to the looser, freer one:

> The shadow of Newfoundland lies flat and still.
> Labrador's yellow, where the moony Eskimo
> has oiled it. We can stroke these lovely bays,
> under a glass as if they were expected to blossom,
> or as if to provide a clean cage for invisible fish.
> The names of seashore towns run out to sea,
> the names of cities cross the neighboring mountains
> —the printer here experiencing the same excitement
> as when emotion too far exceeds its cause.
> These peninsulas take the water between thumb and finger
> like women feeling for the smoothness of yard-goods.

The simile of the last two lines of the stanza projects the tactile response back onto the personified land and increases the humanity of the figure by giving it a gender. The metaphysical distance in the comparison between peninsulas and women's hands produces a startling effect; rather than making the land more comprehensible, the simile makes the apparently familiar image of women feeling fabric seem strange. It makes the body seem foreign, other.

Helen McNeil discusses this reversal as a tendency in Bishop's poetry to see or create something awry in an apparently familiar place, and she links that tendency to Freud's theory of the uncanny (1987, 410). The uncanny, often manifesting itself in dreams and sometimes in what Bishop called "the always-more-successful surrealism of everyday life" (Stevenson 1966, 66), surfaces as a feeling that the known world possesses the deepest secrets, the most horrifying undersides, that it is actually unknown and unknowable. Like the familiar barn cat whose face suddenly becomes a bare skull in Richard Wilbur's poem "Walking to Sleep," Bishop's uncanny images reproduce the mixture of the familiar and the odd that dreams often produce. McNeil suggests that the Freudian uncanny in Bishop's poems often surrounds femininity and motherhood, and in "The Map," women testing fabric suggests women who are also mothers, women who create homes. Yet on a still more fundamental level, the most powerfully uncanny images—in the Freudian sense—combine home, the familiar, and death, the otherworldly. Helen Vendler suggests that in Bishop's work domestication is part of the force of love, the force of this world, that we use to counter death, the force of the other world (1980, 34). The tension of this struggle, the juxtaposition of home, the known, and death, the unknown, creates a rift in the certainty of perception. This juxtaposition also seems to arise naturally from Bishop's own experience, from her early, shattering losses, especially the loss of her mother, and her constant preoccupation with the connection between home, the familiar, and loss, the movement from the familiar to the otherworldly.

In "The Map," the sense of the uncanny derives from the deepening sense of the limits of human perception and the way those limits define choice and mortality. Wherever the gaze of the poem shifts, the poet's imposition of bodily existence supplants accurate vision. All the boundaries of the map—the shape of Norway, the seacoasts—define bodily boundaries, look like the body of a hare, the profile of a face:

> Mapped waters are more quiet than the land is,
> lending the land their waves' own conformation:
> and Norway's hare runs south in agitation,
> profiles investigate the sea where land is.

Sybil Estess notes that the characterization of Norway as a hare reveals the centrality of perception to the interpretation of the poem: "Bishop suggests in these lines that what one sees depends on how one looks" (1983, 220). The definition of bodily boundaries in this stanza is whimsical, teasing, tests the possibility that every boundary acts like skin, defines an individual entity, an individual will. Bishop moves then from personification that describes visually to personification that posits human emotion and the human responsibility of choice:

Are they assigned, or can the countries pick their colors?
—What suits the character or the native waters best.
Topography displays no favorites; North's as near as West.
More delicate than the historians' are the mapmakers' colors.

Again, the personifying line is phrased as an almost playful question:
"Are they assigned, or can the countries pick their colors?" This
question, like those that open the poem, toys with seemingly inno-
cent problems of choice and perception, teasingly invites the reader
to participate, to examine the true source of preference, which is
the mechanism of human perception and perception's effect on
choice. The intimate involvement between perception and choice
surfaces again and again in Bishop's work as she struggles with the
question, "If we cannot know how can we choose, act, how can we
live?" But, as the fanciful tone of the poem suggests, this struggle
is not pathetic or even unmitigatedly serious; the final stanza implies
that the effects of perception's limitations are both crippling and
strangely beneficial. Though it necessarily limits and distorts, becomes a "clean cage" that separates seer from seen, human perception can also magically transform through the imposition of imagination: "North's as near as West."

The realization that perception both limits and transforms makes
the last sentence less straightforward and more ironic than most
critics allow. The line has proved problematic to many readers. Many
critics of Bishop's career take this line as gospel, as expressing a real
preference, and use it, as Thomas Travisano points out, as a foundation to explain all of Bishop's poems, early and late, as though they
reject the flow of history in favor of the controlled and controllable
world of the mapmaker (1988, 9). Travisano himself accepts the
literal reading of the last line but suggests that Bishop rejects the
philosophy of antihistoricism in her late work. But in a basically
comic poem that explores and dismantles the human power of perception and choice to the degree that "The Map" does, is it reasonable or prudent to accept as absolute truth a last line that makes
what appears to be a choice? I think the confrontation between
mapmaker and historian in the final line of "The Map" is an ironic

one. How can the poet, or anyone, choose between the two ways of knowing when both ways reflect a reality that is deeply flawed and magically transformed by being filtered through human bodies? Further, I do not take "more delicate" to mean "more true," or even necessarily better in any way.

The inversion of the final line, the only near-archaism of the poem, makes the sentence sound almost like the playful and evocative questions that the reader has already answered: "Does the land lean down to lift the sea from under?" and "Are they assigned, or can the countries pick their colors?" Are the mapmakers' colors more delicate than the historians'? Perhaps. Perhaps the mapmaker's art is more limitable, more accurate, or, as James Merrill suggests, "a more lovable enterprise than the cataloging of human deeds" (*Voices and Visions*), but both mapmaker and historian, as human individuals, possess the same gift and curse as the poet: whatever they look at wears the mark of their looks. Both delicately transform and give human meaning to apparent chaos, and both cannot help but distort and limit, and perhaps make accurate knowing impossible. The poem neither makes a choice nor asks the reader to make a choice; however, it does explore the problem of choosing, the difficulty of perceiving. By delaying the mention of human history until the final line, Bishop carefully leads the reader to accept a line of questioning that might otherwise prove unsatisfactory. If we have acknowledged that the supposedly accurate task of mapmaking can be colored by the perceptions, prejudices, and senses of the mapmaker, then in acknowledging that the same must be true of the historian we challenge our own ability to understand our past and, therefore, our present. Moreover, we acknowledge that nothing we create—neither maps, nor histories, nor even, or especially, poems—can represent absolute or eternal truth. Estess notes, "Bishop seems to make a judgement in 'The Map' concerning the efficacy of all 'maps,' of all invented, artistic images" (1983, 221). "The Map," like Bishop's experiments with personification, seriously and comically questions the value of its own enterprise.

Bishop continues, throughout *North & South* and throughout her career, to question the worth of embodiment in poetic form, and she consistently relates those questions to meditations on the self, or considerations of embodiment in the concrete, isolated human flesh. Robert Pinsky suggests that the value of mapping and poetry is similar because they both restore the self by "defining what we are not" (1983, 52). I think it is more accurate to say that mapping, like history, poetry, or any art, restores the self by turning the self outward, toward the self's own reflection in everything sensed and created. Karl Malkoff, in his book *Escaping the Self,* defines this dialectic, the tension between internal and external, the desire simultaneously to escape and establish the self, as the characteristic feature of contemporary American poetry. The poem that follows "The Map" in *North & South,* "The Imaginary Iceberg," dramatizes a paradoxical search for the self through the imagination and through the imagination's reproduction of physical reality. By introducing a human character, the sailor, to act as one protagonist of the poem (the other being the iceberg), Bishop dramatically defines questions of perception she had addressed in "The Map." The title "The Imaginary Iceberg" proves crucial because it functions as the reader's best clue to the complexity of the poem's perspective. The title immediately calls attention to the degree to which the iceberg is imaginary: it is placed in the poem by the poet's imagination, but as a phenomenon it also exists outside the poem as an object that is wholly other.[4] Imagination is the source of the poet's and the sailor's vision of the iceberg, but they also paradoxically imagine an iceberg that finally resists their imaginings. It remains both ineffable and the mirror of human understanding.

The otherness of the iceberg, the way its distance promises a reflection of the self, makes it much more desirable than even necessary and useful human contrivances, like ships:

> We'd rather have the iceberg than the ship,
> although it meant the end of travel.
> Although it stood stock-still like cloudy rock,
> and all the sea were moving marble. (*Poems,* 4)

The inanimate quality of both iceberg and sea expressed in the phrases "cloudy rock" and "moving marble" will change dramatically, in the second stanza, as the poet's imagination draws the iceberg closer to human apprehension by giving it a human body.

Bishop's repetition of the phrase "We'd rather have the iceberg than
the ship" in the latter part of the first stanza increases the sense of
the mind struggling to apprehend and draw in the external object.
Of course, however, the iceberg has been co-opted by the imagination, becomes internal; the life that endows it is the life of the mind
itself. Thus the imagination inspires, in the exact sense of that word,
and suddenly the iceberg begins to breathe, to feed; the sea becomes
a pasture:

> We'd rather have the iceberg than the ship;
> we'd rather own this breathing plain of snow
> though the ship's sails were laid upon the sea
> as the snow lies undissolved upon the water.
> O solemn, floating field,
> are you aware an iceberg takes repose
> with you, and when it wakes may pasture on your snows?

The "solemn, floating field" could refer to the pasture of the imagination as well as the pasture of the sea, because the iceberg feeds
on both elements. Both as an internal creation and as an external
phenomenon, the iceberg is beautiful, ineffable, cold, and terribly
distant. It is a strange and forbidding image for bodily desire, one
that suggests the peril of connecting with any longed-for object,
imaginary or real.

   In the second stanza, Bishop focuses on the sailor rather than the
iceberg and makes dramatic the act of perception that underlies the
figure of the first stanza. Kalstone suggests that the cliché "give his
eyes for" applies exactly to the situation of the sailor or the situation
of any human being dazzled by perception and desire; the desire to
find the truth, a true reflection, is simultaneously the desire to stop
looking (1977, 27):

> This is a scene a sailor'd give his eyes for.
> The ship's ignored. The iceberg rises
> and sinks again; its glassy pinnacles
> correct elliptics in the sky.

As in "The Colder the Air," sightlessness is the state of perfection.
The iceberg, with its "glassy pinnacles / correct elliptics," reflects
that state of changelessness, elliptical in its geometrical perfection,

a closed plane that seeks no addition, and also elliptical in the sense of linguistic precision, extreme verbal economy. The ship, the means of motion through space and time, is ignored in favor of stillness that suggests the inertia and silence of perfection. To the sailor in the second stanza, as to the poet in the first, the iceberg initially appears completely other, nonhuman. The distance of the iceberg draws both sailor and poet because it promises an opposite that might define and annihilate the self, a way to stop looking, to escape the body. This desired annihilation of the self revolves around a desire for bodilessness, fixation on a terribly cold object that turns out to be a projection of at least the idea of a soul. However, the sailor does not find a perfect antithesis, a bodiless spirit, in the iceberg. Sailor, poet, and reader, in fact, find no unbodied, absolute perfection at all, only the reflection of the entire, imperfect, living self, body and soul indivisible. The iceberg, like the map, takes on human qualities in the eye of the human perceiver; the act of looking draws the iceberg away from otherness and draws it through the distorting and enlivening lens of human perception. In the latter part of the second stanza, then, the sailor and the iceberg become two players on one stage, the stage of the imagination:

> This is a scene where he who treads the boards
> is artlessly rhetorical. The curtain
> is light enough to rise on finest ropes
> that airy twists of snow provide.
> The wits of these white peaks
> spar with the sun. Its weight the iceberg dares
> upon a shifting stage and stands and stares.

The iceberg's actions have been invested with human will, and now they exactly mirror the actions of the sailor; both dare their weight on the shifting stage of the sea, and both stare at each other intently.

The result of this personification is that the iceberg fails to liberate and annihilate the self; neither the sailor nor the poet can stop looking and forget the ship:

> Good-bye, we say, good-bye, the ship steers off
> where waves give in to one another's waves
> and clouds run in a warmer sky.

This movement seems ambivalent; although poet, sailor, and, by implication, reader have failed again to find any true reflection of a self beyond the distortion of bodily perception, we are headed for a warmer sky, and the waves' giving in to each other offers a soothing promise of calm seas. While the description of the iceberg in the final stanza resonates with human significance, Bishop's return to the poet's perspective and the details she emphasizes suggest an attempt at distance, a relational view that looks for difference. As the stanza begins, the iceberg is seemingly as isolated in subjectivity as the sailor; it "cuts its facets from within." However, the iceberg is different in that it does not search out its own reflection, cannot move, change, or be changed by the adornment of the perceiver's gaze:

> This iceberg cuts its facets from within.
> Like jewelry from a grave
> it saves itself perpetually and adorns
> only itself, perhaps the snows
> which so surprise us lying on the sea.

In each stanza, the poem moves back and forth between perspectives that attempt to differentiate the iceberg from the human observers and perspectives that invest the iceberg with human form. This vacillation illustrates the problem of perception and calls into question the worth of attention; why should observation continue if meaningful looking is inaccurate and accurate looking is meaningless? The last three lines of the poem seem to rephrase this implicit question without resolving it. Although the iceberg does not reflect the perfection and changelessness the soul desires, for that would annihilate the self and mean the end of looking, the iceberg reflects another, perhaps more useful, truth:

> Icebergs behoove the soul
> (both being self-made from elements least visible)
> to see them so: fleshed, fair, erected indivisible.

The word "behoove" is crucial and paradoxical because it both distances the poet from the iceberg and strangely anthropomorphizes the iceberg; it is a cold word, implying not desire or identification but correct action, propriety. While the iceberg is incapable of advantage through observation, the soul gains by observing the iceberg. However, in interpreting the final lines of this poem, some critics have substituted "is" for "behoove," suggesting that the soul equals the iceberg. Anne Stevenson suggests that the iceberg is "creative imagination" (1966, 73). Bonnie Costello argues that the iceberg corresponds directly to the invisible human soul (1983, 109). The construction of the sentence around "behoove," however, makes the parallel more relational than equal. The iceberg relates more to the human desire for the soul than to the soul itself. Though the iceberg does not equal or symbolize the invisible, unbodied substance of the soul, it calls on the soul to recognize a parallel: both the soul and the iceberg create themselves from what is "least visible," and neither the creation of the soul nor the creation of the iceberg can be separated from what is most visible, from bodily, physical existence. Both iceberg and soul are "erected indivisible," not from each other but within themselves. Inasmuch as the iceberg and the soul are the invisible made visible, they are both metaphors, embodiments of what is and can perhaps be sensed, but cannot be known, or resolved.

Having separated body and soul, reason ends and the comparison with the iceberg breaks down; in Bishop's poems the objects of the phenomenological world will be drawn only so far into human understanding and no further. The paradox the poem wrestles with is a paradox of embodiment; the soul is by definition not-body, but to know or imagine the soul we must embody it in the phenomenological world. Thus Bishop's fantastic and nightmarish iceberg reveals the coldness, the forbidding distance, of any bodiless and perfect other. The poem explores, not the iceberg itself, but the paradoxical human reaction to the iceberg. The imaginary iceberg represents both what we seem to want, what we would "give our eyes for," and what we most avoid and fear, the end of looking. This paradox of embodiment in "The Imaginary Iceberg" centers on the double nature of the flesh as simultaneously a living organism connected to the contingent world of other organisms and objects, and also the mediator through which the invisible self comprehends the visible world.

In both "The Map" and "The Imaginary Iceberg," Bishop explores the distortions and colorings caused by the body acting as the mediator between internal and external reality. Doubt about the senses' ability to perceive maps and icebergs implies more doubt about the senses' ability to perceive anything, including the form they occupy, the body itself. In the "The Gentleman of Shalott," Bishop explores the implications of this insight in a light-handed, comic tone that manages to keep a graceful balance between parody of the Gentleman's situation, which we all share, and respect for his attention, which few risk.

Tennyson's Lady of Shalott has been cursed with a life of indirect perception: "moving thro' a mirror clear / That hangs before her all the year, / Shadows of the world appear" (Houghton and Stange 1968, 15). The Lady makes beautiful tapestries from the shadows, but she cannot participate directly in life lest her mirror crack and she be condemned. Some Tennyson critics compare her predicament to the situation of the artist, doomed to a life of observation. In contrast, Bishop's Gentleman of Shalott theorizes that indirect perception is the universal curse. Though "The Gentleman of Shalott," like Tennyson's "The Lady of Shalott," revolves around the question of "true" sight and its price, for the Gentleman there is no possibility of not looking in the mirror:

> Which eye's his eye?
> Which limb lies
> next the mirror?
> For neither is clearer
> nor a different color
> than the other,
> nor meets a stranger
> in this arrangement
> of leg and leg and
> arm and so on. (*Poems*, 9)

The first lines of "The Gentleman of Shalott" echo the first lines of Tennyson's "The Lady of Shalott" and make the same play on the word "lie." For both Tennyson and Bishop, the pun suggests the eternal appearance/reality dichotomy. However, Tennyson's lines,

"On either side the river lie / Long fields of barley and of rye" (Houghton and Stange 1968, 15), emphasize the doubleness existing in the construction of reality, the reality that will be ironically doubled again, that will "lie" in both the sense of being placed and the sense of being reversed and represented falsely in the mirror. On the other hand, Bishop's poem questions how we can know that reality is doubled in the first place, and it suggests that the conviction that reality is doubled, the trait of self-consciousness, ends up strangely cutting reality in half. The meter and rhyme of "The Gentleman of Shalott," numerous variations on a rollicking two-foot couplet, recall and poke fun at Tennyson's even and sonorous rhymed tetrameter and tone of allegorical certainty. The form of Bishop's poem, its rapid motion and flat tone, heightens the comedy and increases the unsettling effect of the poem; we end up amused by an uncertainty that we share with the character.

The report of the senses and its relative correspondence to truth is the crux of the Gentleman's theorizing. Having ascertained that he is symmetrical, he attributes his arrangement to a falsely or artificially doubled singleness rather than a symmetrical or organically doubled singleness:

> To his mind
> it's the indication
> of a mirrored reflection
> somewhere along the line
> of what we call the spine.

The phrase "what we call the spine" demonstrates the grave risk implicit in his odd vision. The Gentleman must discard or at least form a new relationship to the language that defines and mediates his own body for his understanding; the spine cannot properly be called the spine if it is actually an edge. The line seems partly to mock the Gentleman for the self-consciousness that isolates him and partly to explore his real predicament.

Moreover, the tone of the whole sentence imitates and mocks the language of scientific certainty that must rely, like the Gentleman of Shalott, on the application of data attained by human senses, that must always qualify with phrases like "the indication of" and "what we call." All such data, the next stanza suggests, can be swayed by internal or emotional circumstance. The Gentleman's novel perspective derives not only from what seems like empirical data—"For neither is clearer / nor a different color / than the other"—but also from a rather subjective, although perhaps self-conscious and false, sense of humility:

> He felt in modesty
> his person was
> half looking-glass,
> for why should he
> be doubled?
> The glass must stretch
> down his middle,
> or rather down the edge.
> But he's in doubt
> as to which side's in or out
> of the mirror.

Denis Donoghue points out that one of the most important words in all of Bishop's poems is the preposition *in*. *In* calls up its opposite, *out,* and indicates the presence of boundaries, the tension between presence and absence, between the present moment and the inevitable loss of houses, people, and love (1984, 247). The speaker in Bishop's 1938 short story "In Prison" says, "One must be in, that is the primary condition" (*Prose,* 182); however, in "The Gentleman of Shalott," "In Prison," and throughout Bishop's work, doubt surrounds the condition of being in. Getting to the interior, in so many of her poems, can be achieved through the force of attention, the power of perception. Yet reliance on perception brings the corresponding risk of uncertainty, as the latter part of the second stanza of "The Gentleman of Shalott" indicates:

> There's little margin for error,
> but there's no proof, either.
> And if half his head's reflected,
> thought, he thinks, might be affected.

The hilarious couplet, the comic paradox, at which the Gentleman arrives marks the turning point of the poem and illustrates the problem of self-conscious perception. When he thinks thought might be affected, the Gentleman falls into the nested loop of human reasoning, the distorted knowledge that perspective distorts knowing. The character, the poet, and the reader are in crisis. But Bishop does not take any of us so seriously that we must collapse under the weight of uncertainty. Jarrell writes, "Instead of crying 'This is a world in which no one can get along' Miss Bishop's poems show that it is barely but perfectly possible" (1983, 181). The Gentleman of Shalott does not, like the Lady of Shalott, paint his name around the prow and head downstream to death. Instead, he gets along, even enjoys living with the uncertainty of his own perception:

> But he's resigned
> to such economical design.
> If the glass slips
> he's in a fix—
> only one leg, etc. But
> while it stays put
> he can walk and run
> and his hands can clasp one
> another. The uncertainty
> he says he
> finds exhilarating. He loves
> that sense of constant re-adjustment.
> He wishes to be quoted as saying at present:
> "Half is enough."

Of course, according to his own perception, the Gentleman is not "half"; he is a reflected whole. Bishop's mock newspaper reporter tone, "He wishes to be quoted as saying at present," another swipe at a style of language reliant on "fact," emphasizes the degree to which language influences perception. The need to readjust constantly, especially to readjust language so it reflects the perception of the fleeting present rather than recycling the stale or expected, is the paradox of the Gentleman of Shalott that Bishop both mocks and also revels in.

In "The Gentleman of Shalott," as in "The Map" and "The Imaginary Iceberg," the question of truth centers on the metaphor of the body and the way the body functions as a barrier between internal and external, between self and not-self. Although the content of these early poems involves more contrived, invented, or "poetic" material than Bishop will tend to employ in her later work, these poems do not represent what Travisano calls "sealed imaginary worlds" (1988, 3). Rather than projecting a wish for control that Travisano's statement implies, they create a microcosmic reality that is as uncertain, unstable, and unmanageable as the human reality on which they comment. Although occasionally threatened by the uncertain world, Bishop, like the Gentleman of Shalott, often enjoys the uncertainty, the instability, and often treats it comically. These poems and poems like "Chemin de Fer," "Seascape," and "Little Exercise" wrestle with the paradox of knowledge and the way the senses, the body, make it possible and impossible; but, though they insistently question the worth of the poet's task, they do not collapse into despair or into any tempting but one-sided resolution.

While "The Map," "The Imaginary Iceberg," and "The Gentleman of Shalott" begin to suggest the importance of attention and its relationship to the movement toward and understanding of the interior, other poems in *North & South* move toward a fuller realization of these themes. "Large Bad Picture" and "The Monument," two poems about two very different works of art, suggest a movement beyond realizing that perception is a "clean cage" and toward dramatizing possible actions in the face of our constant uncertainty. Both use different dialectical forms that draw no conclusions, achieve no certain resolutions, but posit the form itself as a means of enlarging and perhaps escaping momentarily the claustrophobia of the single perspective.

In a letter to Anne Stevenson, Bishop wrote this often-quoted assessment: "What one seems to want in art, in experiencing it, is the same thing that is necessary for its creation, a self-forgetful, perfectly useless concentration" (1966, 66). The desire to connect with something or someone outside the self, to escape momentarily the confines of an egocentric vision, like, perhaps, the self-consciousness of the Gentleman of Shalott, motivates both the appreciation and creation of art. "Large Bad Picture" concerns the possibility for connection inherent in the created form, the obstructions to that

connection, and the transforming power of the human imagination. As Penelope Laurens suggests, "Large Bad Picture" juxtaposes
Bishop's desire to connect, not just with another artist, but with a
member of her family and a part of her own past, with her understanding that she may be, both personally and artistically, beyond
contact (1983, 82). The tone of the first stanza bears out Laurens's
reading, as the flat, remote quality of the voice parallels the flat,
remote quality of the great-uncle's painting:

> Remembering the Strait of Belle Isle or
> some northerly harbor of Labrador,
> before he became a schoolteacher
> a great-uncle painted a big picture. (*Poems*, 11)

Here the galumphing couplets and the awkward, funny "Isle or /
Labrador" rhyme create a light, comic tone, as rollicking couplets
and rhyme did in "The Gentleman of Shalott." However, there
is the characteristic serious underside. The tension of the first five
stanzas derives from Bishop's attention to and desire for connection
with the painting played off against the failure of the painter's technique, and her tone of artistic condescension in the light of this
failure. The opening couplets change to quatrains, and Bishop's mi-
nutely detailed descriptions of the painting contrast with the painting's lack of detail and flat exposition:

> Receding for miles on either side
> into a flushed, still sky
> are overhanging pale blue cliffs
> hundreds of feet high,
>
> their bases fretted by little arches,
> the entrances to caves
> running in along the level of a bay
> masked by perfect waves.

The quality that the "flushed, still sky" lacks is precisely the quality of vividness that Bishop admires in her essay about the Mexi-
can "primitive" painter Gregorio Valdes. Bishop's description of
Valdes's painting reveals not only the lack she finds in her uncle's
work but the strategy she employs in her own: "It was a view, a real

View, of a straight road diminishing to a point through green fields, and a row of straight Royal Palms on either side, so carefully painted that one could count seven trees in each row. . . . The sky was blue at the top, then white, then beautiful blush pink, the pink of a hot, mosquito-filled tropical evening" (*Prose*, 51). The great-uncle paints a view, but his is not a "real View" because it is missing the uniqueness of vision that would allow the viewer to feel as though she had connected with something outside of herself, seen the world as someone else had. Expectations, clichés of knowing, like the "perfect waves," the "pale blue cliffs," the "spars like burnt matchsticks," dull the senses and prevent both escape from the self and, paradoxically, self-realization. What Bishop seems to admire and aspire to is what her great-uncle's "Large Bad Picture" lacks, the "primitive" insistence on detail, a technique that holds tenaciously to verisimilitude, to the details of the concrete world, not because they are externally certain but because they provide the best possibility for some internal connection, communication. Bishop once wrote to Lowell: "My passion for accuracy may strike you as old-maidish—but since we do float on an unknown sea I think we should examine the other floating things that come our way very carefully; who knows what might depend on it" (Kalstone 1989, 213). For Bishop, the "other floating things"—the details, large or small, animate or inanimate—offered a vital if momentary chance for connection and communication on which a great deal depended.

In another autobiographical piece, "The U.S.A. School of Writing," Bishop explains that her experience as a correspondence school teacher made her realize that, in contrast to the often overwhelming detail of the primitive painter, the mark of an untutored writer is missing, inadequate, or inappropriate detail: "There seems to be one thing in common to all 'primitive' writing, as I suppose it might be called, in contrast to primitive painting: its slipshodiness and haste. . . . the primitive writer seems in a hurry to get it over with. Another thing is the almost complete lack of detail. The primitive painter loves detail and lingers over it and emphasizes it at the expense of the picture as a whole. But if the writers put them in, the details are often impossibly or wildly inappropriate" (*Prose*, 46). Bishop's observations about craft provide insight into the strategy of her form in "Large Bad Picture." Though she is by no means a primitive writer, in this poem, and in others through the course of her career, she adapts the techniques of the primitive painter, particularly the accretion of numerous vivid details, in order to arrive at a moment of connection, however transitory, between artist and audience. As I noted in the introduction, *detail* has become a loaded word in Bishop criticism, and I am in no way aligning myself with some of Bishop's critics, who accuse her of amassing "charming little stained glass bits" (Williams 1983, 185) or working in the "feminine art of the miniature" (McNeil 1987, 397). Instead of shrinking reality to manageable size, Bishop's vital details relate to the whole work in a paradoxical way similar to the senses' relation to the body or the individual's relation to the species, a relation that is at once circumscribed and unmanageably vast and complex. The form of "Large Bad Picture" employs a verse technique that resembles the technique of a primitive painter, building through accretion of detail to a moment in which the work of art transcends the physical detail in which it is and must be grounded and moves toward a more complete—more spiritual, if you will—integration of the concrete and abstract, the visible and invisible.

The off rhymes and variable meter of "Large Bad Picture" cause the reader to readjust repeatedly, pulling back from what Laurens calls "lyric intensity that might allow sentimentality" (1983, 88). Laurens argues that the form cultivates roughness to ridicule the great-uncle's artistic attempt, that it relies on "imitation roughness" or a "mock naive tone" (83). However, I think Bishop's rough-edged music, vivid details, and refusal to sentimentalize do not mock the painting's technique by imitation so much as reveal by contrast the qualities the painting lacks, the benefit of fresh vision that refuses to be swept along, to smooth out the vivid and specific. Bishop's roughness, in all but the couplets of the first stanza, comes closer to imitating the dense technique of the primitive painter than the flattened technique of her great-uncle's bad picture.

However, in both the poem and the painting, technique stands in the way of connection. The uncle's failed brushstrokes, relentlessly cataloged by the poet's evaluative, artistic eye in the first five stanzas, do not seem to progress toward anything. It is not until the evaluative eye locates the weakest, most simplistic element in the painting's technique—the "scribbled . . . black birds / hanging in *n*'s in banks"—that a new perspective intervenes. In the sixth stanza the scene suddenly comes alive through the force of the new vision, the imaginative eye:

> And high above them, over the tall cliffs'
> semi-translucent ranks,
> are scribbled hundreds of fine black birds
> hanging in *n*'s in banks.
>
> One can hear their crying, crying,
> the only sound there is
> except for occasional sighing
> as a large aquatic animal breathes.

Bishop makes an imaginative connection by overcoming the painter's technique and her own catalog of visual detail. In the sixth stanza, when she stops looking and begins listening, the painting, like the "large aquatic animal," breathes, suddenly comes to life. Although the poem does not sufficiently forecast this shift to make it as profound as it might be (and will be in later pieces, such as "Poem"), the movement from the evaluative to the imaginative vision nevertheless transforms failure and makes fleeting connection possible.

In the final two stanzas of "Large Bad Picture," the poet seems to report from inside the painting, and the particulars of this strange pink world become more compelling. Though the painting has little sense of real ships or harbors, what in "The Bight" Bishop calls "the untidy activity," the poet's attention has opened a path to the interior of the contemplative reality of her great-uncle's admittedly bad picture:

> In the pink light
> the small red sun goes rolling, rolling,
> round and round and round at the same height
> in perpetual sunset, comprehensive, consoling,
>
> while the ships consider it.
> Apparently they have reached their destination.

It would be hard to say what brought them there,
commerce or contemplation.

"Large Bad Picture" is a dialogue between two visions that, without canceling each other out, complement each other and enlarge the possibility for connection, for penetration. The final sentence both gently rebukes the painter, harkening back to the first stanza, and also suggests the heretofore tacit connection between the poet and the painter: they have both contemplated and restored this scene by internalizing it in their imaginations. "Large Bad Picture" combines two simultaneous and opposing realizations—that connection with the great-uncle and his painting is both impossible, because of the barriers of time and technique, and perfectly possible, because of attention and imagination.

"The Monument" demonstrates similar possibilities. The movement inward in "The Monument" parallels the movement into the painting in "Large Bad Picture." Also inspired by a visual artifact, a wood rubbing by Max Ernst, "The Monument" presents a dialogue between seer and seen, perception and reality, and suggests not only the road to the interior, as "Large Bad Picture" did, but what one can hope to find having taken this road. The dialogic structure of "The Monument" is integral to the poem's themes. While the first voice acts as a spokesperson for the monument, a sort of priestess of its imaginative meaning, the second voice continually asserts its otherness, the reality of the monument's appearance, and questions its relationship to the viewer. Though the poem gives over more space and sympathy to the first voice, the voice of imaginative apprehension, both are dramatically necessary to reach the climactic moment, the direction "Watch it closely." Like the first five stanzas of "Large Bad Picture," the first voice of "The Monument" gathers vivid visual detail that calls attention to the act of perception. The first voice leads us to the monument:

Now can you see the monument? It is of wood
built somewhat like a box. No. Built
like several boxes in descending sizes
one above the other.

> Each is turned half-way round so that
> its corners point toward the sides
> of the one below and the angles alternate. (*Poems,* 23)

As the description progresses, the sheer number and complexity of details begin to disorient rather than clarify; the intersection of angles, holes, fretwork, fleur-de-lys, fishing poles, flagpoles, and ornament becomes bewildering. And, we find, as the details multiply and we struggle for accurate vision, that we are not beyond the monument and looking at it from a distance, as though looking at a painting, as it first appeared we were; rather, we are part of the picture, our perspective is "within the view":

> The view is geared
> (that is, the view's perspective)
> so low there is no "far away,"
> and we are far away within the view.

As the poem progresses and we are drawn deeper in, "the monument" of the first line becomes "our lonely monument," and the first voice reveals that everything "within the view," foreground and background, appears to be made of the same substance as our monument:

> A sea of narrow, horizontal boards
> lies out behind our lonely monument,
> its long grains alternating right and left
> like floor-boards—spotted, swarming-still,
> and motionless. A sky runs parallel,
> and its palings, coarser than the sea's:
> splintery sunlight and long-fibred clouds.

Just when the first voice threatens to dissolve all otherness, all separateness, by asserting that the cloud, the sky, and the sea are all made of the same wood as the monument, the second voice intervenes and interrogates the first, asking for particular place-names and locations:

> "Why does that strange sea make no sound?
> Is it because we're far away?

Where are we? Are we in Asia Minor,
or in Mongolia?"

The dialogue between the voices pits an imaginative view that prefers suggestion against an accurate view that demands facts. To the second voice's direct question "What is that?" the first voice gives an answer that implies the structure's meaning: "It is the monument." The second voice replies by insisting on sense data: "It's piled-up boxes, / outlined with shoddy fret-work, half-fallen off, / cracked and unpainted. It looks old." While the second voice insists on the monument's death, "I am tired of breathing this eroded air, / this dryness in which the monument is cracking," the first voice emphasizes how the details endow it with life:

> The monument's an object, yet those decorations,
> carelessly nailed, looking like nothing at all,
> give it away as having life, and wishing;
> wanting to be a monument, to cherish something.

Helen McNeil points out that the monument is a signifying structure, that it "has an inside and an outside like the body" (1987, 406). Throughout the poem, the subtext of the descriptions of the monument, particularly in the words of the first voice, is a personification that endows the monument with human characteristics, perspective. In the same way that within the perspective of the monument everything appears to be wood, within human perspective everything appears to be human. The dialogue between the two voices, perhaps two internal voices of one speaker, resembles the dialogue between the monument and what it signifies and the viewer. Here, as in "The Map," "The Imaginary Iceberg," and "The Gentleman of Shalott," perspective limits and distorts. However, like "Large Bad Picture," "The Monument" offers a moment of connection and transformation brought about by close attention, a glimpse of

> what is within (which after all
> cannot have been intended to be seen).
> It is the beginning of a painting,

a piece of sculpture, or poem, or monument,
and all of wood. Watch it closely.

The innermost place, the sanctum of art, is the secret that perspective denies access to, the secret of origins to be sought by moving
through the seen toward what was not "intended to be seen." The
movement of the poem toward the climactic exhortation, "Watch
it closely," comes through the interaction between the two voices,
and, spoken in the first voice, does not discredit but rather reinforces
the second voice's demands for accuracy.

"Large Bad Picture" and "The Monument" move beyond the inescapable circularity of Bishop's experiments in personification and
even beyond the certainty of uncertainty expressed in "The Map,"
"The Imaginary Iceberg," and "The Gentleman of Shalott." These
poems suggest the possibility of action, assertions of human will,
that could define and counter the uncertainty of the human body
and senses. Both poems concern the journey out of the self and into
another vision, a willingness and desire to connect with the contingent world through passionate attention. However, in both cases it
is a vision that is held strangely still, or, as in "The Monument,"
"swarming-still," by the artifact. These poems establish the necessity of attention and connection for the journey toward the inner
world, toward the origin that "was not intended to be seen." However, Bishop does not seem content to rest with the connection
to the artifact; in poems such as "The Man-Moth," "A Miracle for
Breakfast," and "The Fish" she offers different possibilities for connection and explores more fully the risk of self-actualization and
self-destruction in the act of attention.

"Pure Enough to Drink": Internalizing the Other

In "Large Bad Picture" and "The Monument," the opportunity
for connection comes about through passionate attention that draws
the self outward and into another perspective. In other poems in
North & South, Bishop almost reverses this outward movement in
favor of a strange and passionate attention that ends in internalization, an enlargement of, rather than escape from, perspective, the

self. Robert Pinsky suggests that Bishop's "great subject is the contest—or truce, or trade agreement—between the single human soul
on one side and, on the other, the contingent world of artifacts and
other people" (1983, 49). *North & South* establishes what will become Bishop's continuous struggle with the world beyond the isolated self, a struggle that is not linear, but rather, as Pinsky suggests,
vacillates, at one moment a contest, followed by an uneasy truce, a
necessary trade agreement, followed by another mortal battle. Some
of Bishop's most complex and beautiful explorations of connection
with the contingent world occur in the poems in *North & South* in
which she posits internalizing as a means of connection—taking the
outside into the self rather than abolishing the self or projecting
the self onto the other.[5]

In "The Man-Moth" Bishop explores the mortal battle between
the individual and the contingent world, and between the individual
and his or her own desires. Typical of Bishop's love of surprise, of
the unexpected, the title and inspiration for "The Man-Moth" came
from a newspaper misprint for "mammoth." Bishop includes this
fact as a note to the original publication of the poem because, I
think, the genesis of the creature reveals an important path to the
origins of meaning in the poem. The creature created by a combination of inspiration and accident challenges the boundaries of
word and thing and becomes, as Costello suggests, "perhaps a symbol of the repressed psyche of urban man" (1991, 51). The poet,
speaking from the "Here, above," shares Man's locale but not his
perspective; Man, separated from men, becomes another kind of
imagined creature, created partly by inspiration and partly by accident. Man and Man-Moth gain identity through relationship with
their surroundings and through the interrelationship created in the
mind of the reader and the structure of the poem. The two creatures are differentiated by their relative awareness of and attempt
to connect with their surroundings. Man belongs to a topography
that he cannot fathom:

> Here, above,
> cracks in the buildings are filled with battered moonlight.
> The whole shadow of Man is only as big as his hat.

It lies at his feet like a circle for a doll to stand on,
and makes an inverted pin, the point magnetized to the moon.
He does not see the moon; he observes only her vast properties,
feeling the queer light on his hands, neither warm nor cold,
of a temperature impossible to record in thermometers. (*Poems,* 14)

The "battered moonlight" prefigures the battering the Man-Moth
will take as he tries to connect with something beyond his natural
state, tries to gain access to some other world. Man resembles the
things he creates—a hat, a doll, a pin—but the things he creates
are impotent to control any portion of the world he lives in, the
world the Man-Moth regards with such attention. The temperature
of the moon is "impossible to record in thermometers." In contrast
to Man, who "does not see the moon," Man-Moth not only sees it
but finds that this primary sense experience forces further investigation, an investigation that involves risking fear and harm:

But when the Man-Moth
pays his rare, although occasional, visits to the surface,
the moon looks rather different to him. He emerges
from an opening under the edge of one of the sidewalks
and nervously begins to scale the faces of the buildings.
He thinks the moon is a small hole at the top of the sky,
proving the sky quite useless for protection.
He trembles, but must investigate as high as he can climb.

The difference between Man and Man-Moth is a difference of
attention. Narcissism limits Man's view; he sees only the "vast properties" of the moon where it directly touches his body, "feeling the
queer light on his hands." In contrast, the Man-Moth recognizes
the moon as other, a phenomenon outside himself that has implications for his existence. The Man-Moth's belief that the moon is not
an object but an opening, "proving the sky quite useless for protection," makes his reality much more precarious than Man's. Allowing that the immensity of the sky could be punctured and
worthless admits the possibility that other barriers or protections,
like homes and bodies, are suspect, made, like "Jerónimo's House,"
of "perishable clapboards" (*Poems,* 34). Yet this perspective also suggests, to the Man-Moth at least, that the limits that protective bar-

riers like homes and bodies impose on understanding can be over-come, that it is possible to be "forced through" into freedom. Be-cause of the paradox of his belief, the Man-Moth risks the annihi-lation implicit in the objects to which he has paid attention. But his great risk, his quest, is undercut by the comedy of the Man-Moth's own appearance and body, his creaturehood, by his fundamentally mistaken idea that the moon is a hole, and still further by the tone of Bishop's description, which suggests that a successful ending to his endeavor, or even a correction of his misapprehension, was never a possibility:

> Up the façades,
> his shadow dragging like a photographer's cloth behind him,
> he climbs fearfully, thinking that this time he will manage
> to push his small head through that round clean opening
> and be forced through, as from a tube, in black scrolls on the
> light.
> (Man, standing below him, has no such illusions.)
> But what he fears most he must do, although
> he fails, of course, and falls back scared but quite unhurt.

Thomas Travisano cites this stanza to prove that, in the earlier po-ems, Bishop creates worlds that lack the potential for communica-tion, that suffer from the sterility of enclosure—"the empty hero-ism of her Man-Moth, the useless beauty of her imaginary iceberg" (1988, 28). And, if "The Man-Moth" ended with the third stanza, the accusation of "empty heroism" would be justified. The reader would be left with a semicomic figure whose quest, whose failed attempt at knowledge, changed nothing and proved nothing. How-ever, in the context of the whole poem, the Man-Moth's heroism is no more empty than the imaginary iceberg's beauty is useless. Like "The Imaginary Iceberg," "The Man-Moth," rather than illuminat-ing one act of heroic investigation or a single beautiful phenome-non, concerns a dramatic series of actions and perceptions, the quest to establish and know the self, to connect the isolated being to the external world through attention. The "photographer's cloth" of the second stanza emphasizes the Man-Moth's attention, prefigures the importance of his huge eye. The fact that the portal resembles a tube presages the inevitable failure, the return to the subway, and suggests the birth canal imagery that pervades the end of the poem. The Man-Moth's heroism is not in the attempt to be forced through the hole of the moon but in his return to the subway—his resignation, like the Gentleman of Shalott's, to living with the uncertainty of perception:

> Then he returns
> to the pale subways of cement he calls his home. He flits,
> he flutters, and cannot get aboard the silent trains
> fast enough to suit him. The doors close swiftly.
> The Man-Moth always seats himself facing the wrong way
> and the train starts at once at its full, terrible speed,
> without a shift in gears or gradation of any sort.
> He cannot tell the rate at which he travels backwards.

The "f" and "s" sounds in these lines mimic the flittering of the Man-Moth and the hissing of the train, and the lines rush along as the reader struggles to "get aboard," starting at once at "full terrible speed."

The return home, both more disorienting and more frightening than the attempt at escape, proves truly heroic. In Sisyphean determination, the Man-Moth parallels the artist whose fate it is to risk constantly "whatever her concentration turns up" (Donoghue 1984, 262), to fail always and fall back "scared but quite unhurt," and to go on living in uncertain and perhaps terrifying realities, unable to judge "the rate at which [s]he travels backwards." The image of the subway conveys the inevitability and relentlessness embodied in the Man-Moth's quest, in the artist's work, or, for that matter, in the expression of any creature who risks attention.

What the Man-Moth longs to discover in the moon's bright opening, a reverse image of the dark birth canal, is his own transformation, his rebirth. The fact that his annihilation is implicit in this transformation becomes apparent on comparing the celestial birth canal, the moon, to the subterranean birth canal, the third rail. The third rail is dangerous because it is well within reach, even intertwining with the dreams and experiences of the Man-Moth's subway home. To keep from reaching for his transformation and achieving his annihilation, the Man-Moth dulls his acute senses:

> Each night he must
> be carried through artificial tunnels and dream recurrent dreams.
> Just as the ties recur beneath his train, these underlie
> his rushing brain. He does not dare look out the window,
> for the third rail, the unbroken draught of poison,
> runs there beside him. He regards it as a disease
> he has inherited the susceptibility to. He has to keep
> his hands in his pockets, as others must wear mufflers.

The danger is not in the external reality but in the Man-Moth's senses: "He does not dare look" and "He has to keep / his hands in his pockets as others must wear mufflers." The difference between Man's and Man-Moth's reasons for wearing mufflers illustrates the fundamental difference between the two creatures. Man notices and protects himself against only those elements that, like the cold, immediately affect his physicality, while the Man-Moth must muffle himself against his own perceptions, his own desire to know.

Up to the final stanza, the poem delineates the distance between Man and Man-Moth. However, this boundary, like the other boundaries in the poem, proves permeable. The final stanza shifts surprisingly; the poet, speaking in second person, seems to turn her head and directly address the reader, who appears at this juncture to be standing in for Man. Though we feel throughout the poem that the poet's sympathies are with the Man-Moth, in the final stanza she gives instructions for overcoming the protective enclosure of the Man-Moth's body, instructions for a moment of connection with the Man-Moth:

> If you catch him,
> hold up a flashlight to his eye. It's all dark pupil,
> an entire night itself, whose haired horizon tightens
> as he stares back, and closes up the eye. Then from the lids
> one tear, his only possession, like the bee's sting, slips.
> Slyly he palms it, and if you're not paying attention
> he'll swallow it. However, if you watch, he'll hand it over,
> cool as from underground springs and pure enough to drink.

The image of the flashlight relates to the central image pattern of the moon, the third rail, and the eye; like these, it represents and conducts energy. Holding up the flashlight to the Man-Moth's eye, a kind of anti-moon, reveals both complete isolation, "all dark pupil, / an entire night itself," and the presence of a permeable membrane, a portal or hole that proves protection useless and connection possible.

The connection between Man and Man-Moth in the final stanza differs from the Man-Moth's earlier attempts at connection because it involves a kind of strict attention that does not investigate outward, but drinks in. By comparing the tear that may be drunk to the bee's sting, Bishop makes explicit the implicit threat of each opportunity for connection and transcendence. The tear resembles a bee's sting, which poisons the receiver and kills the giver; the vulnerability in any moment of connection—sexual, natal, or even intellectual—is equally dangerous. Elsewhere in Bishop's work, in poems like "Chemin de Fer" from this book and "Sestina" from *Questions of Travel,* the poet is especially interested in tears as the external emissaries of an internal state, unique in their capability to join two worlds. In a notebook entry made in 1934 or 1935, Bishop explored the strangeness of tears as emissaries; she describes a window that one evening is "covered with hundreds of long shining drops of rain": "Each [drop] bore the trace of a relative or friend: several weeping faces slid away from mine; water plants and fish floated within other drops; watery jewels, leaves and insects magnified, and strangest of all, horrible enough to make me step quickly away, was one large long drop containing a lonely, magnificent human eye, wrapped in its own tear" (Vassar Notebook V). Tears can be terrifying, and she relocates the tears in both "Chemin de Fer" and "Sestina" onto objects of the environment surrounding the grieving characters. The Man-Moth's desire to palm his tear manifests this desire for displacement, the desire to hide and protect the internal self, like a coin he'd rather not pay. It also connects the Man-Moth with strange legendary creatures like genies and leprechauns, who must surrender their treasure when caught or summoned. In each case, attention can reveal the openings in the external facade and make connection with the internal or other world possible. The suggestion that the tear be drunk, that the other be internalized, relates to the image of the moon as birth canal; the mortal risk and the possibility for true connection through internalization seems to me a profoundly feminine image.

The Man-Moth's tear belongs to a pattern of images in Bishop's poems that concerns abolishing the self in order to preserve it (Motion 1985, 322), or, in Malkoff's terms, escaping the self in order to realize it. Earned by painful attention, the moment of connection concerns giving over control and enlarging perspective, rather than making reality small, manageable, and egocentric. The tear is, as Lloyd Schwartz says, "a clarifying vision for whoever asks for it" (*Voices and Visions*). To the criticism of readers who, like Mazzaro, complain about Bishop's restraint, who lament, "if only she had given up her 'one tear' " (1980, 193), the poem answers, "You're not paying attention." The price of attention is pain and vulnerability to pain, and the gift of attention is sensuous perception. "Cool as from underground springs" recalls both the subway home and the "entire night" of the Man-Moth's self. "Pure enough to drink" suggests that the tear is not otherworldly, perfectly pure, but human, sufficient. In the act of imbibing the tear, Man risks the attention and the connection that the Man-Moth risks, the danger of self-annihilation, transcendence, and understanding.

Another poem in *North & South*, "A Miracle for Breakfast," deals with these same themes of attention, connection, transcendence, and internalization. However, "A Miracle for Breakfast" centers on the naturalness of the transcendent process, moves toward the process of natural transfiguration, a process that combines physical transformation and spiritual transcendence. "The Man-Moth" and "A Miracle for Breakfast" bespeak a natural movement in thought. Like the Man-Moth's tear, which is "pure enough to drink," sufficiently human and imperfect, the food in "A Miracle for Breakfast" is not made by the expected divine intervention but by the constant, natural miracle of the body—interdependence, connection. In an interview with Ashley Brown, Bishop said of "A Miracle for Breakfast": "Oh, that's my Depression poem. It was written shortly after the time of souplines and men selling apples, around 1936 or so. It was my 'social conscious' poem, a poem about hunger" (1966, 12).

Although Bishop characteristically downplays the deeper significance, the sestina, like "The Man-Moth," concerns not just actual poverty but the poverty of Man, the poverty of attention, and spiritual as well as physical hunger. From the first stanza, Bishop juxtaposes the cold, darkness, and hunger with natural transformation, like the sunrise:

> At six o'clock we were waiting for coffee,
> waiting for coffee and the charitable crumb
> that was going to be served from a certain balcony,
> —like kings of old, or like a miracle.
> It was still dark. One foot of the sun
> steadied itself on a long ripple in the river. (*Poems,* 18)

Even the repeated words of the sestina mix human-made and natural phenomena: coffee, crumb, and balcony stand against sun and river. The exception, miracle, is the matter for definition. The man standing on the balcony has "the makings of a miracle," but he does something unexpected with them. Instead of multiplying them miraculously like the biblical loaves and fishes, he makes enough by dividing them naturally, giving each "communicant" one hard crumb and one drop of coffee. While some flick the charitable crumb "scornfully into the river," refusing to accept the natural as miraculous, the speaker in the poem, presumably Bishop, stands attentively, "waiting for the miracle." She sees what others fail to through attention to the natural:

> I can tell what I saw next; it was not a miracle.
> A beautiful villa stood in the sun
> and from its doors came the smell of hot coffee.
> In front, a baroque white plaster balcony
> added by birds, who nest along the river,
> —I saw it with one eye close to the crumb—

Minute attention to the little she is given brings about not only a lavish vision but a fresh understanding of the nature of miracles. Bishop takes possession of, connects with, the miraculously complicated processes that make even the smallest crumb possible. She has a vision of independent bodies working together to produce the miracle bread of which her crumb is a part. It is this vision of interdependence, the incredible connections between isolated bodies, that makes the crumb into a miracle:

> My crumb
> my mansion, made for me by a miracle,
> through ages, by insects, birds, and the river
> working the stone. Every day, in the sun,
> at breakfast time I sit on my balcony
> with my feet up, and drink gallons of coffee.

The phrase "Every day, in the sun" squints to describe both the speaker and the chain of "insects, birds, and the river" that makes the crumb possible; the phrase connects the speaker to the natural miracle she has seen "with one eye close to the crumb."

The envoi of "A Miracle for Breakfast," like the last lines of "The Man-Moth," involve risking complete connection with the object of attention, internalizing the miracle:

> We licked up the crumb and swallowed the coffee.
> A window across the river caught the sun
> as if the miracle were working on the wrong balcony.

The final image connects the natural and the miraculous; the flashing light from the sunrise becomes another kind of miracle. The central paradox once again derives from the nature of the body that is at once singular and isolated and also completely connected to and reliant on the contingent world of creatures and objects. "A Miracle for Breakfast" is, in the deepest sense, a "social conscious" poem, a poem about the universal hunger. Nemerov's argument that Bishop's sestinas are "particularly ineffective" because they move "by means of accumulated detail" (1955, 180) overlooks the importance of accretion of detail to a poem that gathers the force of sensuous experience to arrive at what Estess calls an "epiphanic vision" (1983, 219), an instant of transfiguration.

"The Fish," one of Bishop's most well known and widely anthologized poems, builds to a moment of epiphany that acknowledges the common lot, not just of all humankind but of all the creatures who inhabit bodies. Like "The Man-Moth" and "A Miracle for Breakfast," "The Fish" posits a means of connecting through attention and internalization. The structure of the poem represents a kind of inverted fish story, in which the "normal" sequence—one in which the inconceivably enormous fish and the brave fisherman fight fiercely until the fish is lost—is replaced by an obviously female speaker whose mental and spiritual struggle to see the fish replaces the physical struggle to land him. The repetition of the pronoun "he" in the first lines of the poem emphasizes the degree to which the speaker struggles, and does not struggle, with another entity, an outside will:

> I caught a tremendous fish
> and held him beside the boat
> half out of water, with my hook
> fast in a corner of his mouth.
> He didn't fight.
> He hadn't fought at all.
> He hung a grunting weight,
> battered and venerable
> and homely. (*Poems,* 42)

The fish has clearly disappointed the expectations of the speaker, has challenged her preconceptions, and this challenge sets up a dichotomy. This poem, like "The Monument" and "Large Bad Picture," uses dialogic structure to chronicle the struggle between two views of the fish: a solely objective one and an anthropomorphized one. The descriptions modulate between objective and anthropomorphized descriptions, and this modulation has the effect of preventing a completely distanced view, which sees the fish as meaningless "other," and a completely sentimentalized view, which covers the fish's reality with a cloak of human motivation:

> Here and there
> his brown skin hung in strips
> like ancient wallpaper,
> and its pattern of darker brown
> was like wallpaper:
> shapes like full-blown roses
> stained and lost through age.

The effect of this comparison, like the effect of the comparison between peninsulas and women's hands feeling yard goods in "The Map," is a sense of something awry, a strangeness in the domestic. Bishop juxtaposes accurate report of visual stimuli with simile and metaphor—beautiful images, like "He was speckled with barnacles, / fine rosettes of lime," with ugly truth, like "infested / with tiny white sea lice." This juxtaposition of contrasting descriptions parallels shifts in perspective, as the speaker vacillates between the fish's viewpoint, "his gills were breathing in / the terrible oxygen," and the human perspective, "the frightening gills, / fresh and crisp with blood, / that can cut so badly." This back-and-forth movement, this tension, expresses the struggle of the speaker to "land" the fish, to comprehend and see him accurately.

However, the mention of the "frightening gills . . . that can cut so badly" marks a turning point in the poem. As if the mention of the wound, the vulnerable reality of the human body, propels the speaker to a consideration of the internal reality of this other body, the speaker moves beyond comparing the external appearance of the fish to the external reality she has known and begins to imagine inward, into the fish's body, letting the comparison expose the unseen. Through attention to the exterior, the imagination moves to the interior:

> I thought of the coarse white flesh
> packed in like feathers,
> the big bones and the little bones,
> the dramatic reds and blacks
> of his shiny entrails,
> and the pink swim-bladder
> like a big peony.

Imagination, which gives the power to sentimentalize and distort, also gives the power to move inside the other being, without sentimentality. Throughout the remainder of the poem, the struggle between the two dialectically opposed possibilities for comprehending the fish is mediated through a new awareness, a new attention. Bishop repeats over and over the verbs of visual attention:

"I looked," "I admired," "I saw," and, most importantly, "I stared."
Her references to the fish's eyes connect her perspective to the fish's
while simultaneously refusing to anthropomorphize him:

> I looked into his eyes
> which were far larger than mine
> but shallower, and yellowed,
> the irises backed and packed
> with tarnished tinfoil
> seen through the lenses
> of old scratched isinglass.
> They shifted a little, but not
> to return my stare.
> —It was more like the tipping
> of an object toward the light.

The isinglass recalls the distortion of the human perspective, tar-
nished by human senses, and refers to the fish, both directly, because
isinglass resembles the lens of his eye, and indirectly, because isinglass is made from fish bladder.

As the poem moves toward epiphany, Bishop balances the two
warring views of the fish, the subjective and objective perspectives.
As Prunty argues, letting the fish go overcomes both of the individual will's desires—to hold itself apart and to dominate or overwhelm (1990, 248). Thus, having imagined "into" the body of the
fish—as the speaker in "Large Bad Picture" moves into the painting, and as both speakers in "The Monument" are within the
view—the speaker takes the fish into herself, internalizes it, through
the force of her scrutiny and her attempt at empathy. The riveting
visual exactness of Bishop's description of the "five old pieces of
fish-line" moves into a metaphoric description comparing the line
to military medals and a beard of wisdom, a comparison that differs
from the earlier comparison between wallpaper and the fish's skin
because it attempts empathy, internalizing the other, rather than
projecting the known onto the unknown:

> from his lower lip
> —if you could call it a lip—
> grim, wet, and weaponlike,

hung five old pieces of fish-line,
or four and a wire leader
with the swivel still attached,
with all their five big hooks
grown firmly in his mouth.
A green line, frayed at the end
where he broke it, two heavier lines,
and a fine black thread
still crimped from the strain and snap
when it broke and he got away.
Like medals with their ribbons
frayed and wavering,
a five-haired beard of wisdom
trailing from his aching jaw.

The balance of the vision, the movement out from the self and into the self, creates a moment of epiphany, of connection, a victory. It is, as Prunty argues, a "relational victory" (1990, 249) in the sense that no single perspective, objective or subjective, and no single actor, fish or woman, wins. The victory that fills "the little rented boat" is unascribed and unascribable; everything has won. The image of "the little rented boat" also reveals how brief, how transitory, this victory is. In the image of the rainbow, the sun hitting "the pool of bilge," Bishop creates extraordinary beauty out of the terribly transitory and apparently ugly reality, as she has done in describing the body of the fish. In the final lines, all contingent reality is briefly transfigured:

I stared and stared
and victory filled up
the little rented boat,
from the pool of bilge
where oil had spread a rainbow
around the rusted engine
to the bailer rusted orange,
the sun-cracked thwarts,
the oarlocks on their strings,
the gunnels—until everything
was rainbow, rainbow, rainbow!
And I let the fish go.

Although Parker objects to what he calls the "cheerily sentimental word *rainbow*," saying it "violates the modesty and indirection that [Bishop] was to win such admiration for" (1988, 58), the image of the rainbow and Bishop's ecstatic repetition of the word becomes a microcosm of the entire theme. Like a tear, a rainbow is an external or visual sign of an internal or invisible condition. It is the Western Christian symbol of both the great destruction of the world by flood and the restoration of the Christian God's covenant with humankind, a transient image of a lasting promise. More, the rainbow transfigures the reality of the little boat not by its own light but by imprinting itself on the eyes of the perceiver; everything is rainbow because she sees rainbow. Thus the final lines of "The Fish," like the final lines of "The Man-Moth" and "A Miracle for Breakfast," offer a clarifying vision purchased through attention and connection and letting go.

Many of the poems in *North & South,* in addition to the ones I have concentrated on in this chapter, concern the problem of human knowledge and center on the metaphor of the human body as the mediator of truth. In her experiments with personification, her examination of the "clean cage" of human perception, and her exploration of possibilities for connection and internalization, Bishop searches for ways to discuss and discover how we know. None of her later books exhibits as much sheer experimentation as this first one, for it is here that Bishop works out her own idiom, finds a language for the joyful and painful uncertainty of all human perception.

2

A COLD SPRING
The Moving Self in the Moving World

IN THE YEARS immediately following the 1946 publication of *North & South*, Bishop divided her time between Key West in the winter, living in the house she owned with her friend Louise Crane; extended visits to New York, staying in hotels; and summers in Nova Scotia, living in what she considered her childhood home, the farm of her maternal grandmother in Great Village. Bishop, typically paradoxical, seemed to have settled down to a life of unsettledness—a life, not of home, but of homes, of constant travel. Her letters from this period reveal a moody uncertainty about her ability to combine work and travel; she constantly chides herself for her relatively slow rate of production, her odd creative process, and her estrangement from the general round of readings, lectures, and reviews in the New York literary world. She wrote to Robert Lowell in January of 1948:

> I take your remarks about writing a lot now very much to heart & I'd like to look forward to a long stretch of nothing but work. I've been sick most of the month—asthma—it doesn't completely incapacitate one but is a nuisance. Well—I was asked to speak at Wellesley, too, on March 22—and at the time I accepted. Now I am wondering if it is really worth it to go all the way back North at that time of year. (Giroux 1994, 154)

Bishop had been introduced to Lowell by Randall Jarrell just a year before, in January of 1947. As Kalstone points out, this was an exceptional moment in the careers of both poets (1989, 111); both had published successful first books, and both were uncertain and restless about elements of their own styles and strategies. They were, perhaps, attracted to each other as much by curiosity about their respective differences as by congenial feelings of similarity. Bishop's love of the particular and desire for the accurate challenged Lowell's love of the mythic and desire for the romantic. Lowell states the case against himself somewhat too harshly when he writes in April of 1952 that Bishop makes him feel that he possesses a "breezy, impersonal liking for the great and obvious" that contrasts with her "adult personal feeling for the odd and genuine" (Vassar Box 6). A better comparison, perhaps, comes in a much later exchange of letters in which Lowell reminisces, recalling for Bishop their first meeting at Jarrell's. He remembers Bishop as "rather tall, long brown-haired." He sees them both reveling, "swimming" in youth and laments the "steel cord stretch [*sic*] tense at about arms-length above us" and the threat of "less grace and strength" with passing years (Vassar Box 6).

Bishop characteristically bristles at Lowell's romanticizing of their first meeting and, still more characteristically, balks at the elegiac, dark mood of his remembrance. Her reply illustrates the differences between Lowell and Bishop that energized both poets as their relationship developed:

> Never, never was I "tall"—as you wrote remembering me. I was always 5 ft 4 and 1/4 inches—now shrunk to 5 ft 4 inches. The only time I've ever felt tall was in Brazil. And I never had "long brown hair" either!—It started turning gray when I was 23 or 24—and was probably somewhat grizzled when I first met you. I tried putting it up for a very brief period, because I like long hair—but it never got even to my shoulders and is always so intractable that I gave that up within a month or so. . . . What I remember about that meeting is your dishevelment, your lovely curly hair, and how we talked about a Picasso show then on in N.Y., and we agreed about the Antibes pictures of fishing, etc.—and how much I liked you, after having been almost too scared to go. . . . You were also rather dirty, which I rather liked, too. And your stories about the cellar room you were living in and how the neighbors drank all night and when they got too rowdy one of them wd. say "Remember the boy," meaning you. (Giroux 1994, 592–93)

Throughout their friendship, Bishop and Lowell squared off over the relative importance of the facts, the necessity for accuracy. They also fought over a poet's right to assume other voices and to exploit the pain of other lives. I think both Jarrell and Lowell challenged Bishop to explore voices, although she was never convinced, as Lowell seems to have been, that a poet was made free by his or her art to demolish utterly the boundaries between his or her life and other lives. However, in *A Cold Spring*, Bishop seems influenced by her deepening friendship with both Lowell and Jarrell, as they were themselves influenced by W. D. Snodgrass and others who were exploring the limits of the personal voice in poetry.[1] In her second book, Bishop allows herself a greater range of tones, demonstrates a greater freedom in exploring her own voice, than she had in *North & South*. Although Lowell's influence appears much more broadly in the next book, *Questions of Travel, A Cold Spring* demonstrates Bishop's desire both to connect with and set herself apart from the literary world surrounding her in the United States. Lowell and Jarrell often acted as the mediators of that world for Bishop. It was Lowell who in 1950 suggested that Bishop be appointed the Consultant in Poetry to the Library of Congress, a job he had held during 1947 and 1948. Both men urged Bishop to accept readings, though she seldom did, and to join them in meeting other poets. Bishop's reticence about the literary "scene" and about becoming part of that milieu reflects a much deeper reticence, an uncertainty about connection in general, a deep realization of the peril to the self that any connection entails.

North & South primarily concerned perception, the body as the mediator of reality, the body as a boundary that both distorts and makes possible any human connection with the contingent world of people and things. *A Cold Spring* does expand these themes, but it does so in ways that would have been impossible in the first book. Now Bishop's explorations of poetic form as the skin that holds thought become both more risky and more deeply ambiguous. In this book, for the first (and really the last) time in her career, she directly confronts the sexually charged feelings that surround the poems. *A Cold Spring* concentrates specifically on love and knowledge as the forces that make self-realization possible by, paradoxically, enlarging or escaping the isolated self. But, this book also examines love and knowledge as the forces that threaten to annihilate the self by offering that very possibility of escape. Love and knowledge for Bishop are, of course, distinct forces but are also related expressions of the human desire for connection. The desire for love and the desire for knowledge are both reactions to the external world that express a deeper desire to escape the isolation of the physical body. The poems of *A Cold Spring* demonstrate Bishop's ambivalence about this escape: at one moment she dreads love and knowledge and fears the change, the destruction of the self that change promises; in the next she desires love and knowledge deeply, despite their dangers. At her best, Bishop achieves the sense of simultaneous desire and dread; she manages to express two opposing things in the same poem or even the same word.

In *A Cold Spring,* much more than in *North & South,* time plays a central role in Bishop's consideration of human connection, in her ambivalence about the forces of love and knowledge, and in the ambiguity and evasiveness of her tone. *A Cold Spring,* more than *North & South,* is a body of poems moving in time. Over and over, these poems allude to the difficulty of connecting with others and the world when both the body and the world the body inhabits are in constant motion. Love and knowledge, as integral expressions of the same desire to connect, must fight through the constant change and uncertainty that time creates. In *A Cold Spring,* Bishop is not content simply to re-create the transient but stilled, almost snapshot, moments of connection that she illustrated so powerfully in "The Fish" and "A Miracle for Breakfast." Instead, she uses metaphors of the body, particularly of the body in motion in time, to explore the difficulty of human knowing and human loving, both because knowledge is mediated by human senses (the overriding theme of *North & South*) and because human senses and the human body are subject to time and mortality, to death. The repeated images of birds, the moon, and water, images that appear in nearly every one of the nineteen poems in the second book, emphasize the passing of time and the certainty of change. Her choice of a seasonal title further emphasizes this consideration. Bishop's ambivalence about knowing and loving comes directly from ambivalence about change, the single aspect of human lives that makes all other aspects uncertain, the change that loving and knowing bring, which is most dreaded, most desired, and most certain.

"If Never With": The Love Poems of *A Cold Spring*

Many critics of *A Cold Spring* have claimed that the addition of love poems to Bishop's repertory of themes endangered the integrity of her work; they assert, as Ashbery does, that Bishop's life "threatened to intrude on the poetry in a way that didn't suit it" or that "a couple of the new ones veered dangerously close to the sentimental ballad of the Millay-Teasdale-Wylie school, to one's considerable surprise" (1983, 203). More recently, feminist and lesbian theorists have expressed disappointment at what they see as Bishop's "timidity," her refusal in her love poems to acknowledge openly and celebrate her homosexuality.[2] At opposite ends of the political spectrum, both of these criticisms come from prescriptive aesthetics, a desire to say what love poems "should" be like, and not from careful analysis of what Bishop's love poems *are* like. Although the love poems are not, with the notable exception of "The Shampoo," among the strongest poems in *A Cold Spring,* they do not seem unsuitable in the way I think Ashbery means, that is, by being, like some of Millay's or Teasdale's poems, undigested recountings of powerful emotion, sentimental because they are nearly unchecked by intellect. Instead, the love poems of *A Cold Spring* seem ambiguous, intellectually dense, and emotionally elusive. They range on a continuum from dreading love and its power to dehumanize (in "Varick Street"), to making a pact with days and distance to accept the "gentle battleground" of love (in "Argument"), to a cautious desire for love and connection (in "The Shampoo"). And though they are not as explicitly lesbian as they might be if Bishop had written them in the 1990s instead of the 1940s, they do deal with the wonder and danger of complete connection with the lover, a merging without heterosexual difference, in ways that impugn both the traditional love clichés and the ability of the ordered structure of language to express the disordered chaos of emotion.

In "Varick Street" Bishop's search to comprehend love and its power to create connection centers on images of the human body. The images of the body in "Varick Street," like the images of the body in *North & South,* suggest not only the centrality of the body to human knowing and loving but the way its centrality both betrays and makes possible every human endeavor. In the first stanza of the poem, mechanical creation, human creation, usurps the natural human form. As in much post–World War II literature, this juxtaposition creates a tone of black comedy. With its lilting refrain and exaggerated images, "Varick Street" is funny in the darkest sense. I am reminded of Joseph Heller's *Catch-22* or Terry Gilliam's film *Brazil,* and of Henri Bergson's definition of comedy as something mechanical encrusted on the living. The factories of the first stanza are surreal images of the body awaking to the ugliness of itself. This connection between the body, especially the female body, and the factories was even more explicit in the earlier drafts of the poem as Bishop vacillated between the opening phrase "At night my factories" and "At night the factories" and, in one draft, wrote "their veins show" in place of the more elusive final version, "veined with pipes" (Vassar Box 29). A kind of inverse aubade, the first stanza anthropomorphizes the factories, but to emphasize the indignity of the human form; rather than granting human dignity to the machines, it illustrates the mechanicalness of bodily functions:

> At night the factories
> struggle awake,
> wretched uneasy buildings
> veined with pipes
> attempt their work.
> Trying to breathe,
> the elongated nostrils
> haired with spikes
> give off stenches, too. (*Poems,* 75)

The added "too" creates an explicit comparison between the factory's and the body's stench; it underlines the ugliness, the soiledness of the body's mechanical operations. Like the comparison between women's hands and peninsulas in "The Map," the personification of the factory in the first lines of "Varick Street" makes the familiar more foreign, creates the sensation of something awry and unsettling.

The songlike refrain lines that repeat at the end of each stanza, "And I shall sell you sell you / sell you of course, my dear, and you'll sell me," juxtapose the personification of the mechanical with the mechanization of the personal. That is, just as the factories become bodies in the first stanza, in the refrain the bodies become factories, become salable themselves, objects for attaining profit. The future tense of the refrain line suggests that this mutual objectification is inevitable with the passing of time, that time will sell out the lovers just as they sell out each other. However, Bishop couches this horrifying vision of the future in an almost unpunctuated and liltingly songlike refrain. This effect resembles the potentially frightening sound in the singsong repetition of nursery rhymes like "Ring-a-Round-the-Rosey" or "London Bridge Is Falling Down," blackly comic jokes made into folk rhymes in which horrifying content becomes still more horrible through a simple, childlike medium. Consider Jarrell's poems about World War II in the voices of children or the opening of Fritz Lang's *M.,* in which German children dance in a circle while singing a simple, cheerful little rhyme about a child murderer. In Bishop's poem the horror resides both in the embodiment in the verse and in the embodiment in the flesh, in the ugliness of the body's own form.

The mechanized nature in the second stanza parallels the objectified body of the first. The technique of internalizing the natural world, which seemed so positive in the poems of *North & South,* becomes in "Varick Street" a means of distortion rather than connection. Interestingly, Bishop chooses two of the central images from important poems in *North & South:* an iceberg from "The Imaginary Iceberg" and the moon from "The Man-Moth." As in the earlier poems, these images remain elusive:

> On certain floors
> certain wonders.
> Pale dirty light,
> some captured iceberg

being prevented from melting.
See the mechanical moons,
sick, being made
to wax and wane
at somebody's instigation.

The moon that in "The Man-Moth" was an object and an opening, representing a singular ideal, a passage into new life, here becomes plural, moons, that are both stilled and forced to move. Similarly, the iceberg, once the sailor's antithetical and unattainable "other," has been captured. Like the tone of the lines "The Seven Wonders of the World are tired / and a touch familiar" from "Over 2,000 Illustrations and a Complete Concordance" (*Poems*, 57), "On certain floors / certain wonders" is touched with a jaundiced view of possibility for connection, or wonder. The terrible distance of the voice creates a bitterly comic tone. There can be no surprise, no wonder, no scene "a sailor'd give his eyes for," because the moons and the iceberg have been dragged into human factories, have been internalized. The artificial and mechanical waxing and waning of moons again highlights the passage of time, and the repetition of the refrain line seems more frenzied somehow for this insistence on time's movement.

The third and final stanza opens with a strange Elizabethan construction whose meaning is oddly elusive:

Lights music of love
work on. The presses
print calendars
I suppose; the moons
make medicine
or confectionery. Our bed
shrinks from the soot
and hapless odors
hold us close.

In earlier drafts of the poem, Bishop alluded more openly to *Twelfth Night*, beginning the stanza with "If music be the food of love / play on" (Vassar Box 29). However, the published version both retains the allusion to Orsino's romantic vision and simultaneously demolishes that romanticism by mechanizing it, replacing "play on" with "work on." "Lights music of love / work on" is grammatically elusive; it could be an exhortation or a statement. A comma after "lights" would suggest that Bishop means both "lights" and "music of love" as double subjects of the exhortation "work on." An apostrophe before or after the "s" in "lights" would mean that they create the music. But Bishop inserts neither. The exact meaning of the phrase eludes the reader, just as, in the following lines, the exact function of the factory eludes the speaker.

The speaker's weary supposition that the presses print calendars reintroduces the concept of time as betrayer. The image suggests a factory/body that creates purposely cheap and transient calendar art; the act of printing calendars itself involves, both in its repetitive nature and in its content, marking off time. The phrase "the moons / make medicine / or confectionery" proves more elusive. In earlier drafts Bishop had made the ugliness clearer, the moons made "medicine, confectionery, money" (Vassar Box 29). In the final version, medicine, perhaps necessary or important, is equated with confectionery. The lovers join because they shrink from the factory/body's ugliness, "Our bed / shrinks from the soot," without any apparent will to connect, "hapless odors / hold us close." The reappearance of the refrain at the end of this final verse seems so weary as almost to collapse. Certainly, "Varick Street" cannot be said to fall into the "Millay-Teasdale-Wylie school" of unchecked emotion. In these lesser love lyrics (e.g., Millay's "Hyacinth"), the rejected lover most often bemoans the wounded self and sees the cause of love's failure in the insensitive other. The underlying and unstated hypothesis is that love is the most desirable state. In "The Hyacinth," Millay concludes that her lover's failure is the failure to listen to her pain and not the failure of love generally—"the gnawing at my heart he does not hear" (Millay 1951, 135). In Millay's construction, the hyacinths, or the concerns that the hyacinths symbolize, have supplanted the lover, and the beloved's failure to notice her agony at this usurpation means the failure of the benevolent power of love. In Bishop's "Varick Street," the underlying hypothesis about love is more elusive; Williamson suggests that Bishop has "a ground conviction that reciprocal love is, almost metaphysically, impossible" (1983, 96). This is half of it; the other half, however, seems to suggest paradoxically that love is perfectly possible, but wearying, terrifying, and not necessarily desirable or benevolent, and all this not because of metaphysical disconnection but because of the potential horror of the physical form.

In "Four Poems," a series of short love lyrics, Bishop continues to explore the paradox of love—simultaneously possible and impossible, desirable and horrible. The first section, "Conversation," concerns the speaker's unhappiness with the repeated internal dialogue, the conversation, that constantly fails to find distinction and answer and, instead, collapses into tumult and interconnection:

> The tumult in the heart
> keeps asking questions.
> And then it stops and undertakes to answer
> in the same tone of voice.
> No one could tell the difference.
>
> Uninnocent, these conversations start,
> and then engage the senses,
> only half-meaning to.
> And then there is no choice,
> and then there is no sense;
>
> until a name
> and all its connotation are the same. (*Poems*, 76)

The poem's conversation is also not a conversation, both in the sense that it is not a dialogue and in the sense that the internal conversation, such as it is, collapses into one voice almost before it begins. The "tumult" that "keeps asking questions" and then "undertakes to answer" makes the question and answer sound exactly the same, like the tumult: "No one could tell the difference." This collapsing of barriers in a love poem should and does promise a kind of connection, but the connection has the same sense of will-lessness and weariness that the lover's connection in "Varick Street" had: "Uninnocent, these conversations start, / and then engage the senses, / only half-meaning to."

As in "Varick Street," in "Conversations" love seems simultaneously impossible, because the speaker shows no identifiable volition or strong desire, and yet also inevitable, fated: "And then there is no choice, / and then there is no sense." Finally, the last two lines, with their ambiguous grammatical construction, both call attention to the barriers between self and other, between thought and thought, and, paradoxically, collapse those barriers: "until a name / and all its connotation are the same." Bishop's use of the singular "connotation" in place of the more usual and expected plural says two simultaneous and opposing things, says that the boundaries have collapsed, that all connotations have become one connotation, and yet says that the boundaries are real, calls attention to the differences. The ambiguity, the strangely distanced emotion of "Conversation," comes from this kind of doubleness, this refusal to choose or to define love's connection, even for a moment, as either beneficial or injurious, life-giving or deadly.

The second section of "Four Poems," "Rain Towards Morning," reverses the collapsing motion of "Conversation" but evinces the same tension, the same feelings of ambiguity:

> The great light cage has broken up in the air,
> freeing, I think, about a million birds
> whose wild ascending shadows will not be back,
> and all the wires come falling down.
> No cage, no frightening birds; the rain
> is brightening now. The face is pale
> that tried the puzzle of their prison
> and solved it with an unexpected kiss,
> whose freckled unsuspected hands alit. (*Poems*, 77)

The images that begin the poem remind me of the beautifully elusive images of an Escher print; "The great light cage" of night breaks up to become the black shadows of ascending birds. This dissipation of darkness, the ascending motion of the birds, the brightening rain, though they are all literally images of dissipation and disconnection, are nevertheless positive, brought about by a moment of connection, an unexpected gesture of human love, a kiss. However, the tone of the poem does not resolve itself to rejoice. Instead, the poem seems to capture the numbness of that moment between the blackest hour and the coming of the light, between the

awful night's "great light cage" and morning made by the hands
and kiss that alight in place of the "wild, ascending birds," the moment of near disbelief and almost paralyzing uncertainty. The sameness of the series of declarative sentences, the qualifying phrase "I
think," and the contrasting "now" all demonstrate the speaker's
uncertainty. The final word, "alit," captures in one utterance the
duality of the moment of transition, the ambiguity that informs the
voice of the speaker, for though the word literally means to come,
descend, or land, its archaic meaning and the connotation retain the
sense of chance, the possibility that the connection is merely accidental and perhaps momentary.

Both "Conversation" and "Rain Towards Morning" avoid expressing or eliciting a definitive emotional response; instead, the images remain elusive and intellectually difficult. Similarly, the third
poem in the series, the sonnet "While Someone Telephones," depicts
a moment of transition, a movement from a black hour into a gray
one. The octet establishes the speaker's annoyance and frustration,
a tension that, at moments, verges on panic:

> Wasted, wasted minutes that couldn't be worse,
> minutes of a barbaric condescension.
> —Stare out the bathroom window at the fir-trees,
> at their dark needles, accretions to no purpose
> woodenly crystallized, and where two fireflies
> are only lost.
> Hear nothing but a train that goes by, must go by, like tension;
> *nothing*. And wait: (*Poems*, 78)

Once again, the force that opposes and harries the speaker is time.
Bishop embodies the invisible force of time in the visible world that
is subject to it; she projects her conflict with it onto the world beyond the bathroom window. Thus, the moments, like the needles
on the fir trees, are "accretions to no purpose" and "woodenly crys-
tallized." Bishop embodies the feeling of tension in the sound of
the train and in the breathless, long line that relates the sound of
the train: "Hear nothing but a train that goes by, must go by, like
tension." The irritability of the phrases "must go by" and "are only

lost," the annoyance implicit in the initial repetition of the word "wasted," and the final "And wait" create that sense of tension that verges on panic, create the feeling that the speaker holds back overwhelming emotion at some cost.

However, the volta in the sestet unexpectedly and suddenly undermines or reverses the tension of the speaker's conflict with time that was established in the octet:

> maybe even now these minutes' host
> emerges, some relaxed uncondescending stranger,
> the heart's release.
> And while the fireflies
> are failing to illuminate these nightmare trees
> might they not be his green gay eyes.

The speaker suddenly envisions a reality in the same details of the tense one she sees; still staring out the same bathroom window and still waiting, she embodies different emotions and possibilities in the concrete reality of the landscape. However, these new possibilities are tentative ones, qualified and qualified again by "maybe" and "might they not be."

The word "host" seems particularly odd and surprising in this stanza, indicating both the beloved's power over time, his presence being the source of meaning and defining force, and his vulnerability to time, since "host" connotes also that the beloved is preyed upon by time, by the wasted minutes themselves. In the final image of the poem, the speaker suggests that the fireflies may be "his green gay eyes" and thereby simultaneously approaches a solution and refuses to resolve the duality of the image. Though, in the sestet, the fireflies still fail "to illuminate these nightmare trees," by imposition of the imagination the speaker figures the failure as success, imagines that the fireflies are the eyes of her lover, "the heart's release." In the sestet, Bishop embodies new emotions in the same images that, in the octet, embodied annoyance, discomfort, and panic. The result is a sonnet in which the octet and the sestet demonstrate remarkably similar figurations of remarkably separate internal realities, a sonnet that uses the same landscape and concrete details to depict

two opposing emotional states. Although the movement from conflict to consolation or solution in "While Someone Telephones" suggests the traditional Petrarchan sonnet structure, Bishop refuses in
the sestet to define or resolve the conflict that the octet has established. The volta reminds me of Shakespeare's "Haply I think on
thee" from Sonnet 29, but the poem ends with none of the Shake-
spearian conviction of "then I scorn to trade my state with kings."
Instead, the sestet calls attention to its own device, offers a qualified
consolation of imagination and image, emphasizes the uncertainty
of the poem's endeavor. The title "While Someone Telephones" amplifies this uncertainty. On a first reading, one might expect that the
someone who is telephoning in the title will appear in the sestet and
release the speaker from the loneliness and tension of the octet's
wasted minutes. However, Bishop, characteristically elusive, refuses
to reveal the identity of the caller or the destination of the call. The
title may suggest that the poem ends at the moment just before the
phone rings, but this is suggestion at best, and the poem proper
focuses only on the longing for contact, for connection, and the
problem of embodying the conflicting emotions of that longing
either in a concrete image, like the firs or fireflies, or in the poetic
structure itself.

In the final section of "Four Poems," called "O Breath," the
speaker's search for a means of connection comes through the same
kind of passionate attention to another's body that Bishop explored
in "The Fish." The breath, like the rainbow of "The Fish" or the
tear of "The Man-Moth," acts as an external emissary of an internal and invisible phenomenon, the life force of the other, even,
the heart. The speaker must bargain with, must "make a separate
peace   beneath / within" the external and visible body in an effort
to connect somehow with the internal and invisible, the thing that
is original, that, in the words of "The Monument," "cannot have
been intended to be seen":

> Beneath that loved   and celebrated breast
> silent, bored really   blindly veined,
> grieves maybe   lives and lets
> live, passes   bets,

> something moving   but invisibly,
> and with what clamor   why restrained
> I cannot fathom   even a ripple. (*Poems*, 79)

Although it may look strange in such a short piece, the loose, Anglo-Saxon verse form allows Bishop to explore visually, in a way she has not done elsewhere, the boundary between the self and the other that is the theme of the poem. The caesura acts as a kind of visual gulf that separates alliterative or sometimes equivalent sounds and mirrors the separation between the speaker and the beloved, with whom she tries to find equivalences. The alliterative verse form, used so often in heroic poetry to portray the clash of actual battle, here depicts a more figurative war, the desire to storm the walls of the other and to conquer and comprehend the interior. As in "The Gentleman of Shalott," the questions and tensions in "O Breath" concern the distinction between in and out. The structure of the poem visually re-creates the struggle both to distinguish the self from the other and also to connect over the distance that this distinction creates; it also re-creates the exact physical sensation of pausing, or better, struggling for breath, that Bishop's own asthma constantly necessitated (Millier 1993, 227).

This tension in connection comes, not just from the alliterative form, but from the dual and often opposing meanings of the linked half lines. For example, the crucial line, "and with what clamor   why restrained," is, like all alliterative verse, strongly linked across the caesura by the sensuous repetition of sound—here by the repetition of the "w." But in Bishop's hands, the link between the two half lines seems still more complex; the lines are simultaneously held together and held at a tense distance by the opposition of "clamor" and "restrained." The opposition parallels not just the imagined emotions of the beloved but also the emotions of the speaker and the tension in the poem's voice.

The caesura also indicates negative space, gives Bishop the opportunity to re-create visually the presence/absence dichotomy, the push-pull of desire and dread, that so powerfully informs the reactions to love in all four poems in the series. As in "The Gentleman of Shalott," here differentiating between in and out is both crucially important and impossible. The breath, the invisible and internal, becomes the only visible, external indication of commonality, of the possibility for connection, for equivalence. The second half of the poem, filled with conditionals and qualifiers, demonstrates the speaker's uncertainty in the face of this difficult connection:

> (See the thin flying   of nine black hairs
> four around one   five the other nipple,
> flying almost intolerably   on your own breath.)
> Equivocal, but what we have in common's   bound to be there
> whatever we must own   equivalents for,
> something that maybe I   could bargain with
> and make a separate peace   beneath
> within   if never with.

The play on "equivocal" and "equivalent" reveals the struggle both to connect and to avoid connecting, to discover equivalence without becoming equal to, losing identity. The odd break before "bound" emphasizes this same point and enriches the meaning of the word itself, recalling both of its meanings: connection, ties, and also a leap—and perhaps also suggesting the word "boundary."

That love is, as Bishop says, a "bargain," and a precarious one, becomes even more apparent in her choice of the startling and strange adverbial phrase "almost intolerably" to describe the black hairs surrounding the nipple as they move with each exhalation of the beloved's breath. In that phrase Bishop captures the feeling of overwhelming tenderness and dread that accompanies the minute and careful observation founded in a desire to connect with, to comprehend, and yet, simultaneously, the understanding that complete connection is impossible and probably undesirable. The final lines of the poem express both a frustrated awareness of boundaries and a prudent understanding of the necessity of the separation they create, a desire to "make a separate peace   beneath / within   if never with."

Each of the "Four Poems" expresses this double sense of dread and desire, the need to make a peace that is somehow connected to the very breath, the inmost self of the beloved, and yet separate, equivalent, "never with." All four poems seem internal musings on the speaker's part rather than expressed thoughts meant to forge the vital connections they consider. The tone of the series is cagey, cautious, sometimes bewildered or panicked. However, most often, caught at a moment of transition, the speaker is in motion between two feelings, somehow considering, distanced from both, and weighing the options to negotiate or try to negotiate a compromise between the two, often opposite, emotional responses.

The necessity to "bargain" a love, to negotiate a perilous but necessary connection, comes up again in "Argument." Here, Bishop personifies Distance and Days, the elements that separate the lovers, and they argue with her, insisting on their own power to forestall human connection. The first stanza of the poem, like the octet of "While Someone Telephones," endows Distance and Days with obstinance and malice and possesses a similar tone of annoyance in response to this perceived malicious intent. However, the explicit personification and the more relaxed diction make "Argument" more whimsical and humorous:

> Days that cannot bring you near
> or will not,
> Distance trying to appear
> something more than obstinate
> argue argue argue with me
> endlessly
> neither proving you less wanted nor less dear. (*Poems*, 81)

The stubbornness of Days and the fake nonchalance of Distance are figures that seem both amusing and annoying, their arguments tedious but ineffective. Both Days and Distance try to intimidate the speaker and prove the impossibility of human connection by stressing the physical limitations of the human body, the body's vulnerability to time and space. In the second stanza, Distance emphasizes human smallness in comparison to the vastness of the land that separates the two lovers:

> Distance: Remember all that land
> beneath the plane;

that coastline
of dim beaches deep in sand
stretching indistinguishably
all the way,
all the way to where my reasons end?

"Dim" and "indistinguishably" both point up the failure of the human senses to function over distance. The repetition of "all the
way" and the suggestion that these "dim beaches deep in sand"
would be impossibly wearying to cross point up the single body's
inability to overcome the barriers that distance can impose. However, the situation is not hopeless, perhaps not even very serious;
distance gives itself away from the start when it begins its argument
by mentioning the plane, the human invention for vanquishing distance. Though certainly the plane cannot overcome felt distances,
the "dim beaches deep in sand," it is nevertheless an emblem of
hope, a sign of connection. Thus, Distance's "reasons end" in two
ways, both because Distance's argument is complete and because
that argument turns back on itself and suggests its own counterar-
gument. This contradiction was more evident in an earlier draft of
the poem in which Bishop had both Days and Distance comment
on their own inscrutability, in which Distance explicitly said, "I'm
as difficult to see / all the way / all the way to where my reasons
end" (Vassar Box 29). By personifying Distance, Bishop can simultaneously argue and disprove the argument that connection is hopeless, can embody two opposing ideas in a single structure.

Days' arguments also rely on intimidation, a rhetoric based on
the frailty of the human form and its inability to conquer time. If
the human body cannot cross the "dim beaches deep in sand," then,
according to Days, neither can the human mind fathom the impossibly contradictory relationship between never and forever, between
chronology and eternity:

Days: And think
of all those cluttered instruments,
one to a fact,
canceling each other's experience;
how they were

like some hideous calendar
"Compliments of Never & Forever, Inc."

Like the presses that print calendars in "Varick Street," in "Argument" there is something insidious about time's effect on human connection, on love. Part of this insidiousness comes, according to the argument that Bishop has Days make, from the profusion of contradictory information about the nature of time, contradictions that the intellect cannot grasp. Days exhorts "think," but thinking leads only to greater confusion. Chronometers and calendars succeed in "canceling each other's experience," and, like the thermometers that cannot register the temperature of the moon in "The Man-Moth," human inventions to understand and to accurately perceive fail. But while the relationship between human love and human invention in "Varick Street" becomes a source for bitterness and pain, the tone of "Argument" verges on the comic. The personification of Days and Distance seems whimsical, imaginatively playful, never seriously threatening. The "hideous calendar / 'Compliments of Never & Forever, Inc.' " demonstrates both the hopelessness of human attempts to untangle time and the hope for human connection in time. Never and forever are incorporated both in the sense that they are thoroughly united and absolutely opposing, a relationship that staggers human logic, and also in the sense that they are made corporeal, embodied, at least in the poem and perhaps in the love itself. But if this embodiment joins opposites, in Bishop's work, it rarely unites them. Instead, especially in these love poems, Bishop cultivates and explores the tensions of opposing emotions or ideas, of oppositions that remain distant although held in one form.

In the final stanza of "Argument," the tension derives from the desire to be united with the beloved and the ultimate dread of, and perhaps awareness of the impossibility of, that complete union. The "intimidating sound" of the voices and annoying arguments of Days and Distance can be silenced eventually; they are no real threat. However, the real threat, the heart of the conflict, emerges:

The intimidating sound
of these voices
we must separately find

can and shall be vanquished:
Days and Distance disarrayed again
and gone
both for good and from the gentle battleground.

Once Days and Distance have been vanquished, the "gentle battleground" remains. The lovers find Days and Distance separately and
"disarray" (with all the word's beautiful connotation of undressing)
their arguments by coming together, yet the sense of separation
does not vanish. The skewed, almost awkward, final lines—"and
gone / both for good and from the gentle battleground"—combine a sense of unity and separation, a coming together that suggests a fresh definition of boundaries. Bishop breaks up the cliché
"gone for good" by allowing "both" to intervene, a word that defines number and barrier. "Both" suggests, on the most literal level,
that Days and Distance are both "gone for good." However, on another level, the line break after "gone" makes the phrase "both for
good" stand out, which seems a comment on the separation in
union of the lovers themselves, in the same way that the final phrase,
"gentle battleground," is. The projected reunion of the lovers is
not romanticized or idealized in the final lines of "Argument." Instead, Bishop rejects the overwhelming rush of powerful emotion
for the more confusing and perhaps truer tension of emotions in
opposition.

Although Williamson argues that Bishop's love poems possess a
"tyrannical assertiveness" (1983, 96), "Varick Street," "Four Poems," and "Argument" seem to me more bewilderingly evasive than
tyrannically assertive. They are elusive, avoiding bald assertions of
truth or expressions of overwhelming emotion in favor of exploring
a more puzzling and contradictory emotional response to the frightening and desired human connection, to love. Interestingly, these
three poems appear in *A Cold Spring* in the order in which I have
discussed them, an order that demonstrates a progression. The tone
of the poems moves along a line, from the nearly unqualified pessimism and seriousness of "hapless odors / hold us close," in "Varick
Street," to the whimsical personification of Days and Distance, the
qualified optimism of "the gentle battleground," in "Argument."
However, only the final love poem, and, importantly, the final poem

in the book, "The Shampoo," achieves a beautiful balance between dread and desire, creates a moment of connection between the self and the lover despite the inexorable forces of space and time. Significantly, "The Shampoo" is also, as Victoria Harrison points out, the closest Bishop comes to openly expressing a lesbian love (1993). The *New Yorker* rejected "The Shampoo," and, in a letter to May Swenson, Bishop hinted at the "indecencies" to which she felt the editors objected. If it was, as Bishop suspected, because of the poem's oblique hints of lesbian affection that it was rejected, then we have an object lesson about what happened to women who dared such expressions: they lost their readership, their chance at connection.

"The Shampoo" seems significantly different in many ways from the rest of the love poems in *A Cold Spring*. The first stanza takes a perspective on the human condition different from the perspective in all of the previous love poems; it pits human perception of time and fear of connection in time against geological or nonhuman time, pits the illusion of stillness against the truth of constant motion. The oxymoron "still explosions" forces together the seemingly unyokeable opposition of what we see (the lichens on the rocks have not moved in human memory) and what we know (the lichens grow so constantly that their sheer life force will reclaim the rock and make it soil):

> The still explosions on the rocks,
> the lichens, grow
> by spreading, gray, concentric shocks.
> They have arranged
> to meet the rings around the moon, although
> within our memories they have not changed. (*Poems,* 84)

The rhyme scheme, like the lichens, quietly and beautifully spreads, moving outward from the expected, closed abab quatrain to the more open, connected abacbc stanza. The variable line length within the tercets also adds to the sense of gradual growth. Bishop's quiet personification of the lichens makes the opposition between the apparent truth that they are unmoving and the invisible fact of their motion a curious and profound contradiction rather than a jarring or a tense one.

However, the second stanza shifts the consideration from geological to human time and shifts the center of contradiction from the lichens to the lover. The loved one, strangely like the lichens, seems both still and moving, both "precipitate" (hasty, flowing, rushing) and "pragmatical" (careful, considered, constant):

> And since the heavens will attend
> as long on us,
> you've been, dear friend,
> precipitate and pragmatical;
> and look what happens. For Time is
> nothing if not amenable.

While all the other love poems have been interior monologues, "The Shampoo" suddenly directly addresses the lover: "you've been, dear friend." Moreover, time, the force that in the other love poems has been insidious, annoying, betraying, and confusing, is suddenly "amenable"! Part of this difference comes from the possibility for connection. Because the lover is present, something can "happen"; and "look what happens"—the connection, the love itself, creates a world that seems to revolve around human desire, and "the heavens . . . attend . . . on us."

However, the third and final stanza of the poem emphasizes that this seeming attendance comes from human perspective, that the heavens' appointment with the lover is actually frighteningly like the heavens' appointment with the lichen, both rushing off to "meet the circles around the moon," a destination both beautiful and inconceivable:

> The shooting stars in your black hair
> in bright formation
> are flocking where,
> so straight, so soon?
> —Come, let me wash it in this big tin basin,
> battered and shiny like the moon.

The truth that the lover ages and will die in time, the truth and dread of loss, counterbalances the desire for and rejoicing in connection. In earlier drafts of the poem, then entitled "Gray Hairs," Bishop exhorts the lichens to stay and not to rush to their destination—"Those still explosions on the rocks. Oh lichens wait!"—or muses "Those still explosions on the rocks are lichens. / How old are they?" (Vassar Box 29). For Bishop, preserving connection over time, preserving love, involved bargaining with the forces of the universe. In her notes for the third draft of "The Shampoo," she writes, "Eternity could always wait of course" (Vassar Box 29), as though all eternity were what two humans bargained with to achieve their moment of connection.

But "The Shampoo" does achieve this moment of connection, despite, or within, the climate of threat. The simile of the final invitation, "—Come, let me wash it in this big tin basin, / battered and shiny like the moon," draws an equivalence between, without equating, the forces of the universe and change, the moon, and the human artifact, the basin. Similarly, the invitation itself does not cancel or deny the possibility of loss but accepts it alongside the possibility of connection. Octavio Paz, speaking of this poem, says, "Shampoo is a metaphor for love" (*Voices and Visions*). The act of shampooing promises a union of the flesh, a vulnerability; the *Kama Sutra* lists shampooing among the kinds of sexual embraces (1962, 99). In this poem, the act of shampooing also represents a physical embracing of the loss represented by the "shooting stars" in the black hair. The tone does not seem to me, as Travisano argues (1988, 104), reminiscent of a seventeenth-century metaphysical love poem, such as Marvell's "To His Coy Mistress," in which the lovers must react to the threat of loss by exerting whatever they have of human power, in which love becomes a contest with eternity: "Thus, though we cannot make our sun / Stand still, yet we will make him run" (Di Cesare 1978, 105). Rather, the tone seems to well up from a profound, quiet acceptance, a willingness to embrace simultaneously the destructive and creative forces of any union with another being. The momentary regret of the lines "flocking where, / so straight, so soon?" is opposed immediately by the openness of "Come."

The movement through the range of emotions surrounding love that Bishop evinces in the love poems of *A Cold Spring* could be connected to her biography, to her growing understanding of her own desire for and dread of human connection, perhaps to her meeting again, in Brazil, with the woman she would eventually fall in love with and live with for many years, Lota de Macedo Soares.[3] However, it seems unfair and misleading to suggest that Bishop's love poems are sentimental and therefore an anomaly, separate from her other work, even from the other poems in the same book, and equally unfair to suggest that, by refusing to consign herself to a life of unpublishable work, Bishop "let down the side" for all women. The same ambivalences that we find in the love poems permeate all the poems of *A Cold Spring* and, really, of her career. For if the love poems of *A Cold Spring* concern the desire for and dread of connection, this is equally true of what I have termed the poems of knowledge, Bishop's explorations of connection with the larger landscape and the world.

"Open the Book": Poems of Knowledge as Connection

Bishop's exploration of the relationship between the self and the other in the love poems of *A Cold Spring* emphasizes the double possibilities of human connection: connection can be the means to self-realization because it liberates the isolated self and grants perspective, as it does in "The Shampoo," or it can be the means to self-annihilation because it threatens to collapse the boundaries between self and other and thereby threatens all boundaries, even the ones between animate and inanimate, as in "Varick Street." The same dichotomies or conflicts, the same tensions between establishing and annihilating the self, inform the poems in *A Cold Spring* that focus on the speaker's attempt to connect through knowledge, to connect with the contingent world, the landscape in motion. Just as Bishop examined the effect of time and change on the promise of love in the love poems, in the knowledge poems she explores the difficulty of human knowing, of seeing accurately, understanding, connecting, when the world we must know is in motion in time, a fact that makes our connection fleeting, precarious, and uncertain.

The title poem, "A Cold Spring," powerfully illustrates the levels of conflict ever present in the landscape we inhabit. The epigraph, "Nothing is so beautiful as spring," from Hopkins's sonnet "Spring," establishes immediately the theme of conflict between the human desire for a tangible, beautiful, permanent "something" with which to connect and the opposing transience of spring, which eventually passes, becomes nothing. Although most critics have followed Anne Stevenson's reading of "A Cold Spring" as a traditional reverie poem in which "all of the images are conventional" (1966, 88), the quotation from Hopkins provides an important clue to the underlying conflict, the strange and deeply unsettling nature of this poem. To argue, as Alan Williamson does, that Bishop uses this epigraph because she feels uneasy about Hopkins's "automatic affirmativeness of the season" (1983, 101) is to suggest that Bishop reads only the surface meaning of Hopkins's sonnet, a suggestion I find unlikely in the light of the fact that Bishop read and studied Hopkins avidly throughout her life and counted him, along with Herbert, as one of her favorite poets and most influential teachers.

The epigraph, for Bishop as for any avid reader of Hopkins's poems, recalls not one disembodied line but the whole passionate conflict of Hopkins's relationship with the physicality and sexuality of spring. While the octet of Hopkins's sonnet could be said to describe a conventional regreening, his diction and use of sprung rhythm nevertheless constantly intimate the threat of spring, its frightening ephemerality: "It strikes like lightening" to hear the thrush sing (Houghton and Stange 1968, 700). The sestet then links the ephemerality of spring to the ephemerality of human life on earth and to humankind in general, unless, for Hopkins, the godhead should intervene:

> What is all this juice and all this joy?
> A strain of the earth's sweet being in the beginning
> In Eden garden. —Have, get, before it cloy,
> Before it cloud, Christ, lord and sour with sinning,
> Innocent mind and Mayday in girl and boy,
> Most, O maid's child, thy choice and worthy the winning.
> (Houghton and Stange 1968, 700)

Newman's sermon lamenting the body's inability to outface time probably influenced Hopkins's "Spring," as the note in Houghton and Stange's text suggests, and influenced Hopkins's description of the passionate conflict between the eternal and the ephemeral.[4] I discuss Hopkins's sonnet here because, if "A Cold Spring" is traditional, this is the tradition it comes from. Bishop's epigraph points the reader not toward the simple pastoral tradition but toward other poets who have felt a profound realization of the conflict between the human desire to connect with something permanent and the natural truth of change and transience.

In "A Cold Spring," Bishop's characteristic ambiguity heightens the tension, the atmosphere of conflict. It seems too simple to argue, as Williamson does, that Bishop casts spring as the ultimate power, a pagan nature god in the pastoral tradition, a god that she can comfortably worship, that will discipline the ego to look (1983, 104). If this were true, the tone of the poem would be placid, calm, lacking divisive egotism or single, engulfing, human perspective. Instead, in "A Cold Spring," the landscape and the speaker, as well as the elements of the landscape themselves, are at war. "A Cold Spring" chronicles a cold war in which traditional images of spring mix with images of soldiers, torture, arms, and conflict. This interest may even be connected in Bishop's mind to the Dewey farm, about which Bishop writes in a letter to Robert Lowell of August 23, 1950: "I think I've told you about Jane Dewey, the physicist daughter of [Dr.] John Dewey? At present she is in charge of 'Terminal Ballistics' at the Aberdeen [Maryland] proving ground, and when I stay at her farm on weekdays the rural scene shakes slightly once in a while as Jane practices her art about 15 miles away, and then there is a faint 'boom.' It seems there are three kinds of ballistics: Internal, External, and Terminal" (Giroux 1994, 205). However, Bishop is evasive about the emotions surrounding the conflict in the poem, unwilling to define a single source of conflict, a single question or perspective that must be answered or adopted. Certainly, the battle to get born and grow is in the forefront, but also important is the conflict between the speaker's expectations and demands for permanence and beauty and absolute truth and knowledge, and the landscape's transience, its changing violently from moment to moment. This atmosphere of hostility and conflict also seems to take a sidelong glance at political concerns; the poem was first published in 1952 in the *New Yorker,* and its title suggests a play on "a cold war" under way with the Soviet Union, as the images of violence and

conflict throughout the poem comment on the atmosphere of conflict throughout the world in the aftermath of World War II.[5]

The tension of the opening lines imitates the tension of the moment before the storm. As the poem opens, everything about the
landscape holds its breath, "waiting," "hesitating," in a kind of no-
man's-land:

> A cold spring:
> the violet was flawed on the lawn.
> For two weeks or more the trees hesitated;
> the little leaves waited,
> carefully indicating their characteristics. (*Poems*, 55)

The odd fifth line points both to the difficulty of growing, the painful birth through which each living thing becomes itself, and also
to the conflict between the speaker and the landscape, the speaker's
desire to see and know pitted against the caution and defense of the
little leaves, indicating, like an army on maneuvers, their counte-
nance and abilities.

The images in the remainder of this first stanza move beyond the
no-man's-land of waiting and hesitating into the central battle of
birth and growth:

> Finally a grave green dust
> settled over your big and aimless hills.
> One day, in a chill white blast of sunshine,
> on the side of one a calf was born.
> The mother stopped lowing
> and took a long time eating the after-birth,
> a wretched flag,
> but the calf got up promptly
> and seemed inclined to feel gay.

When Anne Stevenson quotes from this stanza to prove that "all
of the images are conventional" (1966, 88), she omits, as I think
she must, the line about the cow eating the "wretched flag" of the
afterbirth. The image is unsettling, awry; the flesh becomes a bloody
"flag" of battle in a war with birth and death and time. The image
is also deeply ambiguous: the eating pulls the outward motion of

birth back in, but it nourishes the instrument of the birth; birth
and death are joined and separated by the single action. The afterbirth image acts as the culmination of the birth/death images that
lead up to it—all the puns on birth and death in the phrase "grave
green dust," the mention that the sunshine comes, like a gunshot,
in a "white blast." The speaker impresses all these images of conflict
on the landscape, but they seem, in the moment, to be drawn from
the speaker's coldly emotionless and accurate observation of the
world around her. This ambiguity itself suggests a second and
deeper conflict—one between the speaker's attitude, which reveals
a desire to connect, to know accurately and completely, and the
speaker's discovery of a landscape apparently in motion and conflict.

However, the conflict and violence are also opposed by a strange
joy. Suddenly, amid all the pain of births and the war between the
looker and the landscape comes the report of the calf's qualified joy:
"the calf got up promptly / and seemed inclined to feel gay." The
root of the strangeness and uncertainty of Bishop's spring seems,
not that it is painful, not that it is a war, but that it is also joyful,
that, in Yeats's words from "Lapis Lazuli," "All things fall and are
built again / And those that build them again are gay" (#322). Like
the spring itself, Bishop's tone in describing the landscape seems
cold, distanced; the calf is an oddity to be puzzled over, qualified,
not an indication of the proper mood but instead the depiction of
another mood in opposition to the mood of the speaker.

The beginning of the second stanza explores more explicitly the
war between the observer and the landscape, as the observer, who
desires to describe and understand, discovers increasing elements of
deception and violence in the landscape to be known. Though one
might imagine that a poem about spring moving toward summer
would grow progressively softer, warmer, and kinder, "A Cold
Spring" first grows progressively more unsettling, more evasive, and
more difficult:

> The next day
> was much warmer.
> Greenish-white dogwood infiltrated the wood,
> each petal burned, apparently, by a cigarette-butt;

and the blurred redbud stood
beside it, motionless, but almost more
like movement than any placeable color.

The verb "infiltrate" suggests the kind of military maneuvers meant to facilitate clandestine observation. Here, literally, the dogwoods have "infiltrated," but the word also implies and impugns the speaker's own meticulous description and observation. More startling still, the image of the dogwoods' petals "burned, apparently, by a cigarette-butt" recalls torture and pain, the price often paid for observation and knowledge. Similarly, the "blurred redbud," "motionless, but almost more / like movement than any placeable color," recalls images of camouflage, reveals that the world the speaker observes, the world from which she seeks knowledge, eludes her observations.

However, in the middle of the second stanza, the tone of the poem shifts, and the conflict, though it does not vanish, becomes part of a larger structure of relative peace. Suddenly, personified spring, "the sleeper," is awakened from this dream of itself:

Four deer practised leaping over your fences.
The infant oak-leaves swung through the sober oak.
Song-sparrows were wound up for the summer,
and in the maple the complementary cardinal
cracked a whip, and the sleeper awoke,
stretching miles of green limbs from the south.
In his cap the lilacs whitened,
then one day they fell like snow.

These lines personify everything in the landscape—the deer, the leaves, especially the spring—everything except the birds. Bishop figures the birds as mechanical rather than natural, a kind of alarm clock. The image reminds me again of Yeats's bird "of gold and gold enameling," made "to keep a drowsy Emperor awake" in "Sailing to Byzantium" (#204). And the personified spring appears as a kind of emperor, a force capable of balancing, if only momentarily, the opposing factions of the landscape. The strange adjective "complementary" describing the cardinal suggests the way the opposing factions can be juxtaposed without being blended together, can be held in tension and in check by the structure, both of the season and of the poem.

When personified spring awakens, the images of the poem soften and change. Night falls. The feeling of surface conflict and violence opposed by an underlying joy and peace reverses to become a feeling of peace and contentment opposed by an underlying and hidden sense of covert conflict:

> Now, in the evening,
> a new moon comes.
> The hills grow softer. Tufts of long grass show
> where each cow-flop lies.
> The bull-frogs are sounding,
> slack strings plucked by heavy thumbs.
> Beneath the light, against your white front door,
> the smallest moths, like Chinese fans,
> flatten themselves, silver and silver-gilt
> over pale yellow, orange, or gray.

The profusion of "o" and "u" sounds softens these lines and imitates, to my ear, the bullfrogs' "slack strings plucked by heavy thumbs." The sound is oddly peaceful, and the images in these lines, with their mixture of colors, their synesthesia, possess an almost surreal, somnolent quality.

This movement crescendos in the final stanza in one elusive expression of time and transience, an illuminating and also befuddling explanation of the conflict between the seer and the seen:

> Now, from the thick grass, the fireflies
> begin to rise:
> up, then down, then up again:
> lit on the ascending flight,
> drifting simultaneously to the same height,
> —exactly like the bubbles in champagne.
> —Later on they rise much higher.
> And your shadowy pastures will be able to offer
> these particular glowing tributes
> every evening now throughout the summer.

The end of the poem seems strangely elusive; in a very few lines, time slips away as we move from "Now" to "Later on" to the most ambiguous "every evening now throughout the summer." That final line seems to say both "these tributes will continue for a long time" and "these tributes are terribly transient." The final line impugns the duration of any peace the season promises and simultaneously undermines the speaker's hope of having connected with, of having attained, any absolute or certain knowledge about the contingent world. The cold tone, the attempt at refusing human passion and emotion, which cloud vision, remains to the end of the poem but, in the strange ambivalence of the closing lines, calls attention to its own failure to achieve certainty.

The details of these final lines emphasize the conflict and the movement, the impermanence, of any natural peace. The fireflies' movement, "up, then down, then up again" until they apparently become the stars, seems a glowing tribute, a champagne toast, to the end of the battle for life or to the power of human observation. However, the overwhelming expression of temporality in the last line demonstrates the transience and relativity of any knowledge gained by human looking. Bishop's comparison of the fireflies' movement and a champagne toast also links knowledge and love; the toast links the rites of spring that the speaker observes to the rites of marriage. The comparison is startling and unsettling, like the comparison between women's hands and peninsulas in "The Map." In fact, the comparison is so unsettling that many readers have dismissed it; Gunn writes off the metaphor as excessively clever (1990, 791), and Williamson sees it as stiff, formal, and sad (1983, 102). However, the metaphor works because it is purposefully jarring and clever. It reveals both the speaker's imposition of human perspective on the landscape that she has tried so hard to see coldly and also her awareness of that imposition. The last line of the poem is a continuous expression of time and transience that qualifies itself with each word. The last line says two opposing things simultaneously, exactly like Hopkins's epigraph. This ambiguity undermines all human attempts to see coldly, just as transience undermines human attempts to achieve permanence.

Bishop treats these same themes again and much differently in "Over 2,000 Illustrations and a Complete Concordance," a poem that concerns the human desire to extricate the inextricable relationship between eternity and chronology, connection and loss, knowledge and change. The poem looks at how the human desire for connection with the living world, in motion and constant change, conflicts with the human desire for permanence and peace and absolute understanding. Unfortunately, the poem has most often been read biographically and retrospectively as a musing on the disappointments of traveling when the landscape fails to meet a traveler's expectations, a reading that most often concentrates on the landscape and omits Bishop's complex consideration of human desires and expectations and their basic relationship to the human body. Thomas Travisano's reading of the poem is representative of most; he divides the piece into three movements: (1) Bible engravings, (2) "disappointed glimpses" of Bishop's travel, and (3) return to a fictional "old Nativity" (1988, 115). Bishop, according to Travisano, reverses her original idea that travel should be "serious and engravable" and comes to the conclusion, by the third section, that the answer to her disappointment is imaginative vision (117–19). This reading assumes—mistakenly, I believe—that Bishop searches for and finds a definitive resolution to disappointment. It assumes that Bishop means her pronouncement "Thus should have been our travels" with all its pathos and pomposity.

But, "Over 2,000 Illustrations and a Complete Concordance" is a funny poem. The title alone should alert the reader that the poem will be comic, though perhaps comic in that most serious sense. It is an advertising pitch for a Bible! The tone and diction of the first stanza poke fun at the desire, present equally in both poet and reader, for a knowledge invulnerable to time, a desire to connect with something serious and permanent, to have one true "biblical" experience that can be preserved in a photograph, affirmed by the whole culture—to possess the definitive edition. In the first stanza, the speaker, staring at the Bible engravings, suggests that she, like everyone, longs to know the still, eternal, and changeless—and, of course, there is nothing more still, eternal, or changeless, more "serious" and knowable, than the dead:

> Thus should have been our travels:
> serious, engravable.
> The Seven Wonders of the World are tired
> and a touch familiar, but the other scenes,
> innumerable, though equally sad and still,
> are foreign. Often the squatting Arab,
> or group of Arabs, plotting, probably,
> against our Christian Empire,
> while one apart, with outstretched arm and hand
> points to the Tomb, the Pit, the Sepulcher. (*Poems,* 57)

The word "engravable" is a pun, meaning both "able to be engraved," set down for all time, and also "able to be put in a grave," like the "poor prophet paynim" at the end of the second stanza. The Seven Wonders of the World turn out to be a paradox, not serious enough or engravable enough because they are worn out with knowing, alive in too many imaginations. But there are other scenes, just as dead, "sad and still," but blessedly foreign. It is the deadness and not the life that the speaker seeks in the Bible engravings. When life obtrudes into the desire for absolute knowledge, for permanence and stillness, the syntax jumbles, political factions and multiplicity need to be considered. The guide "plotting, probably, / against our Christian Empire" is a wry joke; the "one apart" turns from plotting actual deaths perhaps, to point to the death, the permanence and seriousness of "the Tomb, the Pit, the Sepulcher." The capital letters and definite articles bang the gong, announce the entrance of the serious and singular.

The landscape that surrounds the Tomb, Pit, and Sepulcher complements the death that dwells there; it is itself a dead landscape:

> The branches of the date-palms look like files.
> The cobbled courtyard, where the Well is dry,
> is like a diagram, the brickwork conduits
> are vast and obvious, the human figure
> far gone in history or theology,
> gone with its camel or its faithful horse.
> Always the silence, the gesture, the specks of birds
> suspended on invisible threads above the Site,
> or the smoke rising solemnly, pulled by threads.

The scene is utterly lifeless and mechanical. The human figure is gone, must be gone, because, like the squatting Arabs, the human figure introduces life and impermanence and change; the human figure makes absolute knowing impossible and makes it necessary to connect with a world in motion in time. The fact that the human figure is "far gone in history or theology" is a joke on two levels: what could be more dead than history or theology, and what disciplines more earnestly seek to know the permanent and absolute?

The silence, the smoke, the birds suspended on threads above the site—all the trappings of death remain when the human figure has departed. But even this stillness, this apparent permanence, collapses because the viewer herself brings to it her living human eye, her perspective. Her desire for absolute knowledge, for the eternal or permanent, is in conflict with her own existence in time, with the necessity of connecting with a world in motion. The images of death, even in the old Bible, are arranged by a living human hand, and these images, when "dwelt upon," are resolved in the grim lunette that the living hand has granted:

> Granted a page alone or a page made up
> of several scenes arranged in cattycornered rectangles
> or circles set on stippled gray,
> granted a grim lunette,
> caught in the toils of an initial letter,
> when dwelt upon, they all resolve themselves.
> The eye drops, weighted, through the lines
> the burin made, the lines that move apart
> like ripples above sand,
> dispersing storms, God's spreading fingerprint,
> and painfully, finally, that ignite
> in watery prismatic white-and-blue.

The dead landscape, caught on the page in all its promising stillness, has every boundary intact. Held on the page, or in "cattycornered rectangles," or "granted a grim lunette," or "caught in the toils of an initial letter," the images of death resolve themselves into themselves, evading ambiguity, impermanence. All these boundaries promise to hold the dead landscape still, to facilitate absolute and changeless knowing, but the eye of the onlooker, the living eye, drops, and its movement also grants life to the "lines / the burin made," just as this phrase looks back to the artist who made the physical line and grants life. The dispersed storm, the blurry fingerprint of God, ignites in "watery prismatic white-and-blue," which recalls both Christian catechism pictures of heaven and what could be the eye itself; it is an eye like the one caught inside a triangle that often appears above Catholic altars as the symbol of the watchfulness of the Lord. "Over 2,000 Illustrations" revolves around the problem of looking and knowing, sensing and connecting.

The second stanza explores, with more detail, this desire to know certainly in the living world of motion and time. The stanza is not a mere recitation of a traveler's disappointments but a catalog of the constant and annoying encroachment of the transient and living upon the serious and dead. The traveler in "Over 2,000 Illustrations," like the sailor in "The Imaginary Iceberg," searches for a scene she can finally give her eyes for, a scene that means the end of travel. However, instead of the certain, the stilled, the moment of complete connection and absolute knowledge, the traveler finds the living, the moving, a human connection vulnerable to time and loss:

> Entering the Narrows at St. Johns
> the touching bleat of goats reached to the ship.
> We glimpsed them, reddish, leaping up the cliffs
> among the fog-soaked weeds and butter-and-eggs.
> And at St. Peter's the wind blew and the sun shone madly.
> Rapidly, purposefully, the Collegians marched in lines,
> crisscrossing the great square with black, like ants.
> In Mexico the dead man lay
> in a blue arcade; the dead volcanoes
> glistened like Easter lilies.
> The jukebox went on playing "Ay, Jalisco!"
> And at Volubilis there were beautiful poppies
> splitting the mosaics; the fat old guide made eyes.
> In Dingle harbor a golden length of evening
> the rotting hulks held up their dripping plush.
> The Englishwoman poured tea, informing us
> that the Duchess was going to have a baby.

The names St. Johns and St. Peter's help connect the biblical engravings and the actual travel, and just as the engravings were brought
to life by the motion of the eye, the places the traveler visits are
alive with motion, with leaping goats and Collegians like ants. As
the stanza progresses, this motion reveals itself as an interruption to
the stillness and seriousness the traveler hoped for in the scenes. The
poppies burst through and undermine the ancient mosaics. "Dripping plush" of live algae and moss overtakes and covers the "rotting
hulks" of dead ships. The "fat old guide" whom the traveler seems
to expect to be serious or solemn is instead flirtatious. The duchess,
a member of an ancient, serious monarchy, is going to have a baby.
Over and over again, the motion of life interrupts and transforms
the stillness of death.

However, the speaker's reaction to life's interruptions is ambiguous. Her tone is both annoyed and interested, bewildered and ex-
hilarated. The interruptions rob her of absolute knowledge and final
permanent connection, but absolute knowledge seems, especially in
the final section of the second stanza, to a kind of death, to
promise self-annihilation. This conflict becomes clear in the following lines, which contrast the "little pockmarked prostitutes," with
all their mixed beauty and ugliness, disease and gaiety, with a scene
of death uninterrupted by life, a scene of unmitigated stillness and
seriousness that seemed, initially, to be the traveler's goal:

> And in the brothels of Marrakesh
> the little pockmarked prostitutes
> balanced their tea-trays on their heads
> and did their belly-dances; flung themselves
> naked and giggling against our knees,
> asking for cigarettes. It was somewhere near there
> I saw what frightened me most of all:
> A holy grave, not looking particularly holy,
> one of a group under a keyhole-arched stone baldaquin
> open to every wind from the pink desert.
> An open, gritty, marble trough, carved solid
> with exhortation, yellowed
> as scattered cattle-teeth;
> half-filled with dust, not even the dust

of the poor prophet paynim who once lay there.
In a smart burnoose Khadour looked on amused.

The juxtaposition of the entire catalog of life and movement, and particularly of the naked and giggling prostitutes, perhaps the least "serious, engravable" element of the catalog, with the "holy grave" creates a tension of opposition that captures and terrifies both the speaker and the reader. Interestingly, in earlier drafts Bishop verbally connected herself to the giggling prostitutes; she wrote, "the fat old guide made eyes and I kept giggling" (Vassar Box 29). Later, she separates the speaker and avoids resolving any of the tense ambiguity of the tone.

The phrase "holy grave" implies both a sacred grave and a "wholly grave" place, one whose deadness is complete. Unlike the mosaics, or the rotting hulks, or St. Peter's, this place shows no indication of life renewing itself. It is the "serious, engravable" thing the traveler mocks herself for searching for. She mocks herself precisely because of her own reaction on finding this grave. Though the scene is reminiscent of "The cobbled courtyard, where the Well is dry," the speaker's reaction is not longing, as before, but horror. Khadour's amusement is a foil for the speaker's fright in the face of the wholly grave. He is separated from the speaker's desires and seems to regard both the grave and the speaker knowingly. In an earlier draft, Bishop limited Khadour's amusement to the sight of the grave: "In his burnoose, Khadour looked on amused, / although it was his sacred place and not mine" (Vassar Box 29); however, in the published version the amusement has greater ambiguity, comments on both the grave, becoming a kind of laugh into the void, and the speaker, becoming a comment on her expectations and her tone.

The giggling prostitutes and Khadour's amusement frame and conflict with the speaker's horror. The grave and the poem, and the old Bible of the opening stanzas, may be, as Williamson argues, a reflection of the desire to save through art, all three "carved solid / with exhortation" but unable finally to redeem any of the lively details they house (1983, 105). Yet, the poem conveys a consciousness of its own enterprise, its own necessarily failed attempts to connect with something permanent and to redeem through this connection all that is transient, a self-consciousness that the engravings (presumably from the Koran) or passages from the Bible cannot have. The poem seems to me not an exhortation but an exploration, an exploration of the conflicting human desire for and dread of connection, the longing for something permanent and absolute and the certainty that permanence and absolutes annihilate the most essential quality that the descriptions of life in the poem demonstrate, change and motion. "Over 2,000 Illustrations" explores and gently mocks the ambivalent and contradictory longings implicit in the human experience of our own bodies.

In the final stanza, Bishop returns to the Bible engravings, but she does not return to the satiric tone of "Thus should have been our travels." Instead, the language of the final stanza is full of wonder. Though many readers have taken the first line of the final stanza as a complaint, to me it suggests a new possibility, a turning away from the search for the absolute, toward the possibility of accepting the conditional and relative, the transient and human:

> Everything only connected by "and" and "and."
> Open the book. (The gilt rubs off the edges
> of the pages and pollinates the fingertips.)
> Open the heavy book. Why couldn't we have seen
> this old Nativity while we were at it?
> —the dark ajar, the rocks breaking with light,
> an undisturbed, unbreathing flame,
> colorless, sparkless, freely fed on straw,
> and, lulled within, a family with pets,
> —and looked and looked our infant sight away.

This final stanza juxtaposes knowledge and change, creates a beautiful ambivalence by holding opposing forces in proximity but refusing to resolve them. The images reflect this tension; the scene of the "old Nativity" both recalls and opposes the scenes of death Bishop has so far described: "the blue arcade," "the holy grave." However, in this scene, instead of either life interrupting death or death alone and frightening, the opposites coexist. Dark and light are joined and yet retain their individuality: "the dark ajar, the rocks breaking with light." The flame burns and does not consume, like God speaking to Moses from the burning bush: "an undisturbed, unbreathing flame." The connection between this Nativity and "the Tomb, the Pit, the Sepulcher" was even more obvious in earlier drafts when Bishop referred to this "unbreathing flame" as a "perpetual flame" (Vassar Box 29). All of the images surround the central paradox of an "old Nativity," a timeless birth into time. This image of fertility without death is the gilt that "pollinates the fingertips," a world we can imagine but never have. Like the imaginary iceberg from *North & South*, the Nativity is a scene a traveler would give her eyes for, a scene that would make any more searching for knowledge, for connection, unnecessary. However, implicit in the absolute connection is the moment of annihilation, "looked and looked our infant sight away." The Latin root of the word "infant," meaning "speechless," reveals the deadliness of this ultimate connection; it engenders permanent silence. (It is Kalstone [1977] who first connects the Latin root of "infant" to its meaning in "Over 2,000 Illustrations," and Doreski [1993] follows up in more detail on the importance of the preliterate in Bishop's work.) However, "infant" also and most commonly connotes birth and rebirth. The one word, like the images that precede it, juxtaposes but refuses to resolve the opposing forces of change and knowledge, connection and loss, birth and death.

The rich ambiguity of "Over 2,000 Illustrations and a Complete Concordance" derives from the unresolved conflict between the human desire for permanence, for absolute knowledge, and the nature of the human flesh, alive in the flow of time, which creates change and uncertainty. The jukebox playing, the fat old guide making eyes, and the duchess having a baby are, like the traveler herself, moving and acting in time, involved in scenes "connected by 'and' and 'and,' " that appear to have no overarching unity, no possibility of resolving themselves into the one experience or dogma, the bookworthy truth. However, Bishop manages both to gently mock the desire for absolutes and to convincingly explain it. She suggests—comically and tragically and perfectly understandably—that what we desire is paradoxical: a serious and engravable revealed truth that can be known by a body that moves through time. Instead of this "biblical" moment, she finds literally over 2,000 illustrations and a complete concordance, or ambiguity, multiplicity, uncertainty.

"A Cold Spring" and "Over 2,000 Illustrations" both concern knowledge, human attempts to connect with the knowable world, the physical landscape. However, each poem depicts a different relationship between the seer and the seen. In "A Cold Spring," the speaker, attempting to see the landscape without the veil of emotion, tries to suppress her perspective. On the other hand, in "Over 2,000 Illustrations," the speaker looks at the landscape to discover a predesigned something, something serious and engravable, that the landscape may possess. In "The Bight," which follows "Over 2,000 Illustrations," the tension of the poem revolves around the speaker's careful observation and apparent insistence on the landscape's separateness and her simultaneous feeling for the landscape as a projection of herself, of her own body.

The understated epigraph tucked in square brackets, "[On my birthday]," like most of Bishop's epigraphs, proves crucial to understanding the poem; it recalls the process of aging and the contemplative consideration of aging often occasioned by a birthday. The opening lines describe a landscape of fragility and desiccation:

> At low tide like this how sheer the water is.
> White, crumbling ribs of marl protrude and glare
> and the boats are dry, the pilings dry as matches.
> Absorbing, rather than being absorbed,
> the water in the bight doesn't wet anything,
> the color of the gas flame turned as low as possible. (*Poems*, 60)

The description seems an attempt to connect with, to know, the bight. Like the landscapes the speaker sees in "Over 2,000 Illustrations," the world of the bight seems dead, still, its ribs of marl protruding through a sheer skin of water. However, this stillness proves not desirable, as before, but stagnating. Even the water does not nourish, does not "wet anything"; it seems noxious, sickly, burning like a low fever, "the color of a gas flame turned as low as possible." The speaker's tone is melancholic or maybe even a little annoyed, but her presence does not obtrude into the description; her tone, like the water in the bight, has been absorbed by and is reflected in the details.

However, in the lines that follow this description, Bishop suddenly shifts tone. She as speaker moves into the foreground of the poem, and the reader becomes suddenly aware of the human perspective that filters this description, the human perspective that has been mediating the scene all along:

> One can smell it turning to gas; if one were Baudelaire
> one could probably hear it turning to marimba music.
> The little ocher dredge at work off the end of the dock
> already plays the dry perfectly off-beat claves.

The impersonal pronoun "one" seems odd in these lines, a sort of overformal sniff at Baudelaire's silliness. However, the reader should not be convinced by this "sniff." On the surface, the lines mock Baudelaire's tendency to impose his own imagination on the scene and never see the truth of the muddy bight. However, Bishop's description of the "little ocher dredge" playing the "perfectly off-beat claves" not only does exactly what she mocks Baudelaire for doing but takes advantage of the beautiful metaphor she mocks him with.

Like so many of the poems from *North & South,* "The Bight" concerns how human knowledge is both created through and distorted by the senses, by the human body itself and by the body's tendency to see itself in every landscape. This question is implicit even in the title of the poem; the archaic meaning of the word "bight" is a bend or curve in the human body. Like the earlier poems, "The Bight" deals with correspondences, with the problem of seeing a correspondence and missing the reality. However, "The Bight" combines this consideration with the quality of self-effacing humor that pervades so many of the poems of *A Cold Spring.* The following lines, describing the overwhelming activity in and around the bight, demonstrate the same whimsical and self-mocking tone Bishop uses in "Over 2,000 Illustrations." These lines point up the difficulty of knowing and describing the world in motion, the problem of human perspective and the possible distortion because of the natural human tendency to see correspondences. This description departs dramatically from the "serious, engravable" opening: "At low tide like this how sheer the water is. / White, crumbling ribs of marl protrude and glare." Here life—the speaker's life and perspective and the motion of all physical bodies—preempts the serious and still and ultimately more knowable world of death. The bight is turning to marimba music, and therefore the music of these lines also shifts away from the quiet, steady iambs of the opening to a more staccato rhythm:

> The birds are outsize. Pelicans crash
> into this peculiar gas unnecessarily hard,
> it seems to me, like pickaxes,
> rarely coming up with anything to show for it,
> and going off with humorous elbowings.

The whimsy of these lines comes not just from their colloquial tone and staccato beat but also from the way they mock the enterprise of the poet herself, especially in her opening lines, who also crashes into this bight like a pickax, trying to know it, to describe it, but perhaps, she feels, "rarely coming up with anything to show for it." This parallel was even more obvious in earlier drafts of the poem, in which Bishop described the pelicans as "semi-human" (Vassar Box 29).

The lines that follow continue in this whimsical tone, relying on similes both to create the description and also to call attention to the poet's artifice in creating it:

> Black-and-white man-of-war birds soar
> on impalpable drafts
> and open their tails like scissors on the curves
> or tense them like wishbones, till they tremble.
> The frowsy sponge boats keep coming in
> with the obliging air of retrievers,
> bristling with jackstraw gaffs and hooks
> and decorated with bobbles of sponges.
> There is a fence of chicken wire along the dock
> where, glinting like little plowshares,
> the blue-gray shark tails are hung up to dry
> for the Chinese-restaurant trade.

The tails of the man-of-war birds are "like scissors"; the sponge boats have the "air of retrievers"; the shark tails are "glinting like little plowshares." Bishop makes all the correspondences, the connections, but allows the similes to hold the correspondences apart, to create a tension. This tension recalls the tension in a love poem like "O Breath," in which the speaker desires equivalences but not equations, similes rather than straight metaphors, a state of correspondence in which the vital identity remains intact. Here, Bishop tries to create another kind of connection, tries to know and describe a landscape, and she resorts to similar equivalences; she must make a separate peace "beneath, within, if never with" the contingent world of bodies in motion.

However serious this connection or knowledge may be, Bishop seems to find the paradox of human desire for connection and knowledge, ours and hers, as amusing as Khadour finds her horror in "Over 2,000 Illustrations." Though the sentence that follows the catalog of life and movement returns to the stillness and death of the opening, this return is punctuated by a joke, a wicked pun:

Some of the little white boats are still piled up
against each other, or lie on their sides, stove in,
and not yet salvaged, if they ever will be, from the last bad storm,
like torn-open, unanswered letters.
The bight is littered with old correspondences.

Here, as in "Over 2,000 Illustrations," attempts to find absolute knowledge or love become attempts to accomplish the impossible, to extricate life and death, the serious and the comic, knowledge and change, stillness and motion. But these are not worthless attempts; they are just comic and, of course, tragic.

The final lines of "The Bight" capture the beautiful ambivalence of any attempt to connect, to know or to love:

Click. Click. Goes the dredge,
and brings up a dripping jawful of marl.
All the untidy activity continues,
awful but cheerful.

The music of these last lines holds the humor and seriousness of the poem together and in tension. For example, the comic rhyme, "jawful" and "awful," offsets the more profound and serious near rhyme, "awful but cheerful." These lines, and especially the word "untidy," almost return to the snobbish sniff of "if one were Baudelaire," but the catalog that precedes them, the colloquial tone, and the variable meter turn the tone into a joke, a pseudosnobbery.

As in "Varick Street," the intertwining of the living and the mechanical in "The Bight" draws near to black comedy. However, while "Varick Street" moves through the blackly comic to the tragic through the forces of its overwhelming sadness, its pessimism, "The Bight" becomes humorous through its cheerful attention to the creature. The connection, the knowledge Bishop seeks in the stilled landscape, is always interrupted by life's force and motion, its constant change, as it had been in both "A Cold Spring" and "Over 2,000 Illustrations." In "The Bight," "untidy activity" intrudes; the knowable changes from moment to moment. This is the kind of "untidy activity" Bishop misses in her great-uncle's "Large Bad Picture," where the stilled and perfected and knowable moment makes it difficult to recognize human motivation or action: "It would be hard to say what brought them there, / commerce or contemplation." But her feeling about the "untidy activity" seems more ambivalent here. In an earlier draft of the poem, she wrote about what she wanted to hear and didn't hear, rather than the "Click. Click." of the dredge:

> No heavenly voice, no organ music plays
> behind this scene
> world
> No soprano shrill (Vassar Box 29)

This failed expectation, this longing for something "heavenly" and permanent beyond the ordinary "Click. Click." underlies the tone of the whole poem. In "A Cold Spring," "Over 2,000 Illustrations," and "The Bight," the same conflicts occur between the speaker and the contingent world, between the speaker's desire to connect and fear of connecting and the world's transience, its violent change. In this sense, the poems about love and the poems about knowledge in *A Cold Spring* deal with the same problems.

In "At the Fishhouses," one of the most exciting poems in *A Cold Spring* or anywhere, Bishop explores the rich ambivalence arising from the conflict between knowledge and change, connection and loss, history and eternity, life and death. Nowhere in the poem do these tensions collapse into chaos or even into order, into resolution. Instead, Bishop draws on the tensions, juxtaposes opposites within the same line, or thought, or word in order to embody in the poem's structure the evasive and elusive quality of knowledge that she finds in the world. Bishop moves from the apparently known to the unknowable, from the land to the sea, from powerful description to the realm where language falls silent, from connection to immersion. "At the Fishhouses" captures the sense that, as Elizabeth Spires says, "what little we know to be true keeps changing" (1984, 23).

From the outset of the poem, the landscape the speaker examines seems both absolutely vivid and on the point of dissolution. Kalstone notes that the old fisherman seems to be wearing away into the scene, seems to be becoming the gloaming, the net, the shuttle (1977, 19). However, Bishop introduces a subtle conflict between the fisherman and the evening in the word "although":

> Although it is a cold evening,
> down by one of the fishhouses
> an old man sits netting,
> his net, in the gloaming almost invisible,
> a dark purple-brown,
> and his shuttle worn and polished. (*Poems*, 64)

Even though the fisherman may seem to be a part of the landscape, his physicality conflicts with the contingent world. His enduring the cold points toward the upcoming conflict between the speaker and the cold, cold sea, the "element bearable to no mortal."

The poem opens with the speaker and the fisherman on the edge between two worlds, the land and the sea, both belonging to the first and yet trying to connect with and know the second. The fact that this knowledge, like all human knowledge, is mediated through

the senses becomes strikingly clear in the lines that follow, in which
the speaker describes the landscape:

> The air smells so strong of codfish
> it makes one's nose run and one's eyes water.
> The five fishhouses have steeply peaked roofs
> and narrow, cleated gangplanks slant up
> to storerooms in the gables
> for the wheelbarrows to be pushed up and down on.

This description seems like a figurative version of the fisherman's
literal net, a device to gather and catch, a way to know. Spires suggests that "netting" is itself a metaphor for the human effort to
know with certainty in a world that is in constant transition (1984,
20). Bishop's passionately accurate and vivid description, the liq-
uid "f" and "s" sounds, paradoxically creates a landscape that is still
enough to connect with and yet pervaded with a sense of motion,
of inevitable change.

In the following lines, however, Bishop seems to differentiate, to
draw a line, between the nature of the things on land, human-made
objects like lobster pots, masts, benches, all silvered translucent as
if with age, and the nature of the sea, silver too but opaque, allowing the light to pass through:

> All is silver: the heavy surface of the sea,
> swelling slowly as if considering spilling over,
> is opaque, but the silver of the benches,
> the lobster pots, and masts, scattered
> among the wild jagged rocks,
> is of an apparent translucence
> like the small old buildings with an emerald moss
> growing on their shoreward walls.

The profusion of "s" and "l" sounds, which seem themselves to
swell and consider spilling over, stands against the more clipped individual consonants of "lobster pots," and "wild jagged rocks." The
sea, like the imaginary iceberg from *North & South* or the prophet
paynim's tomb in "Over 2,000 Illustrations," is "other," absolutely
inscrutable. Again, in order to describe this otherness, Bishop uses

a simile that simultaneously creates and destroys the personified figure of the sea; she figures the sea as a being that could consider spilling over. The tension in this simile echoes the tension between the objects of the land, translucent and knowable, and the sea itself, opaque and inscrutable.

Bishop goes on to describe vividly the details of the land, all touched and changed by the sea but still knowable, still part of the land, the human milieu:

> The big fish tubs are completely lined
> with layers of beautiful herring scales
> and the wheelbarrows are similarly plastered
> with creamy iridescent coats of mail,
> with small iridescent flies crawling on them.
> Up on the little slope behind the houses,
> set in the sparse bright sprinkling of grass,
> is an ancient wooden capstan,
> cracked, with two long bleached handles
> and some melancholy stains, like dried blood,
> where the ironwork has rusted.

The wheelbarrows lined with herring scales and the flies that live off of these scales connect the human-made objects to the natural world of the land. The absolute vividness of this description, Bishop's ability to re-create the physicality of the objects in the landscape, provides a way for the reader and the speaker to know the world, to connect momentarily with each other and with the scene.

This connection is amplified in the lines that follow by the connection the speaker makes between the old fisherman and herself:

> The old man accepts a Lucky Strike.
> He was a friend of my grandfather.
> We talk of the decline in the population
> and of codfish and herring
> while he waits for a herring boat to come in.
> There are sequins on his vest and on his thumb.
> He has scraped the scales, the principal beauty,
> from unnumbered fish with that black old knife,
> the blade of which is almost worn away.

As in the opening lines of the poem, the old man seems both connected with and separate from the landscape that surrounds him. He seems a fixture; he has known the poet's grandfather. He, like everything human in this scene, is covered with the silvery herring scales. Like the speaker, the fisherman negotiates with the landscape he inhabits, by acting, waiting, attempting to find a living in the sea. Both speaker and fisherman are "netting," looking for sustenance from the sea, forging a connection. But for both, this connection is terribly ambivalent. In this stanza, the fisherman interacts with the world around him by scraping off "the principal beauty" of "unnumbered fish." This action parallels the violence and conflict implicit in the relationship between the seer and the contingent world in "A Cold Spring." Similar ambivalence and conflict occur in the relationship between the fisherman and the speaker, as the list of conversational topics demonstrates—all topics of common small talk but tinged with the threat of dissolution, of the failing of the community and the trade, all flatly delivered.

From these ambivalent relationships the poet shifts her gaze, looking out from the shore to the edge where the shore meets the sea. Here again Bishop juxtaposes opposites, and she draws from the tension that opposition creates, like pushing together two opposing magnets:

> Down at the water's edge, at the place
> where they haul up the boats, up the long ramp
> descending into the water, thin silver
> tree trunks are laid horizontally
> across the gray stones, down and down
> at intervals of four or five feet.

The repetition of ascending movements, "haul up" and "up the long ramp," opposes the repetition of descending motions, "Down at the water's edge," "descending into the water," "down and down / at intervals of four or five feet." Spires suggests that Bishop's description of the tree trunks parallels the movement of beats per line in the poem, the lines and the logs laid down at intervals of four or five (1984, 21), both exploring the edge where the known and the inscrutable meet and overlap.

This short stanza is the turning point of the poem, the pivot. From this stanza, Bishop looks—or, more accurately, attempts to look—at the inscrutable face of the sea, the "other," what she called in "Over 2,000 Illustrations" the serious and engravable. The first line of the next stanza is a pronouncement of the speaker's intention to characterize, to describe, to know and connect with the sea:

> Cold dark deep and absolutely clear,
> element bearable to no mortal,
> to fish and to seals . . . One seal particularly
> I have seen here evening after evening.
> He was curious about me. He was interested in music;
> like me a believer in total immersion,
> so I used to sing him Baptist hymns.
> I also sang "A Mighty Fortress Is Our God."

The poetic pronouncement, the catalog of adjectives, breaks down after the second line because, on one level, in announcing that the sea is bearable to no mortal, that the sea is a kind of death, Bishop finds herself once again staring into the "holy grave." By the third line, life—fish and seals, like the poppies in "Over 2,000 Illustrations"—bursts through the mosaic of the inscrutable. Bishop seemingly begins the stanza by trying to describe, to know, the sea, but almost immediately she shifts her focus to another creature, to the seal, who can be anthropomorphized, who makes the sea relational. The poem equates the speaker and the seal; they are both curious observers, both interested in music, and both on the edges of a kind of religion. Bishop's choosing to sing Baptist hymns and "A Mighty Fortress Is Our God," her noting that she and the seal are both "believers in total immersion," points toward another relationship with the inscrutable, a religious attempt to connect with the permanent and eternal.

The seal's reaction to Bishop's singing seems a half-mocking self-parody of her own reaction to the inscrutable, the strange:

> He stood up in the water and regarded me
> steadily, moving his head a little.
> Then he would disappear, then suddenly emerge

almost in the same spot, with a sort of shrug
as if it were against his better judgment.

In the next line, the poet mimics the motion of the seal, beginning
again in "almost the same spot" where she started the stanza, with
an almost audible shrug:

Cold dark deep and absolutely clear,
the clear gray icy water . . . Back, behind us,
the dignified tall firs begin.
Bluish, associating with their shadows,
a million Christmas trees stand
waiting for Christmas.

Again she makes the poetic pronouncement, recites the list of adjectives describing the sea, and again, by the third line, she turns
away from this inscrutable face back toward the apparently knowable
land. Parker suggests that both sets of ellipses in this stanza, as they
follow the description of the sea, are meant to whet the reader's
appetite, to build up our expectations for and our understanding
of the ocean's power, that somehow Bishop feels that the sea is too
powerful and sacred to discuss (1988, 81). However, I don't see this
movement between land and sea as a contrived hesitancy; I think
these assaults on and rebuffs from the inscrutable comprise the center of meaning in the poem. The poem is about how to know and
the relationship between physical connection and human knowledge. The ellipses demonstrate a true difficulty; every attempt to
state the nature of the sea, to capture in language its otherness, to
pronounce poetically something about the eternal, ends in a string
of adjectives held still by forcibly withholding a verb, ends in the
poet's gaze wandering back toward the living, the ambivalent, the
human.

Paradoxically, the complete acceptance of human perspective in
seeing the blue firs as "a million Christmas trees," the surrendering
of the voice to the single perspective as the only available truth,
allows the richly ambiguous and beautiful characterization of the
sea that finally comes in the last lines of the poem:

> The water seems suspended
> above the rounded gray and blue-gray stones.
> I have seen it over and over, the same sea, the same,
> slightly, indifferently swinging above the stones,
> icily free above the stones,
> above the stones and then the world.

The voice suddenly assumes a more intimate tone; the assertion "I have seen it over and over" suggests a sort of weary participation in this sea, weary and frightening because the sea remains indifferent and icy. Suddenly Bishop has abandoned the poetic pronouncement, the timeless and true list of adjectives, and embraced another kind of ambivalence—water that "seems suspended," a sea "swinging above the stones" and also above the world. The rhythm of these lines and the repetition of "s" and "f" sounds reproduce the physical sensation of being at sea, of participating in the sea's motion.

In the last lines of the poem, Bishop switches to the second person and the reader is literally immersed in the poem; the moment of baptism, of connection, broadens to include the speaker's connection with the sea, the speaker's connection with the reader, and the reader's connection with the sea:

> If you should dip your hand in,
> your wrist would ache immediately,
> your bones would begin to ache and your hand would burn
> as if the water were a transmutation of fire
> that feeds on stones and burns with a dark gray flame.
> If you tasted it, it would first taste bitter,
> then briny, then surely burn your tongue.
> It is like what we imagine knowledge to be:
> dark, salt, clear, moving, utterly free,
> drawn from the cold hard mouth
> of the world, derived from the rocky breasts
> forever, flowing and drawn, and since
> our knowledge is historical, flowing, and flown.

The connection with the sea involves physically touching the icy water; this experience is knowledge, but the sea itself is not knowledge, but instead, and more importantly, "It is like what we imagine knowledge to be." Paradoxically, the connection that promised to draw the speaker and the reader out of themselves, perhaps to their own annihilation, actually forces both speaker and reader back into themselves and connects them to their own imaginations. This connection is not only paradoxical but frighteningly ambiguous. "At the Fishhouses" suggests that knowledge and connection may actually be mutually exclusive, that we cannot know what we experience because of our subjective walls, because of our flawed human senses, our tendency to imagine our own bodies everywhere. Thus, the sea Bishop finally put her hand in becomes a woman, has a "cold hard mouth" and "rocky breasts." She finally connects with the sea by taking it into herself, connects with the reader by taking him or her to the sea.

A Cold Spring and North & South are complementary; therefore, it makes sense that Bishop chose to publish the two books in one volume, Complete Poems. Both books use metaphors of the body to explore connection and loss, actualization and annihilation, but in A Cold Spring Bishop allows more intrusion of the poet's personal voice than she does in North & South. Part of this, as I suggested earlier in this chapter, may be from the influence of her contemporaries, particularly Lowell and Jarrell, who were in turn influenced by a younger poet searching for a new direction, W. D. Snodgrass. Yet, the move toward the personal voice, which I will discuss in even more depth in the next chapter, also seems a natural outgrowth of Bishop's colloquial tones. Here, she moves, as she will continue to move in her next two books, toward a poetry that is more personal and less objective and modernist. However, she does not struggle as openly with issues of love and sexuality in either Questions of Travel or Geography III. In many ways, A Cold Spring marks her struggle to find a way to have connection without annihilation, to have a personal voice *and* a readership. A Cold Spring has received little of the critical attention it deserves. The book reveals the complicated and subtle workings of Bishop's thought and craft at a crucial stage in her career. Seeking a way to reach through time and change, to connect the constantly moving self to the constantly moving other, lies at the heart of both the love poems and the poems of knowledge in A Cold Spring.

3

QUESTIONS OF TRAVEL
The Poetics of Evasion

IN NOVEMBER OF 1951, four years before the publication of *A Cold Spring*, Elizabeth Bishop won the first Lucy Martin Donnelly Fellowship from Bryn Mawr College and set out on a journey to the Strait of Magellan. She had long been interested in South America,[1] its tiny hummingbirds and huge fish, and she especially wanted to see Brazil and the fecund life surrounding the Amazon. So great was her love of Brazil that she contended, years later, that E. Lucas Bridges's book *Uttermost Part of the Earth*, a history of Brazil and description of its landscape, should be "classed with Robinson Crusoe for a suspense of strangeness and ingenuity and courage and loneliness" (MS draft introduction of *Brazil-Brasil*, Vassar Box 25). However, while visiting friends in Rio de Janeiro, she ate cashew fruit, had a violent allergic reaction, and was forced to stay in Rio and recover rather than continue on her course to the long-dreamed-of Strait.

As she got over the attack and grew stronger, Bishop found herself "enthralled by the Brazilian geography and landscape, by the paradoxical, affectionate, spontaneous Brazilian people, and the complications of a world at once feudal, 19th century, and contemporary" (Kalstone 1989, 149–50). She decided to live in Brazil. With Lota de Macedo Soares, a woman she had met in New York in 1942, Bishop had a home built forty miles outside Rio near a mountain resort called Petropolis. She and Macedo Soares shared this home, and a small apartment in Rio, for fifteen years.[2] She wrote to Lowell during her second year in her new home: "I am extremely happy, for the first time in my life" (Kalstone 1989, 151).

In what she called "an atmosphere of uncritical affection" (Kalstone 1989, 151), Bishop grew increasingly able to accept her un-connected wanderings, the feeling that she "was always sort of a guest" (Spires 1978, 141) or that her travels were "connected by 'and' and 'and.'" This new Brazilian life—in its domesticity, its sense of combining the ancient and contemporary, and in the new-found atmosphere of unconditional love—seemed an exotic mirror of her dear and familiar childhood home in Great Village, Nova Scotia. Even later in her life, after the tragedy of Lota's death, she wrote: "What I'm really up to is recreating a sort of deluxe Nova Scotia all over again in Brazil. And now I'm my own grandmother" (Kalstone 1989, 152). Her sense of the uncanny connections be-tween her childhood past and her adult present—connections she often alludes to in her letters as strange and unsettling and joyful—translates into *Questions of Travel,* a book published fourteen years after her arrival in her adopted home.

Questions of Travel gathers the wonder and strangeness Bishop felt about the rediscovery of her childhood during her Brazilian years. The book represents fresh explorations of the boundlessness and limits of the body and a new sense of the compendium of questions surrounding the relationship between perception and reality, past and present, imagination and experience, and the mind and the flesh. *Questions of Travel* becomes itself a body that unites and sepa-rates the two worlds of the Nova Scotia childhood and the Brazilian adulthood in the two sections—"Brazil," poems concerning travel-ing to and living in a foreign country, and "Elsewhere," poems about Bishop's other homes, particularly her Nova Scotia home. Yet, these two separate places are joined both by the book and by the images, tones, and emotions of the poems that call to and recall one another across the geographical divide.

In *North & South,* Bishop often posed questions about the body as the mediator of the physical world. She saw human perception as miraculously transforming, causing both terrible distance and amaz-ing proximity. In *A Cold Spring,* she complicated the stilled mo-ments of connection she had achieved in poems like "The Fish" and "A Miracle for Breakfast" by setting them in motion, by considering knowledge and love as they are affected by time. Here, in *Questions of Travel,* Bishop struggles to express the almost inexpressible felt connections between different times, separate places, even opposing ideas. She strives more than ever before to write poems that are both perfectly lucid, almost self-evident, and entirely inscrutable, contradicting themselves and the poems around them. In this struggle to both say and unsay, in her evasiveness and in her gift for beautiful ambiguity, I see still more clues to Bishop's ambivalence about embodiment, both in physical form, the flesh, and in its microcosm, literary form, the poem.

Questions of Influence

The larger structure of *Questions of Travel* itself suggests Bishop's ambivalence about the physical form. Dividing the book into two sections, one limited by the barriers of geography and one moving freely through and around these barriers, signals the kind of contradictory yet interdependent relationships that pervade every level of the work. Although Kalstone is correct in noting that Bishop "made no attempt to interweave Brazil and Elsewhere" (1989, 214) in individual poems, this observation minimizes the strong bonds of opposition that not only connect poem to poem but connect the two major sections. Kalstone's observation also slights the centrality of Bishop's prose piece "In the Village" and overlooks the way the story's narrator, by combining the perspectives of her adult present and her childhood past, implicitly connects the poems of the Brazilian present and the past spent elsewhere.

Bishop's decision to include "In the Village" signals a development from the first two books, a testing of the limits of form and its ability to contain and release essential contradictions. Some of Bishop's developments between *A Cold Spring* and *Questions of Travel*—particularly, her increasing reliance on autobiography—resulted from her sensitivity to the possibilities Lowell had opened up in *Life Studies* and *For the Union Dead*, possibilities Lowell himself had seen in the poetry of W. D. Snodgrass.[3] However, Bishop had already been working on autobiographical prose pieces, and many of her earlier poems, in both *North & South* and *A Cold Spring*, contained a great deal of autobiographical detail. *Questions of Travel* differs, though, in its willingness to speak outright of her childhood loss. The tone of "First Death in Nova Scotia" and some of the peculiarities of the children's voices in other poems seem to owe something to Lowell's "My Last Afternoon with Uncle Devereux Winslow." A desire to correct Lowell's rather melodramatic concentrating of the harrowing details of "In the Village" in his poem "The Scream" (collected in *For the Union Dead*) may have motivated Bishop to include the prose piece in her next book (Kalstone 1989, 212). Or perhaps she took up Lowell's suggestion in his letter of February 9, 1959, that her next book be a verse/prose mixture (Vassar Box 6).

But, questions of Lowell's influence (or Jarrell's, for that matter, or Moore's), like most of the issues surrounding Bishop's work, are more complicated than they at first appear, are a true Gordian knot of suggestion, imitation, coincidence, and shared background. As much as Bishop was influenced by *Life Studies* and Lowell's work generally, she deeply influenced it also. In a letter dated December 3, 1957, Lowell recounts for Bishop the praise some of the poems in *Life Studies* received and says: "You guess how my head is turned. But I've really just broken through to where you've always been and gotten rid of my medieval armor's undermining" (Vassar Box 6). He notes that he will publish "Skunk Hour" and three other poems and tells Bishop that he has dedicated "Skunk Hour" to her.

After Bishop had written "Gwendolyn" (the account of a playmate's death) and "In the Village," her letters exhorted Lowell to write his autobiography. Though both poets found prose a difficult medium—in Lowell's words, "it starts naked, ends as fake velvet" (Vassar Box 6)—they struggled on, testing the limits between verse and prose, exploring the boundaries and the bridges between autobiographical truth and artistic form. In a letter of June 18, 1956, Lowell alludes to the first publication of "91 Revere Street," the autobiographical story that appears in *Life Studies*, saying that he has "a big chunk" of prose autobiography coming out in the *Partisan Review* and hoping that Bishop will approve. He abjures, however, that his "seems thin and arty after your glorious Nova Scotia mad mother and cow piece" (Vassar Box 6). Through their complex, romantic, competitive, protective feelings about each other, Lowell and Bishop forged a literary relationship that, for a while, nurtured and nourished each other's work. *Questions of Travel* chronicles the height of this interdependence and also the strength of the opposition within it; Lowell's versification of "In the Village" demonstrates in microcosm the kind of usurpation that ultimately separated Bishop and Lowell's literary relationship and endangered, if never destroyed, their personal one.

"In the Village"

"In the Village" is the story of Bishop as a young child witnessing her mother's growing insanity, and enduring loss and absence when her mother is finally committed to an asylum. In many ways it is the story of two sounds, disembodied and opposing—the sound of her mother's scream as she tries on the purple dress that will signal the end of her mourning period and the sound of Nate's, the blacksmith's, hammer. The opening paragraph of "In the Village" distills in prose many of the central concerns of the poems in *Questions of Travel*. It explores the felt connections between past and present, struggles with the tension between human perspective and reality, and expresses an underlying ambivalence, an uneasiness, about emotion and thought embodied in sound:

> A scream, the echo of a scream, hangs over that Nova Scotian village. No one hears it; it hangs there forever, a slight stain in those pure blue skies, skies that travelers compare to those of Switzerland, too dark, too blue, so that they seem to keep on darkening a little more around the horizon—or is it around the rim of the eyes?—the color of the cloud of bloom on the elm trees, the violet on the fields of oats; something darkening over the woods and waters as well as the sky. The scream hangs like that, unheard, in memory—in the past, in the present, and those years between. It was not even loud to begin with, perhaps. It just came there to live, forever—not loud, just alive forever. Its pitch would be the pitch of my village. Flick the lightning rod on top of the church steeple with your fingernail and you will hear it. (*Prose*, 251)

The question "or is it around the rim of the eyes?" characteristically calls attention to the centrality of the body, of the human perspective. The sound is alive, embodied in every detail of the Nova

Scotian landscape. But there is an uneasiness about the embodiment of this sound; the final sentence, switching into second person, seems almost menacing, as though the speaker dares the reader to test the truth of the scream. Because of this menace, the reader seems to hear what he or she actually has not heard, the scream itself. The play of perspective, shrinking the village and making the reader a giant, creates a sense of uncanniness, a sense that things are askew.

However, the sound of Nate's hammer at the end of the story stands in direct opposition to the sound of the scream, which we do not actually hear, in the first paragraph. The clang of Nate's hammer has the power to banish the ghost sound of the scream, to unbody it and cause it to float away into the "dark, too dark, blue sky." However, Nate's sound, by being disembodied, is lost, transient, and points up the lostness of everything human, of the "clothes, crumbling postcards, broken china," all the things her mother owned, kept, even the lostness of Bishop's mother, of Nate, of Bishop herself. Denis Donoghue says, "What Bishop's story speaks of in letting the mind play over the two sounds is the desire to be released from the whole human state—from Yeats' 'the fury and mire of human veins,' and at the same time and with no less force, the desire not to be released but to be held within it" (1984, 277). In this desire is the related desire to let go of grief, to let it float away, and to hold onto grief forever, like Tennyson's "In Memoriam," to embody it in the concrete details that seem more stable than our transient human existence. These two simultaneous and opposing desires present themselves with poetic force in the closing paragraphs of "In the Village":

> Clang.
> Clang.
> Nate is shaping a horseshoe.
> Oh, beautiful pure sound!
> It turns everything to silence.
> But still, once in a while, the river gives an unexpected gurgle. "Slp," it says, out of glassy-ridged brown knots sliding along the surface.
> Clang.
> And everything except the river holds its breath. Now there is

no scream. Once there was one and it settled slowly down to earth on a hot summer afternoon; or did it float up, into that dark, too dark, blue sky? But surely it has gone away, forever.

It sounds like a bell buoy out at sea. It is the elements speaking: earth, air, fire, water. All those other things—clothes, crumbling postcards, broken china; things damaged and lost, sickened or destroyed; even the frail, almost-lost scream—are they too frail for us to hear their voices long, too mortal?

Nate!

Oh, beautiful sound, strike again! (*Prose* 274)

The first and last paragraphs of "In the Village," the description of two related and opposing sounds, exemplify in prose the kind of ambivalence and ambiguity that mark the poems in *Questions of Travel*.

Like the two sounds, the matter and form within and among these poems both oppose and recall each other, revealing Bishop's ambivalence about the power of sound (sounds play a central role in the images of almost every poem in the book) and the nature of the body. These poems get their power from the tension between saying and not saying, the nearly evaded—as opposed to the evasive—form or emotion or idea. To explore the ambivalence about bodiliness in these poems and the ambiguous relationships between them, I first discuss the way the opening three poems—"Arrival at Santos," "Brazil, January 1, 1502," and the title poem, "Questions of Travel"—refute and recall each other, creating a verbal triptych. Next, I explore that same ambiguity and evasiveness as it expresses itself in Bishop's use of form in the poems "Sestina," "The Armadillo," and "Visits to St. Elizabeths." When appropriate I discuss how that tension with form connects the two sections, "Brazil" and "Elsewhere."

"Here Is the Church and Here Is the Steeple": The Opening Triptych of *Questions of Travel*

David Kalstone perceptively suggests that the first three poems in *Questions of Travel* can be productively considered in relation to one another as featuring three different expressions of the method-

ology of observation (1989, 214). These three poems pose what
seem like three different sets of questions about the ways we observe, the centrality of bodily experience, and the limits of the
imagination. They are all about the first look around a strange port,
about expectation and impression. But, on the surface, these poems
seem to illustrate three opposing approaches to perceiving the foreign, to having a "new" experience: the casual tourist worried about
personal comfort in "Arrival at Santos," the conqueror and plun-
derer concerned with material gain in "Brazil, January 1, 1502,"
and the anthropologist or cultural observer looking for societal insight in "Questions of Travel." On one level, then, these poems appear to be simple statements about travel and its excitements and
disappointments. They represent distinct and opposing methods of
observing the new, each focusing in different ways on how the body
and this strange reality interact, the voices variously concerned
about comfort, power, wealth, and understanding. However, on another level, these poems, and the voices of the speakers in the poems, although they do oppose each other, also echo and suggest
each other. The voices overlap, touch, and refuse to resolve themselves into three separate and relatively simple perspectives. Instead,
these opening poems become a kind of triptych, separate but touching, each poem suggesting, refuting, and amplifying the other two.
For example, the casual tourist in "Arrival at Santos" is headed, like
the anthropologist on a search for discovery and understanding, toward the interior. The conqueror in "Brazil, January 1, 1502" seeks
lute music and bowers, the same easy pleasure and homey familiarity
sought by the casual tourist worried about her bourbon. The cultural observer in the title poem forces images and meanings from
details of the landscape and yet resists her own constructs in the
same way the Portuguese soldiers unconsciously and even joyfully
see their Catholic philosophy played out in Brazil's nature and then
just as joyfully rip that veneer of civilization away.

I will put the title poem, "Questions of Travel," aside for a moment and discuss the relationship between the first two poems, "Arrival at Santos" and "Brazil, January 1, 1502." Both poems are, of
course, about beginnings, arrivals, and entryways, about how the
expectations we have at our departures influence our perception of

the "new" world. Both describe how we see or miss seeing the unknown landscape because of the remembered or known. Each takes place at the port, the entrance, and ends with a suggestion of moving toward, or, more accurately, being drawn into, the interior. In both poems, the movement from the entrance to the interior, from the orifice to the center, has an insistent element of sexuality. They are poems about connection and about failure to connect, not just with a landscape but with a peopled landscape. As in the poems of *A Cold Spring*, the acts of knowing and loving in *Questions of Travel* are essentially interchangeable in that both require the same risk of connection, of expanding the boundaries of the self. "Arrival at Santos" and "Brazil, January 1, 1502" simultaneously express the indefatigable hope for connection and the utter impossibility of connection, the loss and disappointment and exhilaration of embodying limitless thought in a limited thing, the smallness of the limited imagination in comparison with the power and surprise of the awkward human flesh. They manage to both embody the most complex ideas and emotions and also avoid embodying them by setting these ideas and emotions in opposition to each other, by saying two opposite things in the same breath, or in the same book.

In the opening verse paragraphs of "Arrival at Santos," the speaker's disappointment about the look of the place, conveyed in the adjectives "meager," "harsh," "frivolous," "feeble," and "uncertain," is couched in the sound of a simple children's rhyme, a kind of fairy tale tone and rhythm. The first two lines, in particular, recall the triptych nursery rhyme "Here is the church and here is the steeple; open the doors and see all the people." Bishop admired children's verse ("Manners," the first poem in "Elsewhere," was to open a collection of children's poetry she never completed); she admired writers like Edward Lear,[4] and she had incorporated the entire "Here is the church" rhyme into an earlier, unpublished draft of a Jonsonian masque called "Prince 'Winsome' Mannerly," which dealt with similar themes: the possibility of finding new life, the disappointment of what was sought after and is now achieved, the invasion of the unexpected, and traveling and returning home. In "Arrival at Santos," the combination of adult disillusionment and the underlying suggestion of childlike wonder manages to impart a number of seemingly opposed meanings at the same time. We hear the expectant excitement of the tourist before arriving and the disappointed catalog of details that failed these expectations, and we also get a sense of the world beyond the tourist's perspective, of the reality of the port, the commerce, the "untidy activity":

> Here is a coast; here is a harbor;
> here, after a meager diet of horizon, is some scenery:
> impractically shaped and—who knows?—self-pitying mountains,
> sad and harsh beneath their frivolous greenery,
>
> with a little church on top of one. And warehouses,
> some of them painted a feeble pink, or blue,
> and some tall, uncertain palms. (*Poems*, 89)

A part of Bishop's ability to impart multiple meanings, her gift for ambiguity, stems from a willingness to rephrase, to rethink—to apparently reveal the motion of her thought behind the characterizing image. For example, in the first draft of "Arrival at Santos," she had written, "impractically pointed mountains, self-pitying / decorated with a frilly, dainty greenery" (Vassar Box 29). This description erects a completed facade of perspective; the reader unselfconsciously sees the mountain through Bishop's gaze. However, the phrase "who knows?" cracks that facade; the reader becomes conscious of the fact that he or she is looking through someone else's perspective, becomes conscious of the motion of thought behind the image. This consciousness creates a kind of double vision, an irony, as we see through both the speaker's eyes and our own. The first draft of the poem also lacked the apostrophe to the tourist that follows the opening description and performs much the same function as the phrase "who knows?"—creating self-consciousness, cracking the facade, and harassing the reader into uncomfortable participation:

> Oh, tourist,
> is this how this country is going to answer you
>
> and your immodest demands for a different world,
> and a better life, and complete comprehension

of both at last, and immediately,
after eighteen days of suspension?

The reader may seem, at first, to be the accused tourist. The reader,
then, becomes aware of and outside of the speaker and of comfortable participation in the speaker's perspective. However, the question could literally be directed to the hypothetical tourist-speaker
who uttered the first disappointed description. It could be self-ref-
erent, or, at least, refer to a particular side of the self, the one with
the "immodest demands." The tone is schoolmarmish, the question
rhetorical in the motherly vein of "Are you going to stop that?" or
"Do I have to tell you again?" or "You certainly didn't believe that,
did you?"

However, the question delves deeper, undercuts and opposes the
schoolmarmish tone, because the answer to "is this how this country
is going to answer you" is not as evident as the tone suggests. The
first "this" emphasizes the literal fact of the port; it asks, "Is the
entry all there is?" It questions our ability to know anything with
certainty, questions the mind's capacity to imagine the answers.
Would the tourist know if this was the longed-for change, the better
life? How would she know? Would the palms look certain? Would
the mountains rise confidently? This confident landscape, the pic-
ture-postcard beauty, is, perhaps, the imagined or expected answer.
And yet, there may be an answer in this imperfect scenery to the
tourist's demand for a different world and a better life and complete
comprehension.

In the same quasi-certain, schoolmarmish tone, the speaker gives
the only answer in the poem, the motherly non-answer, "Finish your
breakfast." That phrase has all the implications it has when any
mother uses it—"You have to wait"; "I don't know"; "First things
first"; "Be nourished." It is a classic evasion of the most difficult
questions, an evasion that reveals the intricacy of the question it
evades. However, it is also a counsel of patience. This answer is followed by a complete change in voice; the wonder—the wonder that
the landscape has disappointed, the wonder that causes the disillusionment of the opening description—returns to the surface as the

tourist realizes that this place is more than what she imagined, that it exists outside of and independent from her thought of it:

> Finish your breakfast. The tender is coming,
> a strange and ancient craft, flying a strange and brilliant rag.
> So that's the flag. I never saw it before.
> I somehow never thought of there *being* a flag,
>
> but of course there was, all along. And coins, I presume,
> and paper money; they remain to be seen.
> And gingerly now we climb down the ladder backward,
> myself and a fellow passenger named Miss Breen,

The realization that there has been a flag "all along" is a realization that this new world is not stilled and waiting to present itself as the "new life" but is a world in motion, a world with money, an operating economy, other people. Miss Breen, the fellow passenger, is part of that surprise, part of the unimaginably alive world outside of the speaker's control. She and the tourist-speaker climb "gingerly" or, as in earlier drafts of the poem, "awkwardly" "down the ladder backward." Both are symbolically born or reborn into the moving world of the port:

> descending into the midst of twenty-six freighters
> waiting to be loaded with green coffee beans.
> Please, boy, do be more careful with that boat hook!
> Watch out! Oh! It has caught Miss Breen's
>
> skirt! There! Miss Breen is about seventy,
> a retired police lieutenant, six feet tall,
> with beautiful bright blue eyes and a kind expression.

The boat hook catching Miss Breen's skirt is unimagined, plays no part in the tourist's preconception of a different world and a better life. The incident is punctuated with four exclamation points, completely alive, a surprise! While the speaker's imagination, her imagined landscape, can cause the real landscape to disappoint, the body, the unimaginable awkwardness of being reborn into "twenty-six freighters / waiting to be loaded with green coffee beans," because it is unthinkable, is alive, cannot fail her preconceptions. The poem has moved away from the distancing effect of the imagined landscape, from the unreality of "uncertain palms" and "self-pitying mountains," to the absolute reality of the unexpected, the awkward creatureliness of the body.

In my imagination of her physicality, Miss Breen has something in common with the soldiers of "Brazil, January 1, 1502." The mention that she is a "retired police lieutenant, six feet tall" encourages the imagination to dress her in a uniform, a kind of military uniform, different from but still akin to the armor of the Portuguese soldiers. There is also something strangely sexual about the boat hook pulling up her skirt. The picture of the female lizard in "Brazil, January 1, 1502"—"back-to, / her wicked tail straight up and over, / red as a red-hot wire" (*Poems,* 92)—seems almost a gloss, an overlay, on the more awkward, accidental sexuality of Miss Breen, descending the ladder backward, skirt raised by a clumsily swung boat hook. These two scenes oppose and recall each other. Bishop imagines that the soldiers connect the appearance of the lizards and man's Fall: "Still in the foreground there is Sin: / five sooty dragons near some massy rocks" (91). She whimsically connects Miss Breen with the Fall by dropping the "s" from the name of her hometown—not just a line, but a stanza:

> Her home, when she is at home, is in Glens Fall
>
> s, New York. There. We are settled.
> The customs officials will speak English, we hope,
> and leave us our bourbon and cigarettes.

In this configuration, Bishop not only plays on "Fall" but, by setting the "s" apart, begins the next line with a strange and comical hissing sound.

In this seventh stanza, the repetition of "There," this time without the exclamation point, reinforces the play on its opposite, "here," and insists on the questions at the center of any meditation on travel—scientific, practical, or literary—the questions of defining home and away, here and there, familiar and foreign, all questions that the phrase "when she is at home" playfully begs. In this stanza, "There." actually becomes an antonym for the earlier "There!" and conjures the surprise and movement of the new and unexpected. However, the same word followed by a period recalls the quieting phrase "there, there," and means "We are here, still, settled." In this one word, Bishop embodies the simultaneous and opposing desires—for home and away, for the familiar and the new—that underlie the poem. Yet, by setting "There." and "There!" in opposition to each other, she also cancels, or at least resists, that embodiment. In the poem's first verse, the speaker seemed to feel disappointed because the landscape was not set apart enough from everyday concerns, was not exotic enough. However, while the speaker desires the "there-ness" of exotic landscape, she also desires, later in the poem, the "here-ness" of creature comforts—"bourbon and cigarettes," customs officials who speak English. The combination of these desires, simultaneous and apparently opposite, informs the speaker's musing on the nature of ports and the announcement, at the end of the poem, that she will be moving on, or, more accurately, in:

> Ports are necessities, like postage stamps, or soap,
>
> but they seldom seem to care what impression they make,
> or, like this, only attempt, since it does not matter,
> the unassertive colors of soap, or postage stamps—
> wasting away like the former, slipping the way the latter
>
> do when we mail the letters we wrote on the boat,
> either because the glue here is very inferior
> or because of the heat. We leave Santos at once;
> we are driving to the interior.

The poem forecasts but does not explore the movement inward. Instead, it concentrates on the complex of paradoxical emotions surrounding entry and initiation. Travisano sees this concentration as purely purposeful: "By right of attention to the exterior, one can drive to the interior" (1988, 174). However, the duality of the verb "driving," casually noncommittal but also forceful and powerfully sexual, captures the doubleness of the poem's metaphor. Driving to the interior seems both desirable and terrifying. The suggestion of inward movement in both "Arrival at Santos" and "Brazil, January

1, 1502" recalls the poems of internalization in *North & South,* only here the body moves into another body—on a literal level, a body of land—rather than taking something into itself; ever present is the risk of self-annihilation. And yet, in "Arrival at Santos" this inward movement seems casual on the surface; the language nearly evades, but still suggests, the philosophical and sexual undertones beneath the poem's casual facade. The insistently casual tone masks—or better, almost masks—the more threatening and serious sexual and philosophical undercurrents. This near masking in itself sets up another opposition from which the poem draws creative energy. The reader feels the electricity that jumps between what the speaker says and what seems to be at stake in the poem.

Reading "Arrival at Santos" and "Brazil, January 1, 1502" in the context of one another deepens the sexual and philosophical suggestions in the former and increases the duality, the sense of humanity and connection, in the latter. Written eight years after "Arrival at Santos," "Brazil, January 1, 1502" takes up the same themes, the same paradoxes, from a different viewpoint. The human figures in the two poems seem, on the surface, to be opposed: the casual tourist means no harm, has come to sightsee; the soldiers have come to plunder, rape, and usurp. The two poems comment on two different approaches to experiencing the foreign. But the first line of "Brazil, January 1, 1502" inextricably and uncomfortably links the perspective of any middle-class American tourist/observer with the perspective of the soldier/plunderer. The first verse gathers our perspective and the soldiers' perspective and sets them in opposition to a female nature. All of nature as "she" is an unusual construction in Bishop's poems, and the effect of this male/female opposition is something like the effect of the apostrophe to the tourist in "Arrival at Santos"; it harasses and accuses the reader, whether man or woman. The construction figures us all as male invaders plundering a female nature:

Januaries, Nature greets our eyes
exactly as she must have greeted theirs:
every square inch filling in with foliage—

big leaves, little leaves, and giant leaves,
blue, blue-green, and olive,
with occasional lighter veins and edges,
or a satin underleaf turned over;
monster ferns
in silver-gray relief,
and flowers, too, like giant water lilies
up in the air—up, rather, in the leaves—
purple, yellow, two yellows, pink,
rust red and greenish white;
solid but airy; fresh as if just finished
and taken off the frame. (*Poems,* 91)

As in the opening stanzas of "Arrival at Santos," in the first verse of "Brazil, January 1, 1502" the expected or known overtakes and undermines the new and foreign. However, while in the first poem this situation evokes the speaker's disappointment, here there is a strange comfort in the fact that the rain forest looks like a tapestry. The epigraph to "Brazil, January 1, 1502," from Sir Kenneth Clark's *Landscape into Art,* explains this comfort, exemplifies the human tendency to make the unknown less frightening by seeing it in terms of the known, or to make it even more manageable by seeing it in terms of human creation: " . . . embroidered nature . . . tapestried landscape." While the scenery in "Arrival at Santos" fails by being "meager," "feeble," and "uncertain," the scenery in "Brazil, January 1, 1502" overwhelms with its sheer multiplicity of colors and shapes, its frightening fecundity. However, the careful catalog of detail, the movement by square inches across the overwhelming scene, represents a kind of human control. Limiting perspective limits panic. The phrase "fresh as if just finished / and taken off a frame" reduces the scale of the fecundity to a manageable size, delimits it, and demonstrates how human perspective, particularly human art, can embody the limitless fecundity of nature in concrete form, both making it manageable and imaginable and also robbing us of the accurate and overwhelming experience of its multiplicity, its rawness.

The second verse works out this embodiment, the tapestry metaphor, revealing how the mental frame readjusts the actual picture.

More and more relationships develop—foreground, background, geometric arrangement. The verse almost seems like instructions for embroidering the tapestried landscape that the outsiders see:

> A blue-white sky, a simple web,
> backing for feathery detail:
> brief arcs, a pale-green broken wheel,
> a few palms, swarthy, squat, but delicate;
> and perching there in profile, beaks agape,
> the big symbolic birds keep quiet,
> each showing only half his puffed and padded,
> pure-colored or spotted breast.

This geometric arrangement, wrought by the imposition of human perspective, not only allows the soldiers and us to tame the landscape, so frightening in its raw multiplicity, but also allows the possibility that the landscape has human meaning. What the Portuguese see in their new surroundings is an allegory of the ideas they carried with them; they impose on nature the terms of their Catholic philosophy and sensibility:

> Still in the foreground there is Sin:
> five sooty dragons near some massy rocks.
> The rocks are worked with lichens, gray moonbursts
> splattered and overlapping,
> threatened from underneath by moss
> in lovely hell-green flames,
> attacked above
> by scaling-ladder vines, oblique and neat,
> "one leaf yes and one leaf no" (in Portuguese).

It is important that the name of the scaling-ladder vine, "one leaf yes and one leaf no," is Portuguese and not native Brazilian, for it is the Catholic Portuguese and not the native Brazilians who, in the European Christian tradition, read this kind of morality in nature, see in nature's fecundity not only sin but their own temptation, their simultaneous attraction to and repulsion from sin. The ladder vines say two things at once. They might be Bishop's struggle with and ambivalence toward embodied meaning in miniature, a small version of her larger technique. They are, for the Portuguese, the embodiment of moral dilemma, just as the lizards, and really all of female nature, embodies sin:

> The lizards scarcely breathe; all eyes
> are on the smaller, female one, back-to,
> her wicked tail straight up and over,
> red as a red-hot wire.

Like the boat hook lifting Miss Breen's skirt in "Arrival at Santos," the female lizard's raised red tail represents the inescapable surprise of bodily nature, alive and unimaginable. Both events are accidental, but they are charged with meaning by the human perspective, specifically by the male observers. Human perspective, and especially the perspective of the soldiers, the overlay of Catholic philosophy on the natural body, creates the imposition of meaning, of will. This imposition may distance the self from the other, block the perception of the actual, cause us to read the new always in terms of the old and, thereby, prevent our finding the different world and better life. However, imposition of meaning also creates a kind of necessary familiarity, a way into comprehending the foreign, the disturbingly raw and multiple, that could draw us, like the soldiers, into the interior.

Although, in the third verse, the Portuguese certainly look ridiculous, small and insignificant in the overwhelming landscape, they are just like the tourist in "Arrival at Santos," who hopes that the customs officials will speak English; they are not without our sympathy. Lowell, in his letter of January 4, 1959, comments on the success of "Brazil, January 1, 1502" and Bishop's attitude toward the Portuguese plunderers. He compliments the poem's beauty and notes that the description stands at the edge of reason, "the jungle turning into a picture, then into history, and the jungle again" (Vassar Box 6). He also hears Bishop's wonderful modulation of voice, "with a practical, absurd, sad, amused and frightened tone for the Christians" that Lowell connects with one of Bishop's favorite authors, Edward Lear, and suggests that Lear would have approved of "your disciplined gorgeousness, your drawing, your sadness, your amusement" (Vassar Box 6). This "disciplined gorgeousness" is precisely what becomes sad and amusing, because it is the disciplined gorgeousness that belongs, not just to the poet, but to the soldiers, to the human perspective. It is less gorgeous, presumably, but more comprehensible and human than the jungle itself. By imposing the "old dream of wealth and luxury" on the new reality, the soldiers and the poet embody the known in the unknown, a practice that simultaneously distances them from the new experience and, by providing surface comfort, draws them deeper into the mystery of the unfamiliar:

> Just so the Christians, hard as nails,
> tiny as nails, and glinting,
> in creaking armor, came and found it all,
> not unfamiliar:
> no lovers' walks, no bowers,
> no cherries to be picked, no lute music,
> but corresponding, nevertheless,
> to an old dream of wealth and luxury
> already out of style when they left home—
> wealth, plus a brand-new pleasure.
> Directly after Mass, humming perhaps
> *L'Homme armé* or some such tune,
> they ripped away into the hanging fabric,
> each out to catch an Indian for himself—
> those maddening little women who kept calling,
> calling to each other (or had the birds waked up?)
> and retreating, always retreating, behind it.

Although many reviewers simply see these final lines as a condemnation of the actions of the plunderers, or, as Parker suggests, a condemnation of the male language's appropriation of female nature, "Brazil, January 1, 1502" avoids any such simple or political statement. The Portuguese soldiers and the tourist in "Arrival at Santos" both desire "a different world, / and a better life, and complete comprehension / of both at last, and immediately" (*Poems,* 89); this is the fruition of the "old dream of wealth and luxury" and "a brand-new pleasure." The irony of the soldiers heading straight from Mass to catch themselves Indian women is not lost, but, as readers, our own dreams and desires for a better life, for connection, our own questions of travel, place us all in complicity with the soldiers. The comma in the line "came and found it all, not unfamiliar" means that "not unfamiliar" modifies not the soldiers' finding a version of lovers' bowers but our experience and the speaker's with the soldiers'. The experience is what is "not unfamiliar."

I think it is shortsighted to argue, as many critics do, that Bishop attempts to speak in the ironized voice of the male doer but somehow falls into her own trap; as Parker writes, "even she who will criticize it [the language] cannot help being infected by it" (1988, 92). Bishop's evasiveness of tone, her ambiguous phrasing, rules out any such one-dimensional answer. It is significant that the poem opens, not with the word "January," but with the plural, "Januaries," indicating that this event has taken place, not once, but often, over time. The fact that "Nature greets our eyes" as she greeted theirs distances us from the passive receiver role and lumps us in with the glinting, creaky Portuguese who have become accustomed to a northern January and found an amazingly fecund summer. The opening words of the third verse, "Just so," are also equivocal, meaning both the event happened just so and the event happens just so to any of us.

The final scene, of the soldiers "ripping away into the hanging fabric," recalls the tourist "driving to the interior." Though on the surface the two actions seem in opposition, in movement and motivation they are essentially the same. Like the tourist's better life, the soldiers' "brand-new pleasure" is pleasure made brand new, a stripping of, or more accurately, ripping through the civilized pleasures of lute music and bowers to rediscover the animal pleasure of lust, of forced connection. However, this desire for brand-new pleasure seems to draw them toward something more primal, stronger than their creaky armor can defend against. As Costello says, "The landscape, which originally greeted the beholders, turns its back on them, inviting pursuit into its illusory depths" (1991, 147). It is this feeling more than any other that suggests to me that the poem is not finally about the evils of rape—rape of women, the land, or language—but about the soldiers, the tourist, all of us, being drawn into what we draw in. To see the soldiers' action as utterly reprehensible belies the tone of the poem, the experience of reading it, and its relationship to "Arrival at Santos."

"Arrival at Santos" and "Brazil, January 1, 1502" oppose but do not cancel each other. They are two explorations of the human desire to connect and the fear of connecting with new surroundings, of the human dream to find the better and different, and of the strong desire to embody the invisible in the visible, the old in the new, as well as the equally strong ambivalence about the body and the act of embodying, the way the body can distance us from accurate perception. The title poem, "Questions of Travel," follows "Brazil, January 1, 1502" and unites and deepens the themes the other two poems explore, acting as the central poem in the opening triptych.

"Questions of Travel" begins with the same disappointed tone as "Arrival at Santos," Bishop's characteristic impatience with herself or her surroundings that is related, in its surface censoriousness, its whistling-in-the-dark quality, to her tone of motherly quasi certainty, tones that never appear without being undercut by a strange and telling word or a deeper level of meaning that hint at the black hole of uncertainty that the brave voice covers. "Questions of Travel" also recalls the concerns with time's passing that begin "Brazil, January 1, 1502." Like the first two poems, the title poem describes the scenery through an ironic perspective; the mountains from "Arrival at Santos" (or others like them) reappear, as does the shift in perspective from seeing natural multiplicity to embodying that multiplicity in a human-made object. Here the mountain becomes a ship, just as the rain forest became a tapestry in "Brazil, January 1, 1502":

There are too many waterfalls here; the crowded streams
hurry too rapidly down to the sea,
and the pressure of so many clouds on the mountaintops
makes them spill over the sides in soft slow-motion,
turning to waterfalls under our very eyes.
—For if those streaks, those mile-long, shiny, tearstains,
aren't waterfalls yet,
in a quick age or so, as ages go here,

they probably will be.
But if the streams and clouds keep travelling, travelling,
the mountains look like the hulls of capsized ships,
slime-hung and barnacled. (*Poems*, 93)

What Pinsky calls Bishop's "detached and respectable tourist voice" (1983, 59) is completely missing here. The tone instead is personal, almost petulant; too many waterfalls for whom? why? The sense of motion created by the repetition of words and sounds, by the crowded lines, is as overwhelming as the waterfall itself. However, in the final lines of the stanza Bishop rephrases this sense of motion, and by comparing the mountain, at first crowded, rapid, hurrying, to the "slime-hung and barnacled" capsized ship, she catches the waterfall in a glass, as it were, resists the movement, undermines the description she herself has established.

This ambiguousness, this tendency to say and unsay, resolves itself, as it had in "Arrival at Santos," into a kind of motherly non-answer, but this time a non-answer that incites rather than calms anxiety. The admonition "Finish your breakfast" is replaced in "Questions of Travel" by the admonition "Think of the long trip home." Like "Finish your breakfast," this non-answer is packed with meanings, and Bishop devotes the rest of the second verse to asking the questions that the thought of the long trip home elicits. These questions, each impossible to answer, each revealing the ultimate uncertainty of human perception and the limitation of the human flesh, unite not only these three poems but the opposed sections into which *Questions of Travel* is divided, "Brazil" and "Elsewhere":

Think of the long trip home.
Should we have stayed at home and thought of here?
Where should we be today?
Is it right to be watching strangers in a play
in this strangest of theatres?
What childishness is it that while there's a breath of life
in our bodies, we are determined to rush
to see the sun the other way around?
The tiniest green hummingbird in the world?
To stare at some inexplicable old stonework,

inexplicable and impenetrable,
at any view,
instantly seen and always, always delightful?
Oh, must we dream our dreams
and have them, too?
And have we room
for one more folded sunset, still quite warm?

These questions underlie the emotions and themes in both "Arrival at Santos" and "Brazil, January 1, 1502"—and really all of *Questions of Travel*. The list begins by focusing on the limitations of the body, its ability to be in only one place at any given time, the necessity of being somewhere and thinking about somewhere else, the weariness of the "long trip home," but the catalog moves on to more intricate problems, the problems of correct action ("Is it right?") and motivation ("What childishness is it?").

Bishop's first draft of the poem began with the question of motivation, with a version of the lines as they appear in the published poem but phrased in a statement:

A sort of childishness that makes one rush
while there is life in the body, to see
the smallest bird in the world,
the sun the other way round. (Vassar Box 29)

As is often the case, Bishop revises the lines to avoid statement, fractures the facade of singular perspective and involves the reader. The clue to both the published lines and the lines as first drafted comes in the nearly thrown away phrase "while there's a breath of life / in our bodies." The questions in the three opening poems surround the problem of the life of the body and its relationship to both the world and the people around it and to the life of the mind. All the things we are determined to see leave us with greater uncertainties; how can we know if we are seeing "the sun the other way around" or "the tiniest green hummingbird in the world"? The old stonework is "inexplicable and impenetrable," does not fulfill our wish for "a different world and a better life," but when we as readers expect this revelation of uselessness, this declaration of our failure, we get instead "instantly seen and always, always delightful." The word "delightful," like Miss Breen's lifted skirt, is completely unexpected.

The unexpectedness of the adjective, the way it undermines the tone that the previous questions have established, prompts the two final and strangest questions: "Oh, must we dream our dreams / and have them, too? / And have we room / for one more folded sunset, still quite warm?" The question of dreaming our dreams and having them too is filled with Bishop's gift for the ambiguous, for saying two things in one breath; it contrasts the life of the mind, the dreaming, and the life of the body, the having. But neither operates independently, a fact that the second question—"have we room?"—makes evident. Have we room where? Where do we store sunsets, the landscape we connect with? The question plays on the concept of internalization, as did "Arrival at Santos" and "Brazil, January 1, 1502." In "Questions of Travel," Bishop returns once again to a version of the internalizing metaphor that she used in *North & South;* connection occurs not because the body moves beyond its boundaries into another body but because the body expands its boundaries to take something into itself.

In the long stanza that follows the list of questions, Bishop explores the effect of this internalization, examines the effect of human intellectual processing on raw sense information, questions the relationship between the life of the mind and the life of the body. This stanza is a triumph of elusiveness, evasion, and negative statement. The increasing insistence on negative expressions ("a pity / not to have seen," "Never to have studied," "never to have had to listen") makes the speaker's perspective as she catalogs the sensuous details of the landscape (the sounds of the wooden clogs, the rain, the bird) seem elusive because she both describes and posits her own failure to experience. She vividly recalls the landscape, the sensuous experiences of another country, and simultaneously muses about not having seen or heard it, not having been there. The uncanny sense of opposition here is increased by the fact that the descriptions in this stanza are inseparable from the consciousness of the speaker; we are constantly aware—in metaphor, simile, and semi-scientific observation—that we are seeing this landscape through a screening intellect, but the intellect itself insistently posits its own absence:

> But surely it would have been a pity
> not to have seen the trees along this road,
> really exaggerated in their beauty,
> not to have seen them gesturing
> like noble pantomimists, robed in pink.

The rich ambiguity of this description, then, comes from the combination of opposites, from the suggestion of absence and the simultaneous insistence on presence. Denis Donoghue suggests that this presence/absence dichotomy is central to Bishop's poems; presence understood as presence of mind, of perspective, and absence understood as the loss of the concrete, of loved ones, houses, the death of the body (1984, 247).

Along with the presence/absence dichotomy, this comparison between the trees and actors reinforces the earlier theater imagery: "Is it right to be watching strangers in a play / in this strangest of theatres?" The repetition of the word "pity" as the stanza progresses ties into this theatrical pattern and increases the ambiguity of the negative statement. Pity comes to have two opposing meanings. It literally means, of course, "Wouldn't it be a shame, a pity, not to have seen or heard these interesting things." It is a reemergence of the schoolmarm language. However, pity also means Aristotelian pity, implying sympathy and catharsis. Therefore, the one word says simultaneously that it would be a pity not to have seen these things *and* it is a pity to have seen these things; in other words, we experience pity or catharsis because we have watched these strangers, seen and heard these interesting things.

The clogs that make two disparate noises, and Bishop's comparison between the crude wooden footwear and the finicky, ornate wooden birdcage, the same material used two different ways and present simultaneously, are the images of her own technique and her own deeper ambivalence about the ability of language to resolve thought and embody it in statement:

—Not to have had to stop for gas and heard
the sad, two-noted, wooden tune
of disparate wooden clogs
carelessly clacking over
a grease-stained filling-station floor.
(In another country the clogs would all be tested.
Each pair there would have identical pitch.)
—A pity not to have heard
the other, less primitive music of the fat brown bird
who sings above the broken gasoline pump
in a bamboo church of Jesuit baroque:
three towers, five silver crosses.
—Yes, a pity not to have pondered,
blurr'dly and inconclusively,
on what connection can exist for centuries
between the crudest wooden footwear
and, careful and finicky,
the whittled fantasies of wooden cages.
—Never to have studied history in
the weak calligraphy of songbirds' cages.

"In another country" (a title Bishop considered for the poem) the clogs would have been rhetorical, tested, identically pitched, moving toward a common goal. In another country, perhaps in another language, statement would be possible. But in this country the clogs are dialectical, like Bishop's language, saying yes and no, admitting multiple possibilities. This possibility or ambiguity is not only linguistic but also historical. Bishop connects the clogs and the birdcages, establishes a logical comparison that could be intended to reveal something about the nature of Brazil, about the interaction between the landscape and the Europeans who invaded it. However, while establishing the rhetorical structure, she constantly questions it, insists she is pondering "blurr'dly and inconclusively," phrases the most direct statement about the study of history in a negative construction. "Never to have studied history in / the weak calligraphy of songbirds' cages" both recalls and mocks the recollection of the importance of the historical interaction between the Portuguese soldiers and the South American landscape, the desire to tame, to possess the wild femininity of nature that comes up in "Brazil, January 1, 1502": the way that what the soldiers saw became Brazil, and what was Brazil drew them in, encompassed and overwhelmed their perspective.

This apparent opposition between rhetorical statement and dialectic construction emerges more clearly as a theme in the final paragraph of the third verse, though Bishop's attitude toward the opposition itself becomes muddier. Here her comparison between the silence after unrelenting rain and the silence after politicians' speeches seems to make a direct statement about the evils of rhetoric, and yet it is only the contrast, the presence of rhetoric, that makes the silence "golden":

> —And never to have had to listen to rain
> so much like politicians' speeches:
> two hours of unrelenting oratory
> and then a sudden golden silence
> in which the traveller takes a notebook, writes:

Rhetoric, the "politicians' speeches," joins the list of things it would have been a pity not to have experienced. The poem cannot be said, then, to be a statement against rhetoric, to be a statement of any kind. And yet the poem constantly struggles with statement, and this struggle is perhaps most evident in the final verse paragraphs, the quote from the traveler's notebook:

> *"Is it lack of imagination that makes us come*
> *to imagined places, not just stay at home?*
> *Or could Pascal have been not entirely right*
> *about just sitting quietly in one's room?"*

In this first paragraph, the traveler poses two central questions concerning the power of the imagination, the life of the mind, in comparison with the power of the physical experience, the life of the body. Is it a weak imagination that makes physical travel necessary? Can we go everywhere we need to go sitting quietly in one room? These questions of freedom, of the limitation imposed by the senses and the possibility that the mind could overleap the boundary of the body, are unanswered and unanswerable, but they elicit a kind of statement, a reflection about here and there, that recalls the cen-

tral concerns of all three poems in the opening triptych and recalls
in their form especially "Arrival at Santos":

> *"Continent, city, country, society:*
> *the choice is never wide and never free.*
> *And here, or there . . . No. Should we have stayed at home,*
> *wherever that may be?"*

The drafts of "Questions of Travel" prove that this last verse was
difficult to nail down, mostly because of Bishop's ambivalence about
statement, about rhetoric. Barbara Page notes that Bishop's struggle
here surrounds her desire to leave room for the possibility of change
but to simultaneously make some statement (1981–82, 51). As in
so many other instances, here Bishop wrestles to say two things simultaneously. In the first draft, these lines are prosy; they reveal
Bishop's attempt to say and unsay by qualifying as she had in the
line "Or could Pascal have been not entirely right": "The right
country, the right party, the right society / The choice is not too
great but not so simple either" (Vassar Box 29). In the second draft,
this qualification is itself qualified, becomes "The choice is not too
great and not too free" (Vassar Box 29). The third draft, marked
with the alternate title "Nagging Thoughts of Travelling," reads
"the choice is never too wide and never too free" (Vassar Box 29).
Each of the unpublished versions of the line keeps and amplifies
the negative construction that is so important to the ambiguity
throughout the poem, but none of them risks the kind of statement
that the published version, "the choice is never wide and never free,"
risks. Here complete negation of the adjectives "wide" and "free"
leaves choice, the absolute center, the paradox of human perception
and moral responsibility. Though "never" negates the adjectives, it
does not negate choice, a negation that would have suggested a kind
of easy determinism. Choice remains, limited, maimed by perspective and humanity, but still present, and it is choice finally that
makes the questions of travel most troubling, most important.

The final lines of the poem, "And here, or there . . . No. Should
we have stayed at home, / wherever that may be?" begin in a way
that suggests that the statement will continue, but the statement is
brought to an abrupt halt by the intervening negative. The "No"

seems to answer an unstated question, a question the speaker has silently asked herself. The poem ends in a question that seems, in the context of the other, more philosophical or difficult questions, to be flippant or tossed off. However, in many ways, "Should we have stayed at home, / wherever that may be?" is the axis of all three of the opening poems. The search for the exotic in "Arrival at Santos" and the search for the familiar in "Brazil, January 1, 1502" are two different ways of accomplishing the same act, of locating home. Do we live in the imagination or in the flesh? here or there? This idea resists the rhetorical impulse, refuses to be resolved, to be embodied in concrete forms. Even the word "home" cannot stand without question; the phrase "wherever that may be," calls into question the hope of locating, of identifying, a single home. Bishop constantly wrestles with the problems of expressing this elusiveness, the questions that keep "calling to each other (or had the birds waked up?) / and retreating, always retreating" (*Poems,* 92). This struggle involves, not mere intellectual ambiguity, but deeper emotional and personal ambivalences about the possibility and desirability of finding a home, of connecting with another person, of coming to know any landscape, the contingent world.

In these three poems, Bishop simultaneously embodies these elusive questions in poetic structures and sets the forms in opposition to each other. I think of them, then, not as a trilogy, suggesting three installments of an ongoing story, but as a verbal triptych. In the same way that a visual triptych creates tension because it unites opposing forces in texture, line, or image, Bishop's opening three poems gain power from surface tension or opposition combined with deeper concord, an agreement about ambiguity, about the nature of the questions.

"The Inscrutable House": Form as the Medium of Ambiguity

Bishop's ambivalence about embodiment, her gift for saying and unsaying, is nowhere more apparent or more effective than in the poems in *Questions of Travel* that employ traditional poetic form. In "Sestina," "The Armadillo," and "Visit to St. Elizabeths," Bishop implicitly questions the use of form and manipulates form so that it becomes self-questioning. Though they are similar to her experiments with personification in *North & South* in her exploration of the circularity of formal structures, in *Questions of Travel* her experiments with form are maturer expressions of a poet who can orchestrate form, theme, and detail into an expression of meaning both entirely lucid and complete and also entirely inscrutable and in tension.

One of the best examples of this amazing duality is the poem "Sestina," from the second section, "Elsewhere," of *Questions of Travel*. The vocabulary and grammar of "Sestina" are utterly lucid, generally the simple vocabulary of a children's book or of the voice of the child in the poem. The repeated words—"house," "grandmother," "child," "stove," "almanac," and "tears"—are not only simple in themselves but reappear simply, with none of the play on sounds or words that many sestinas rely on for interest and tension.[5] Instead, Bishop relies for tension on the contrast between the simplicity of the situation and the complexity of the emotion behind it, the conflict between the child's apparent innocence and the grandmother's apparent knowledge, and the way these surface roles are undermined by the poem's voice and tone. All these oppositions are evident from the first lines of the poem:

> September rain falls on the house.
> In the failing light, the old grandmother
> sits in the kitchen with the child
> beside the Little Marvel Stove,
> reading the jokes from the almanac,
> laughing and talking to hide her tears. (*Poems*, 123)

Like the tears at the end of the stanza, the quiet suggestion of death in the phrase "failing light" is hidden, covered. Death and grief can be displaced by the warmth of the Little Marvel Stove, the almanac jokes, and laughter, but they cannot be banished completely. The grandmother's knowledge, her awareness of the displaced grief, apparently separates her perspective and our perspective from the child's, creates a tension that the first stanzas beautifully exploit:

She thinks that her equinoctial tears
and the rain that beats on the roof of the house
were both foretold by the almanac,
but only known to a grandmother.
The iron kettle sings on the stove.
She cuts some bread and says to the child,

The grandmother's knowledge consists of connecting seasons of
the literal year with the seasons of the emotional year, connecting
the rain and the tears, and connecting grief to the passing of the
seasons. On the surface, loss, the inevitable effect of the passage of
time, seems to the grandmother to be her exclusive burden, "only
known to a grandmother." However, in the stanza that follows, the
child performs the same feat of knowledge, makes the same connection that the grandmother had:

It's time for tea now; but the child
is watching the teakettle's small hard tears
dance like mad on the hot black stove,
the way the rain must dance on the house.

The difference between the grandmother's knowledge and the
child's is a difference of control, of projection; the child projects
her grief onto objects, makes images. The sestina form itself parallels the child's grief in comparison to the grandmother's; the same
elements reappear, but they reappear in different locations. The sensitive child understands the wordless grief and makes an image for
the tears, gives them to the teakettle, but nevertheless connects
them with the falling rain. In the next stanza the tears are again
relocated, this time in the teacup into which, perhaps, the grandmother cries:

Tidying up, the old grandmother
hangs up the clever almanac

on its string. Birdlike, the almanac
hovers half open above the child,
hovers above the old grandmother
and her teacup full of dark brown tears.

> She shivers and says she thinks the house
> feels chilly, and puts more wood in the stove.

The almanac hovering above the child and the grandmother, like the suggestion of death in the "failing light" and the grandmother's feeling cold at the end of this stanza, menaces, increases the sense of inevitable loss that the child is trying to understand and control, to project outside herself.[6] In fact, in the first draft of the poem Bishop used the more explicit adjective "heartless" rather than "clever" to describe the almanac (Vassar Box 29). The almanac, like maps or thermometers or any number of recurrent images in Bishop's published and unpublished work, functions dualistically, both to help humans control their environment, or at least give them the comforting reassurance that some control is possible, and also to remind us that we live at the mercy of nature and time. In that paradoxical sense, the child's images themselves, the child's projections, call attention to and augment the very sense of loss they seek to evade. In the same way, the sestina form, by rigidly repeating the simplest words, by evading any mention of the sorrow, the "it" of the next stanza, which caused the grandmother's tears or the child's sadness, makes that very grief the unspoken focus of the poem, makes the absent ever present.

This paradox, the dichotomy between absence and presence, appears in the next stanza in the contrast between the rigid house and the winding pathway in the picture the child draws for the grandmother:

> *It was to be,* says the Marvel Stove.
> *I know what I know,* says the almanac.
> With crayons the child draws a rigid house
> and a winding pathway. Then the child
> puts in a man with buttons like tears
> and shows it proudly to the grandmother.

Once again, the child relocates the tears, but this time making them an element of her own creation, making them manageable. The action is in some ways like the soldiers turning the landscape into a tapestry. The child reduces the scale of the overwhelming things around her. The picture that the child shows proudly to the grandmother contains representations of all the knowledge—the grief, the paradoxes—that seem "only known to a grandmother." But, as the words of the almanac and the stove warn, these representations will fail to ward off the menace of the almanac's moons, the certainty of loss in the passage of time:

> But secretly, while the grandmother
> busies herself about the stove,
> the little moons fall down like tears
> from between the pages of the almanac
> into the flower bed the child
> has carefully placed in the front of the house.

On one level, the "rigid house" reached by a "winding pathway" is a metaphor for the sestina form itself, which is a winding pathway of language and repetition that ends in a rigid structure. But neither of these constructions, the child's or the poet's, can effectively displace and evade the pain, nor do either of them mean to, except on the surface. The mechanism of the sestina and the rigidity of the drawing seek a structure in which to embody the otherwise incomprehensible experience. However, the almanac, itself a kind of paradox—both the source of laughter, a gentle bird, and also a source of pain, a kind of menacing bird of prey—plants moons, a central image in Bishop's poetry for the body's necessary submission to natural processes, time and death. The child will harvest what the almanac has planted, but that harvest will come even more directly from the structures the child has created to manage loss.

The brilliantly ambivalent envoi gathers the paradox of the entire sestina just as it gathers the six end words:

> *Time to plant tears,* says the almanac.
> The grandmother sings to the marvellous stove
> and the child draws another inscrutable house.

These final lines complicate the conflict between the grandmother's knowledge and the child's innocence. The title Bishop rejected for the poem, "Early Sorrow," made this reversal more explicit but perhaps less interesting (Vassar Box 29). Though on the surface the initial knowledge/innocence conflict remains, on another level the tables are turned, and it is the child who carries the weight of knowledge and the burden of turning this loss into some manageable expression of grief. The irony, the paradox of both the child's expression and the poet's, is that they come so close to their goals and just barely fail, fail to alleviate or manage grief and pain. Both structures ultimately are unable to organize thought, to distance emotion, or to make sense of loss. However, this failure is the poem's success. From the moons the almanac plants, the foretold tears, the child will grieve and grow. Because the poem tries so hard to evade the sense of loss, we will feel it acutely and identify its humanity.

Bishop demonstrates how the rigidity of the sestina form can be made to circle back on itself, to undermine its own ends, and, on a larger scale, how any rigid form devised around absence paradoxically makes the absent present. This is part of the paradox of embodiment: the event that the structure was established to evade becomes the center of the poem.

Bishop employs a very different technique to obtain a similar sense of paradox, to explore the dichotomy between absent and present, in a poem from the "Brazil" section, the much anthologized poem "The Armadillo." In this poem Bishop employs a looser form, a quatrain structure with a mainly abcb rhyme in a varied trimeter moving to tetrameter rhythm. It is obvious, even from this brief description, that the structure of this poem, unlike the loosely metered but certain structure of the sestina, experiments with form in another way, as each stanza constantly overlaps the new boundary the previous stanza established. Its wealth of metric variation and the way the variation interacts with the subject matter insist on the serious questions the poem poses about the advisability of embodying life in form, the morality of life's mimicry in art.

Lines one, two, and four of the first stanza of "The Armadillo" establish the trimeter quatrain base, a tight structure, that the third line breaks with the modifiers "frail" and "illegal":

This is the time of year
when almost every night
the frail, illegal fire balloons appear.
Climbing the mountain height, (*Poems,* 103)

Because they break the meter, "frail" and "illegal" insist on themselves, stand out. They also imitate the action of the fire balloons; the word "illegal" itself breaks the rules, and the word "frail" fractures the fragile metric (Ruark 1991). The structure, then, introduces the theme, since this mimicry, the desire to embody emotion and thought in the structures of art, is precisely what is at the heart of "The Armadillo."

The second stanza stretches the structural boundaries established by the first; the abab rhyme scheme becomes the cded rhyme that dominates the rest of the poem, up to the final stanza. In the same way that it expands on the structure, the second stanza stretches the boundary of the poem from suggestive description to explicit comparison. In the final line of this stanza, the poem suddenly shifts ground and hints, in the simile comparing the balloons to hearts, at the unspoken subject beneath the literal one:

> rising toward a saint
> still honored in these parts,
> the paper chambers flush and fill with light
> that comes and goes, like hearts.

The word "chamber" beautifully signals the comparison to the human heart that will follow it, as does the verb "flush," recalling the effect of the blood on the aspect of the skin. The modifier "paper" and the verb "flush" both break the trimeter scheme in the third line, calling attention again to the frailty of the balloons and to the corresponding frailty of the human heart. The figure also adds a note of pathos to the preceding lines, "rising toward a saint / still honored in these parts."

The first two stanzas in conjunction then establish a second pattern, the pattern of breaking the trimeter beat in the third line. However, once that pattern has been established, the next two stanzas break it, moving to tetrameter variations throughout:

> Once up against the sky it's hard
> to tell them from the stars—
> planets, that is—the tinted ones:
> Venus going down, or Mars,

> or the pale green one. With a wind,
> they flare and falter, wobble and toss;
> but if it's still they steer between
> the kite sticks of the Southern Cross,

The breaks in the meter give these verses, even more than the first two, the effect of a mind in motion, a speaker rephrasing and re-thinking. But just as before, the words that overleap the boundary and insist on themselves reveal crucial things about the perspective of the speaker and the unstated subject beneath the surface subject. The phrase "it's hard," which makes the trimeter line tetrameter, recalls the phrase "like hearts" in sound and suggests some failure of human love. The idiom "up against," with its colloquial meaning of failure and adversity, also connotes this destruction of love. Similarly, the extra beat in the line "Venus going down, or Mars" calls attention to the choice of planets, the way human perspective has assigned love to one and war to the other. The first phrase in the fourth stanza, "or the pale green one," reveals the lively mind of the speaker moving over these objects. Sandra McPherson notes, "We're glad she didn't know the name of the 'pale green one.' That wording makes her an observer, not an expert in an observatory" (1984, 10).

In the same way that the balloons imitate the motion of the planets, the poem imitates the balloons. The movement into tetrameter at the end of the fourth stanza mimics the steadiness of the balloons moving away in the still night: "but if it's still they steer between / the kite sticks of the Southern Cross." Then the first line of the fifth stanza continues this imitation, as "receding, dwindling, solemnly" makes a trimeter line of dactyls that themselves recede:

> receding, dwindling, solemnly
> and steadily forsaking us,
> or, in the downdraft from a peak,
> suddenly turning dangerous.

The metric variation throughout this stanza mimics the quiet receding and then the sudden turning of the balloons.

Interestingly, the first two drafts of this poem, then called "The Owl's Nest," read "steadily escaping us" rather than "steadily forsaking us" (Vassar Box 29). Bishop's revision in the third draft strengthens the connection between the balloons and hearts, insists on the ambivalence, the perspective of the speaker, without entirely breaking the facade that the subject of the poem is fire balloons. In the sixth and seventh stanzas, the meter again imitates the splatter of the falling fire balloon and the shriek of the owls:

> Last night another big one fell.
> It splattered like an egg of fire
> against the cliff behind the house.
> The flame ran down. We saw the pair
>
> of owls who nest there flying up
> and up, their whirling black-and-white
> stained bright pink underneath, until
> they shrieked up out of sight.

The only interruption to the sixth verse's iambic tetrameter is the trochee in the word "splattered," which itself imitates the action of something striking the cliff and falling. The shock of the trimeter line that ends the seventh stanza now mimics the shriek of the owls whirling from their burning nest.

This scene of destruction is the upshot of the illegal fire balloons, but the beauty of this scene derives from that other illegality, the real destruction embodied in the "false" contrivance of the poem. The eighth and ninth stanzas concentrate on that odd beauty; the meter expands to include the "pretty" word "glistening," gains power from the double beat of "rose-flecked":

> The ancient owls' nest must have burned.
> Hastily, all alone,
> a glistening armadillo left the scene,
> rose-flecked, head down, tail down,
>
> and then a baby rabbit jumped out,
> *short*-eared, to our surprise.
> So soft!—a handful of intangible ash
> with fixed, ignited eyes.

The owls "stained bright pink underneath," the "glistening" armadillo, and the baby rabbit that looks like "intangible ash / with fixed, ignited eyes"—the fire alters the aspect of each of the animals, colors them with its own colors.

Human perspective, the human heart, and the structure of the poem imitate the fire: coloring, destroying, and also strangely beautifying. The elasticity of the metric form, the levels of mimicry in the poem, progress toward this crescendo, this moment of destruction. The final, italicized quatrain breaks the voice of the poem, much as, to this point, each quatrain has broken the structure of the one it succeeded. Here Bishop risks a rhetorical, poetic, extravagant, and uncharacteristic comment on what the poem has described and on what the structure has accomplished:

> *Too pretty, dreamlike mimicry!*
> *O falling fire and piercing cry*
> *and panic, and a weak mailed fist*
> *clenched ignorant against the sky!*

Bishop's ambivalence about embodiment, her conviction that perception both destroys and creates, makes her react against the very act of embodiment and of mimicry that her poem has magnificently accomplished. This stanza, perhaps more explicitly than anywhere else in Bishop's work, attaches a feeling to that paradox, the feeling of panic. Donoghue notes that this feeling comes from the subject's fixation on an object without hope of comprehension (1984, 255), and that combination is strikingly present in the final lines of "The Armadillo." The line "Too pretty, dreamlike mimicry!" itself mimics the "piercing cry" of the owls' shrieking. In the lines that follow, it is the word "panic" that stops the rush of language, that leaves the poem frozen like a frightened rabbit. So even this stanza, written seemingly in reaction against the "dreamlike mimicry," continues and even amplifies, electrifies, the practice it almost helplessly denounces.

The final line and a half—"and a weak mailed fist / clenched ignorant against the sky!"—have often been taken as an allusion to Robert Lowell, to whom the poem is dedicated, and connected with his status as a conscientious objector in World War II. When the poem appeared in the *New Yorker* in 1957, however, it did not carry the dedication to Lowell, which Bishop added when she collected the poem in *Questions of Travel*. Bishop may have dedicated the poem to Lowell because he admired it so much, writing in his letter of June 10, 1957, "The Armadillo is surely one of your 3 or 4 very best. . . . the little creature, given only 5 lines, runs off with the whole poem" (Vassar Box 6). However, early drafts of the poem suggest Bishop was thinking about war—if not specifically about the firebombs of World War II and Lowell's conscientious objector status, certainly about conflict, and the panic caused by her own conflicting and ambivalent emotions. The first draft of this final paragraph stated this concern more explicitly:

Too dainty mimicry of war—
The falling fire, the furious flight,
and panic and a small
mailed fist clenched against the night. (Vassar Box 29)

The appearance of the armadillo itself recalls the glinting, creaky armor of the Portuguese soldiers; like them, it weakly challenges the world that seeks to engulf it. The animal also, it seems to me, recalls what Lowell said to Bishop about form in his letter of December 3, 1957. He calls the form of poems like "Lord Weary's Castle" "my medieval armor's undermining" (Vassar Box 6). This seems particularly interesting because one of the titles Bishop rejects for the poem is "From a Letter" (Vassar Box 29). The form of "The Armadillo" captures both Lowell's impatience with his old "armor" and Bishop's deep-seated ambivalence about embodiment, about form's ability to carry meaning. "The Armadillo," much like "Sestina," holds opposing and related concepts of form: form appears to be armor, capable of excluding or controlling the wild internal forces of emotion, and yet, by focusing all its energy on evasion, on control, form necessarily calls attention to what it evades. The title "The Armadillo" suggests deep connections between the poem and the animal, connections between their reactions to the contingent world of fire and conflict. The final verse is a version of the armadillo's clenched fist; it is an act of defiance, a statement that nevertheless refuses to resolve itself into an answer. Bishop risks allowing the form to comment on itself, and this risk reveals layer upon layer of rich ambiguity within the poem's structure.

"Visits to St. Elizabeths," a poem about Bishop's visiting Ezra Pound when she lived and worked in Washington as the poetry consultant to the Library of Congress, again uses a structured form, one taken from the repetitive verse pattern of a traditional portion of the *Haggadah*, the book of ceremonies read on the Seder night of Passover. This form is also well known in folk tradition as the "House-that-Jack-Built." Bishop's manipulation of the form to demonstrate the multiplicity of human perception has roots in the form's religious and secular variations. In "Visits to St. Elizabeths," as she had in "Sestina" and "The Armadillo," Bishop orchestrates form, theme, and detail into what is, on the surface, a lucid if formulaic account of her feelings about Pound and her visits to Pound's asylum; but, on another level, she employs the tensions and contradictions among and within the form, theme, and detail to create a disconcerting feeling of uncertainty about what must be evaded to remain only a visitor at the asylum.

The form of "Visits to St. Elizabeths," perhaps more than that of any other poem in this book, explores the experience of travel. Even though the characters in the poem are stilled, trapped between the walls of the ward, the world they inhabit is composed of an accretion of images that gather momentum and movement; the world rushes past. This sense of motion comes, not from the setting, but from the form. The form consists of continuous inward motion, movement through and into description. As in "House-that-Jack-Built," the form in "Visits to St. Elizabeths" works paradoxically, both mimicking the pattern of addition and refinement that builds a structure and simultaneously creating a sense of building motion and speed. The same sense of overload that makes "House-that-Jack-Built" funny makes "Visits to St. Elizabeths" frightening. Time, a growing obsession from the outset of the poem, becomes, as the poem progresses, an almost overwhelming weight. The first lines slowly introduce detail, and, like light opening from a pinhole to reveal a scene in progress, they describe and then modify description:

This is the house of Bedlam.

This is the man
that lies in the house of Bedlam.

This is the time
of the tragic man
that lies in the house of Bedlam. (*Poems*, 133)

The movement inherent to the form does not come from motion or change in the scene but from movement and change in the reader, from our own ever widening perspective. In "Visits to St. Elizabeths," Bishop demonstrates that the frightening multiplicity, illogic, and insanity of human perspective is both absolutely necessary, in order to connect with the world, and absolutely limiting, blocking connection with the world. This paradox becomes increasingly apparent as a reader's perspective shifts from stanza to stanza. In the early stanzas, perspective is comfortable; nothing despoils our view of the "tragic man." Though the form itself reminds us in every stanza that the setting is Bedlam, through the first five stanzas the man and the things surrounding him appear sane:

This is a wristwatch
telling the time
of the talkative man
that lies in the house of Bedlam.

This is a sailor
wearing the watch
that tells the time
of the honored man
that lies in the house of Bedlam.

In the sixth stanza, however, Bishop introduces an image that, because it is askew, creates tension and conflict in perspective. The introductory line, "This is the roadstead all of board," calls attention to the fact that the sailor is defined, and is in turn defining the world around him, by what he is no longer doing. The line points up that metaphor defines the actual by what it is not. However, in its introductory position the metaphor seems harmless or colorful, a way of controlling, like the child did in "Sestina," the unpleasant truth, the incarceration in the asylum:

> This is the roadstead all of board
> reached by the sailor
> wearing the watch
> that tells the time
> of the old, brave man
> that lies in the house of Bedlam.

The sailor and the "old, brave man"—people who have faced some danger and now rest—seem to lie at anchor in this roadstead. The metaphor seems almost a euphemism.

However, when in the following stanza the form opens to allow still more detail, Bishop takes the metaphor further, and the result is frightening. Perspective slants precariously away from reality, and the almost unpunctuated lines build and rush under their own weight:

> These are the years and the walls of the ward,
> the winds and the clouds of the sea of board
> sailed by the sailor
> wearing the watch
> that tells the time
> of the cranky man
> that lies in the house of Bedlam.

The adjective "cranky" immediately calls into question what we have believed to be true about the man, conflicting with "tragic," "honored," and "old, brave," though not with "talkative." This conflict does not so much expand our perspective as unstick and refocus it. As the form rushes on, the earlier veneer of sanity, a veneer we now have something invested in preserving, cracks. The first line of the sixth stanza, "These are the years and the walls of the ward," equates the confinement of the ward with the limitations created by time's passing, equates the outer world, ours, with the inner one, Bedlam.

The equation between Bedlam and the world beyond the walls, this blurring of the distinction between sanity and insanity, becomes more terrifying and ironic in the seventh stanza's allusion to history. I think Parker is right in suggesting that the mention of the Jew underscores the common fate of humanity (1988, 116). But, although the stanza seems implicitly to judge Pound's political beliefs, it also, perhaps more importantly, exploits the paradox of his situation (he is grouped with those he once despised) to point up the danger of embodying thought in word, the irony of the sane world in which genocide is practiced, the sane newspaper that reports worldwide insanity:

> This is a Jew in a newspaper hat
> that dances weeping down the ward
> over the creaking sea of board
> beyond the sailor
> winding his watch
> that tells the time
> of the cruel man
> that lies in the house of Bedlam.

The lack of punctuation, the "ward/board" couplet, and the profusion of consonance and assonance give this stanza an almost breathless speed. However, the motion of the form, like the motions of the Jew and the sailor, do not progress but panic instead, circling back on themselves obsessively. The form creates an opposition of, on the one hand, stable structure, growing, like a house or a tower, ever higher from its foundation line by line, and on the other hand, circular motion, like ripples opening outward from the same pebble. Only the man, only Pound, is physically still. He is the paradoxical cruel, tragic, talkative, cranky center who is lying, both physically and perhaps verbally, and around which we, like all the things and people in Bedlam, are turning.

In the ninth stanza, the first line, "This is a world of books gone flat," ends with a period, stopping the motion of the stanza and imitating the effect of the word "flat":

> This is a world of books gone flat.
> This is a Jew in a newspaper hat
> that dances weeping down the ward
> over the creaking sea of board
> of the batty sailor

>   that winds his watch
>   that tells the time
>   of the busy man
>   that lies in the house of Bedlam.

The end stop of the opening line stops the building motion of the stanza, emphasizes the loss and failure of art and language to redeem, to order, to make sane. It also recalls Pound's own soundings of this theme in "Hugh Selwyn Mauberly" and the *Cantos*. However, the "flat/hat" couplet also connects the opening line to the motion of the stanza and to the world in motion into which it has been introduced. This world in motion is both the world that the form creates and Pound's "busy" world, and he connects the world of books and the world of Bedlam, just as the form connects the business of the sailor and the dancing Jew to his business. All of these connections come through the form's influence on the reader's perception, through the action of the form creating both stillness and motion.

The tenth stanza, by introducing the "boy that pats the floor," directly introduces the questions of perception that lie at the heart of the poem. To perceive two things at once, to perceive motion and stillness, honor and censure, is to question fundamentally, or come to doubt, the mechanism of perception. The boy demonstrates how doubting one perception means doubting all perception, makes the world a frighteningly uncertain place:

>   This is a boy that pats the floor
>   to see if the world is there, is flat,
>   for the widowed Jew in the newspaper hat
>   that dances weeping down the ward
>   waltzing the length of a weaving board
>   by the silent sailor
>   that hears his watch
>   that ticks the time
>   of the tedious man
>   that lies in the house of Bedlam.

The obsessive doubt of the "boy that pats the floor," like the obsessive, repetitive movements of the sailor and the Jew, are deeply connected with Pound, in the adjective "tedious," and with the motion of the poem, circling over and over the same information but each time with a shift in perception. The repetition also connects with the perception of the reader, moving over the same ground, looking at the scene from an ever-widening angle, and the perception of the writer. The plural in the title "Visits to St. Elizabeths" reveals that the writer herself participates in the repetitive returning of the Bedlamites.

The eleventh stanza insists on the realization introduced in the seventh stanza, that the confinement of the ward and the general human confinement in time are linked, that all perception, because it happens in time, is skewed by time's motion. Therefore, each visit to the asylum, each glance at the watch, each touch of the "sea of board," can yield a different impression:

> These are the years and the walls and the door
> that shut on a boy that pats the floor
> to feel if the world is there and flat.
> This is a Jew in a newspaper hat
> that dances joyfully down the ward
> into the parting seas of board
> past the staring sailor
> that shakes his watch
> that tells the time
> of the poet, the man
> that lies in the house of Bedlam.

The line "into the parting seas of board" not only plays on Moses' parting the Red Sea and the history of the Jewish race but evokes Bishop's own history by recalling the poem "The Monument" from *North & South*. In "The Monument," "A sea of narrow, horizontal boards" skews perspective so that it becomes impossible to discern whether we are inside or outside the view:

> The view is geared
> (that is, the view's perspective)
> so low there is no "far away,"
> and we are far away within the view. (*Poems,* 23)

Precisely the same confusion occurs in "Visits to St. Elizabeths." What the point of view is, what the speaker herself has carefully evaded—the realization of her own connection to the subjects in

the poem—becomes, through the evasion itself, the central and unstated subject of the poem. This connection clarifies in the unspoken but obvious relationship between the speaker and Pound in the
line "of the poet, the man."

Parker sees in the final stanzas of this poem an indictment of
Pound, a "suggestion that the house of his decay is his own building" (1988, 116). I think, though, that in the final stanzas Bishop's
sympathy (and ours) grows steadily deeper and more believable than
it was in the stanzas in which we see Pound as honored, old, and
brave. If Pound's decay is "of his own building," that connects
it strongly to the structure the poet is building, the structure of
the poem, and to the structure through which we all mediate reality, the structure of our own perception. The common fate is not
Pound's and the Jew's common fate in the asylum, but the common
fate, Pound's and Bishop's and the Jew's and the boy's and yours
and mine, the common death.

In the images of mortality and conflict in the final stanza, Bishop
points toward this common fate:

> This is the soldier home from the war.
> These are the years and the walls and the door
> that shut on a boy that pats the floor
> to see if the world is round or flat.
> This is a Jew in a newspaper hat
> that dances carefully down the ward,
> walking the plank of a coffin board
> with the crazy sailor
> that shows his watch
> that tells the time
> of the wretched man
> that lies in the house of Bedlam.

The introduction of "the soldier home from the war" underlines
the uncertainty of our perception; it could be an allusion to Pound
and to Pound's unfortunate involvement in the war, thus coming
full circle and creating a neat structure to close the poem, or it could
refer to a new character, in which case the poem's ending remains
open, suggesting that the movement of the poem could go on in-
definitely. The adjective "wretched," which Bishop chooses to finally

describe Pound, evinces that same sort of paradox; it could either mean deeply afflicted, sick, or weak, or it could mean contemptible, miserable, and mean. As in "Sestina" and "The Armadillo," here Bishop uses ambivalence and contradiction within the form itself to suggest the powerful uncertainty about perception and the equally powerful certainty of loss that unite all human situations.

Throughout this book, Bishop expresses her ambivalence about embodiment, both in human flesh and in poetic form, in her tendency to set poems in relation to and in opposition to each other and in her use of forms that leap their own boundaries, their own bodies, or that undermine their own structures. In the opening triptych, "Arrival at Santos," "Brazil, January 1, 1502," and "Questions of Travel," and in poems that use traditional form, like "Sestina," "The Armadillo," and "Visits to St. Elizabeths," Bishop refuses to settle for simple answers, refuses to compromise the inscrutable complexity of her subjects. Although some might argue that this evasiveness ultimately cancels her poems' capacity to convey meaning, Bishop's ambiguity represents not only her courage in admitting that she both desires and loathes answers, wants and does not want the limitations of the body, but also a fundamental respect for the certainty of change and the human capacity for redirection (a capacity she values, as she notes in her review of a biography of Emily Dickinson). She refuses the temptation of the simple answer or the single perspective and instead risks gathering the proliferating, destructive, unanswerable, fecund questions into a dangerous proximity.

4

GEOGRAPHY III
The Art of Losing

IN THE MID-1960s, Elizabeth Bishop bought a house in the beautiful mountain town of Ouro Prêto, Brazil. In this new home, named Casa Mariana partly in tribute to Marianne Moore, Bishop would spend as much as two months alone while Lota de Macedo Soares lived in Rio, mired in what Bishop called "the Brazilian madhouse" (Kalstone 1989, 230) of that city's partisan politics. Macedo Soares had become a political hero after the success of her huge community parks project, but life in the public eye, with its constant scrutiny, demands, and betrayals, proved a tremendous strain on both women. In the winter of 1965–66, unable to withstand the pressures, even by retiring to Ouro Prêto, Bishop accepted a teaching assignment at the University of Washington in Seattle. This decision seems to have forged the first link in the chain of loss, grief, and illness that ended Bishop's Brazilian years and so powerfully informs the feelings of loss, and the strategy and themes, of *Geography III*.

Bishop returned from Seattle in July of 1966 to find that Macedo Soares had been bedridden for more than a month, apparently owing to a nervous breakdown. To revive her spirits, Bishop planned a trip to London and the Netherlands, but this tactic failed (Lota hated everything, especially London) and the two cut short their trip and returned to Brazil (Kalstone 1989, 230). Back in Rio, Bishop suffered an extremely severe asthma attack, one of the most serious since the crippling attacks of her childhood, and several bouts with depression and alcoholism. She checked herself into Casa de Repouso and then into Clinica Botofoga in Rio, where she and Macedo Soares spent a month (Millier 1993, 385–86). Bishop described this difficult time in a letter to Lowell from the spring of 1967: "[Lota] can't stop blaming me for going away in the first place, even if I thought I had to, to get out of the atmosphere here for awhile—& this makes me feel guilty. She was in a clinic here for two stretches—then finally I gave out, too" (Kalstone 1989, 231). When Bishop recovered, she took advantage of a free apartment in New York and left Macedo Soares to be cared for until she recovered enough to join Bishop in America. In September of 1967, Lota de Macedo Soares traveled to New York, where she committed suicide the evening of her arrival.

Until Macedo Soares's death, Bishop's life revolved around Brazil. She had been working on two prose pieces. The first, *Black Beans and Diamonds,* was a collection of short essays set in Brazil that probably would have included stories like "A Trip to Vigia" and "To the Botequim & Back." The second, *Brazil-Brasil: A Scrapbook,* would have combined personal experience and anecdote with a revealing discussion of the history, culture, and landscape of Brazil, much in the way Bishop's Time-Life book about Brazil had done before the editors banalized it and Bishop disowned it. However, after Macedo Soares's death, Bishop abandoned these projects. Brazilian society, former friends of Bishop and Macedo Soares, refused to see or speak to Bishop, blaming her for Lota's death. The Macedo Soares family, particularly Lota's sister Marietta Nascimento, became so incensed about being excluded from Lota's will that they contested it, claiming that she had been mentally unfit when she drafted it (Millier 1993, 397). Though Bishop kept the house in Ouro Prêto for awhile,[1] living amid that loss finally proved too painful. In 1970 she accepted a teaching position at Harvard and moved back to America permanently.

Bishop wrote many of the poems in *Geography III* in the context of these devastating losses. However, as one might expect after having read her first three books, the poems of *Geography III* deal with overwhelming loss the way we all deal with the overwhelming light of the sun—they squint, avoid looking directly at it. Paradoxically, but perhaps not surprisingly, this evasion makes the sense of loss both more pervasive and more deeply realized. Bishop's evasions, and the strategies she employs to accomplish them, explore the mind in motion behind the structure of the poem, the single human will struggling with the pain of loss and the possibility for recovery. At the center of the poems in *Geography III* are the same feelings of ambivalence about embodiment, about the body as the medium of loss, that have been central to Bishop's three earlier books, but the fourth and last book incorporates more insistent and more profoundly unanswerable questions about embodiment in literary form, the poem, as both a vehicle for recovery and a fresh opportunity for loss, a chance for connection and a discovery of almost unbearable isolation.

Bishop's return to America is paralleled in the poems of *Geography III* by a return to the themes, the images, and sometimes the forms of much earlier poems. "Poem," for instance, takes up once again the work of the great-uncle who painted the picture featured in "Large Bad Picture" from Bishop's first book, *North & South.* The comic-surreal description of Bishop's desktop in "12 O'Clock News" first appeared in her drafts and notes when she was studying at Vassar, and was partially responsible for the description of her desktop in the letter to Lowell that she later incorporated into "The Bight." Bishop had worked on "The Moose" for twenty years. By literally recovering or reembodying old themes and forms, many of the poems of *Geography III* reenact the process of loss and recovery about which they speak. They build a bridge between the present and the past. However, Bishop finds the bridge they build precarious. Each embodiment creates an opportunity for both connection and loss, and Bishop's ambivalence and evasion, her attempts to say two things at one time, consistently point up the simultaneous and opposing opportunities present in every attempt to embody thought in form, spirit in flesh, the invisible in the visible.

Through her experiments with parenthetical revelations of the mind in motion, experiments that appear in poems such as "One Art" and "Five Flights Up," her exploration of the paradox of the isolated body in "End of March" and "In the Waiting Room," and her investigation of the process of loss and recovery in the act of embodiment in "Crusoe in England," "Poem," and "The Moose," Bishop expresses her ambivalence about embodiment in form and flesh and unleashes the myriad questions that surround human loss.

Though none of these questions ever resolves itself into an answer, or even into a single question, Bishop achieves a sense of balance or acceptance in the nine poems of *Geography III*, a sense of the circularity of all opposing forces, that her earlier work hinted at or achieved only momentarily. As Prunty says, speaking of "The Moose," "Each condition mirrors its opposite, and, by accepting whichever presents itself at a given time, we call its opposite into presence" (1990, 245). The grandparents "talking, in Eternity" in "The Moose" act out the acceptance of death and then life, as each summons its opposite:

> "Yes . . . " that peculiar
> affirmative. "Yes . . . "
> A sharp, indrawn breath,
> half groan, half acceptance,
> that means "Life's like that.
> We know *it* (also death)." (*Poems*, 172)

By evading loss, the poems of *Geography III* focus on it. By embodying the past in the form of the poem, Bishop recovers it. However, because she can only recover the lost past from the perspective of the present, she also invokes the loss all over again, and, because she must embody the past in a human form that itself is vulnerable to time, she sets up a new possibility for loss—but also, perhaps, for recovery. The poems of *Geography III* turn on these paradoxes of recovery and loss, connection and isolation, holding them always in opposition so that the very tension and power of their opposition makes the absent present.

"Fancy Come Faster": Parenthetically Revealing the Mind of the Speaker

In several of the poems in *Geography III*, Bishop experiments with new techniques to resist the single perspective, to complicate the simple embodying of thought in form, and these experiments demonstrate her ambivalence about the nature of embodiment, her belief in the form's ability to recover the past and her simultaneous fear of form's tendency to create new loss. By inserting a dramatic

aside, a parenthetical phrase that reveals the mind of the speaker
moving in opposition to the tone or the form, Bishop calls attention
to the facade of the poetic structure and illuminates this tension
between recovery and loss; she tips her hand, pulls the curtain so
we see her working the levers. Like "Sestina" and "The Armadillo,"
the poems in *Questions of Travel* that used form as the medium of
ambiguity, "One Art" and "Five Flights Up" from *Geography III*
consider how form and image fail to control loss and grief, how they
can be made to turn on themselves and reveal the very thing they
intended to conceal.

The compositional process of the villanelle "One Art," as it survives in the manuscript collection, demonstrates Bishop's struggle
with form and her penetrating insight into the possibility of simultaneously creating and destroying a facade by forcing overwhelming
emotion into tight structure (see also Millier's [1993, 535] reading
of the drafts of "One Art"). The first draft begins with the same
concentration on small items and the same attempt to achieve a distanced tone that survives in the final draft: "One might begin by
losing one's reading glasses / oh two or three times a day—or one's
favorite pen" (Vassar Box 30). The first draft, a draft of "free verse"
notes, also depicts the same movement from control to loss of control, a movement away from emotional distance toward overwhelming and frightening proximity. However, the lack of formal structure in the first draft allows the deterioration into grief at the end
of the poem to seem less inevitable and more indulgent:

> All gone, gone forever and ever.
>
> One might think this would have prepared me
> for losing one average-sized not ~~especially~~ exceptionally
> beautiful or dazzlingly intelligent person
> (except for the blue eyes) (only the eyes *were* exceptionally
>   beautiful and the hands *looked*
>   intelligent) the fine hands
> But it doesn't seem to have at all . . .
> a good piece of one continent
> and another continent—the whole damned thing!
> He who loses his life etc.—but he who
> loses his love—never, no never never never again. (Vassar Box 30)

The negation in the final line is reminiscent of the "No" in the last verse paragraph of "Questions of Travel." In contrast, this free verse ending, as it deteriorates completely into the negative, provides an unqualified and basically uncomplicated depiction of the devastation of loss—a loss, however, that the reader is outside of and looking in on. Unlike the end of the published version, which uses distancing techniques like "I shan't have lied" that are purposefully and beautifully unbelievable, the end of the first draft holds onto distancing techniques, like the impersonal "One might" and the strange gender difference of "He who loses his life etc.," which work too well, which seem truly alienating.

At the bottom of the page on which she wrote this first draft, Bishop began to play with rhymes, and by the second draft she had established the villanelle as the form for the poem. Bishop perhaps realized that the first draft's deterioration, the gradual loss of control, could be accomplished in a new version with much smaller gestures if she experimented with stricter form. The first triplet of the published poem establishes the foundation of this structure, the basis on which the villanelle operates, or better, fails to operate:

> The art of losing isn't hard to master;
> so many things seem filled with the intent
> to be lost that their loss is no disaster. (*Poems,* 178)

Even within this first verse, the basically iambic pentameter of the first line breaks down by the third line, tripping over itself with extra beats and odd feet. Then, in the second verse, the form deteriorates more severely, deteriorates, as Ruark (1991) notes, into immortality:

> Lose something every day. Accept the fluster
> of lost door keys, the hour badly spent.
> The art of losing isn't hard to master.

The "fluster/master" rhyme, jarring and inexact, undercuts that schoolmarmish tone in the phrase "Lose something every day," a tone that seems to say "I am the expert"; "Listen to me"; "Finish your breakfast"; or "I suppose you want to make some sense of this." The tone accomplishes the distancing effect of the third person in the phrases "One might begin" and "One might think" from the first draft, but the rhyme undermines its effectiveness. In the final draft, structure and tone vie for meaning, become capable of saying two things at the same time. The expert, certain voice that says "Lose something every day" is the same voice that inexpertly rhymes "fluster" with "master." By embodying two meanings in one utterance, Bishop expresses her ambivalence about the power of language to resolve, or to control, the overwhelming questions of loss. The near rhyme, "fluster/master," demonstrates the loss of control that is perilously close, the breakdown of form that both makes the tone of absolute control and expertise necessary and also undercuts that tone's effect.

In the third stanza, the villanelle form itself begins to deteriorate when Bishop fails to repeat exactly the called-for line "to be lost that their loss is no disaster." The words "loss is no disaster" appear only once in the poem; each time they are called for again, the speaker avoids or qualifies them. While she repeats a version of the line and repeats the final word, as the villanelle demands, her failure to repeat the exact words shows her tension with the form, her struggle to overcome her own grief, and her failure to achieve the very control she proposed. This deterioration of the form, then, is linked to the internal deterioration of the speaker's confidence and the opposing and external tone of certainty:

> Then practice losing farther, losing faster:
> places, and names, and where it was you meant
> to travel. None of these will bring disaster.

The crowding effect of the small words in the second line of this stanza increases the speed and sense of urgency, of masked intensity, in the poem. The line imitates what the phrase before has exhorted, the act of "losing faster." Through this imitation, the poem embodies the loss, practices the art of losing.

However, the fourth stanza reveals the potential for comedy in that embodiment, the problem inherent in forcing the loss into the form. The "last, or/master" rhyme and the correction of "last" to "next-to-last" mark a shift as the speaker's tone moves into a kind of self-parody, the expert voice pushed to its farthest limits:

I lost my mother's watch. And look! my last, or
next-to-last, of three loved houses went.
The art of losing isn't hard to master.

In a search for fixity and permanence, the speaker has failed, and
through that failure she has become an expert on loss. In the fourth
stanza she begins to give us her credentials, and a sense of the irony
behind the expertise.

In the fifth stanza this irony becomes dangerous, draws the
speaker into her own structure, and leads to her playing with the
idea of possession, exploring the impossibility of ownership. As the
tone becomes more ironic, the boundaries of loss increase. By expanding the size of the lost objects, moving from watches to houses
to continents, the poem travels from the credible to the incredible
realm. As the irony increases, the speaker simultaneously establishes
and undermines her own argument. Again, Bishop violates the villanelle form by failing to repeat the words "loss is no disaster," and
this violation further damages the speaker's claims that loss can be
turned into an art by those who practice it often:

I lost two cities, lovely ones. And, vaster,
some realms I owned, two rivers, a continent.
I miss them, but it wasn't a disaster.

The phrase "I miss them" marks the first time the speaker admits
any emotion about what has been lost and forecasts the remarkable
collapse that is about to happen.

Bishop has expanded the boundaries of the objects to be owned
and lost, which is to say she has shifted the terms of ownership, for
while one seems to own keys, an hour, or a watch, one does not own
cities, rivers, a continent, or, perhaps especially, a lover. In just this
same way she expands the villanelle form, both by odd rhyme and
by refusing to repeat the number three line, until finally both form
and content burst, and in bursting reveal, in the final stanza, the
center of the loss that the structure sought to evade:

—Even losing you (the joking voice, a gesture
I love) I shan't have lied. It's evident

> the art of losing's not too hard to master
> though it may look like (*Write* it!) like disaster.

The dash before the crucial admission, "Even losing you"—an admission that parades as a denial because it is included in a larger list of things the losses of which do not qualify as disasters—increases the reader's sense of the speaker's desire to evade, to avoid admitting the devastating power of this loss. For the effect of "One Art," Bishop does not have to "rely on a reader aware of her reputation for reticence," as Travisano claims (1988, 177). Instead, by embodying uncontrollable emotion in a form meant to control it and in an utterance meant to deny it, Bishop can create tension, ambivalence, and a poignant recognition of the pathos of human attempts to control the uncontrollable.

In the earlier drafts of this stanza, Bishop struggled with the desire to say and unsay, to say two things at once, both admitting to the truth of the argument that the villanelle has established and admitting to the evasion of the truth that the tone has insisted on. To accomplish this she tried lines such as "of course, I'm lying" and "it's evident I'm telling the truth"; one draft of the verse completely explodes the villanelle form:

> All that I write is false, it's evident
> The art of losing isn't hard to master
> oh no
> anything at all anything but one's love. (Say it: disaster). (Vassar Box 30)

This duality that Bishop works so hard to achieve in draft after draft (there are seventeen drafts of "One Art" in Vassar's manuscript collection) she finally finds in one word, "shan't." This word, with its overformal stiffness, its anachronistic sound, its schoolmarmish precision, says both "I'm lying" and "I'm not lying." Using the future perfect tense allows an ambiguity that no other grammatical structure can provide. Bishop accomplished the feat of expressing her ambivalence about her own endeavor; in the word "shan't," she combined opposite meanings in the same utterance.

Along with her careful diction and ambiguity of tone, Bishop uses parenthetical revelations, a technique she employs often in *Geography III*, to create tension and paradox; here the parenthetical phrase is worked into the structured form of the final stanza. The parentheses in the final stanza of "One Art" are gaps through which the reader sees the mind of the speaker, sees the motion of the mind beneath or within the facade of form and the nearly brave and certain tone. It is possible, as Travisano suggests, that Bishop learned this technique, at least in part, from Hopkins (1988, 71). In the "Wreck of the Deutschland," in particular, Hopkins moves back and forth between describing from the perspective of an omniscient observer and commenting on his own enterprise as poet. The twenty-eighth stanza demonstrates that movement:

> But how shall I . . . make me room there:
> Reach me a . . . Fancy, come faster—
> Strike you the sight of it? look at it loom there,
> Thing that she . . . There then! the Master,
> *Ipse,* the only one, Christ, King, Head:
> He was to cure the extremity where he had cast her;
> Do, deal, lord it with living and dead;
> Let him ride, her pride in his triumph, despatch and have done with
> his doom there. (Houghton and Stange 1968, 698)

Bishop's parenthetical interruption is similar to Hopkins's "Fancy, come faster" (it is also one of her rhymes!); it comments on her play with perspective and communicates her tension with embodiment.

The first parenthetical phrase, "(the joking voice, a gesture / I love)," locates the grief the rest of the poem evades in the physical loss of "you." Like the fine hands and blue eyes of the first draft, the voice and gestures are "gone, forever and ever." Because they are physical, they are irretrievable. The abstract—kindness, love, even loss itself—can be recovered, can be reembodied, but the hands, the voice, the gestures—these *are* the body, and it is the embodiment itself that creates both the feeling of overwhelming loss and the only human possibility for connection. To be communicated, even the loss of the beloved must be embodied in the form of the poem, and that act of embodying itself is a paradox—a partial act of recovery, a new opportunity for loss, a fresh experience of the pain of that loss.

Bishop powerfully illustrates this paradox in the final line of the poem, in the parenthetical phrase "(*Write* it)." The sense of the final stanza is that the form itself has overtaken the speaker and made her face the crushing loss that she created the form to avoid. Beautifully, the word "disaster" becomes both the inevitable ending and the word most desperately to be evaded. Diehl finds the emotional roots of this inevitability in the syntactic necessity of rhymes like the "he loves me / he loves me not" folk game (1985, 128). However, the parenthetical phrase that comes before "disaster," "(*Write* it)," opens a gap in the fabric of the poem so that the reader sees through to the supreme moment of the speaker's tension, the moment in which she is equally repelled and overwhelmed by the truth. In this conflict, this tension of opposition, the phrase is reminiscent of the italicized stanza that closes "The Armadillo." Moreover, "(*Write* it)" puns on "right it" and in doing so calls into question the possibility that poetic form can control or recover, can right, the overwhelming disaster of loss. In earlier drafts Bishop had italicized the entire phrase, but her decision to emphasize only the word "write" suggests its centrality. "One Art" is finally a failed villanelle, the form itself is lost; it collapses, superbly, into the gaps rent by the motion of the speaker's mind beneath and within the form, the tension between feeling and form.

A similar movement occurs in the final poem of *Geography III,* "Five Flights Up." In this poem, however, not traditional structure but traditional figure, personification, is overturned by a final parenthetical expression that illuminates the mind of the speaker creating the figure. In this way, "Five Flights Up" recalls Bishop's experiments with personification in *North & South,* but where Bishop formerly allowed the personified figure to circle back on itself, here she plays the figure, not against itself, but against the single perspective, the mind, that created it. "Five Flights Up" is a strange and interesting poem for Bishop to choose to close *Geography III.* Like most of the poems in the book, it deals with a sense of loss so deep it can hardly be expressed, but unlike most of the poems in the collection,

"Five Flights Up" explicitly focuses on the speaker's struggle with loss. For me, it is an immediate and personal poem about continuing in the face of great odds.

The first stanza moves gradually from description to personification:

> Still dark.
> The unknown bird sits on his usual branch.
> The little dog next door barks in his sleep
> inquiringly, just once.
> Perhaps in his sleep, too, the bird inquires
> once or twice, quavering.
> Questions—if that is what they are—
> answered directly, simply,
> by day itself. (*Poems*, 181)

The movement from description to personification parallels the movement from darkness to day, from meaninglessness to meaning. The personification in the first stanza turns on the word "inquire" and on its movement from an adverb, "inquiringly," to a verb, "inquires." Bishop seems tentative at first about the personification, qualifying the bird's inquiry with "Perhaps" and qualifying the supposition that the bird's call and the dog's bark are questions with the phrase "if that is what they are." These qualifications immediately and startlingly call attention to Bishop's enterprise, to her use of figure, in the poem.

In the second stanza, day arrives without personification, arrives as an enormous entity; in direct contrast to the dog and bird, it arrives without a verb at all:

> Enormous morning, ponderous, meticulous;
> gray light streaking each bare branch,
> each single twig, along one side,
> making another tree, of glassy veins . . .
> The bird still sits there. Now he seems to yawn.

The description of morning veers toward personification in the adjectives "ponderous" and "meticulous," but the phrase trails off into ellipses where the personifying verb would be. Line one is the answer to the moving, lively questions of the bird and the dog;

the morning is description, all participle and noun without action. Because the day is an answer, it is still, permanent. Significantly, however, the stanza does not end with the ellipses but with the continued, though qualified, personified action of the bird, "Now he seems to yawn."

Bishop has arranged a kind of drama in which the questioners, the bird and the dog, move in simultaneously parallel and perpendicular lines against the backdrop of an almost motionless answer, a morning. In the third stanza, the bird's action both parallels and opposes the dog's action. Though the morning exists without action, the bird "still sits there," actively still, and the dog moves in circles:

> The little black dog runs in his yard.
> His owner's voice arises, stern,
> "You ought to be ashamed!"
> What has he done?
> He bounces cheerfully up and down;
> he rushes in circles in the fallen leaves.

In this stanza, the dog acts as any dog does, but the owner's voice attaches human import to his actions, personifies the dog to the extent that all dogs are personified by their owners, without any qualification, in the phrase "You ought to be ashamed!" Like the expanding dimensions of the lost articles in "One Art," the expansion of the limits of personification, the owner's voice exhorting shame, pushes the figure just beyond the bounds of reality. The speaker questions the figure she herself has established: "What has he done?" This question is addressed as much to herself as to the owner, and it is this question that, in the fourth stanza, collapses the figure the speaker has created and, as in "One Art," leaves her facing herself, facing the unanswerable questions she created the figure to evade—"What have I done?"

The fourth stanza implicitly contrasts the speaker's reality and the reality of the animals she has anthropomorphized:

> Obviously, he has no sense of shame.
> He and the bird know everything is answered,
> all taken care of

no need to ask again.
—Yesterday brought to today so lightly!
(A yesterday I find almost impossible to lift.)

Unlike the dog bouncing cheerfully and running in circles, the speaker does have a sense of shame, is subject to the imposition of human meaning. This is the meaning she herself imposes on the noises of the bird and the dog in their sleep. In the figure of the poem, the bird and the dog easily, lightly bring yesterday into today with a single question to which morning is the answer. This is even more explicit in an earlier draft of the final stanza:

The bird knows everything has been answered
—No need to inquire further.
They carry yesterday so lightly
Yesterdays I find almost impossible to lift. (Vassar Box 30)

The change from "They carry yesterday so lightly" to "—Yesterday brought to today so lightly" proves a crucial one. For, while the early version emphasizes the surface personification of the bird and the dog, continues the poetic figure of the first stanza, the published version remains ambiguous, incorporates more of Bishop's ambivalence about the nature of embodiment and the danger of the figure she herself has created. In the final version, it is not just the bird and the dog who bring yesterday to today lightly, but also the poet, in creating the anthropomorphized figures of the bird and the dog. The drama the poet has created in the still dark, five flights above the imagined scene, carries yesterday into today. Thus, the dash before the phrase "Yesterday brought to today so lightly" functions like the dash before the phrase "Even losing you" in "One Art." It punctuates a moment of self-awareness, a moment in which the structure the speaker has created to control loss and pain, to make waking to, or rising to, another day possible, collapses to reveal the motion of the mind in tension with the form.

The final, parenthetical phrase, "(A yesterday I find almost impossible to lift)," parallels the phrase "(*Write* it)" in "One Art." In both cases, the words in parentheses open a chasm through which we can see the speaker's mind at work behind the form she is struggling to create. "(A yesterday I find almost impossible to lift)" brings the reader full circle, back to the title, "Five Flights Up," suggesting the position and condition of the speaker as the poem opens, probably lying awake in the dark room above, listening to the scene she imagines seeing. Like "(*Write* it)," "(A yesterday I find almost impossible to lift)" expresses the tension of dichotomy, the moment in which the despair and resolution exert equal pull. The word "almost" provides hope, suggests that the speaker ultimately will be able to lift yesterday. The infinitive "to lift" suggests all the risings associated with the morning—rising from bed, opening eyes, the sunrise—and the speaker, rising in all these ways to the morning, must heft the past into the present. Burdened with history, the speaker feels human shame, as the dog and the bird cannot.

To lift yesterday, the speaker has created the structure of the poem, but, while the animals only question once, the fourth stanza implies that the speaker needs or wants to ask again. Morning, description without movement, is not an answer to the poem's questions of loss, of history, of shame. The questions the form seeks to evade by concentrating on the cheerfulness and certainty of the natural creatures become the center of the poem when the figure all but collapses at the sound of the voice that created it. In both "Five Flights Up" and "One Art," Bishop employs parenthetical phrases that break the form; this technique allows her simultaneously to embody thought in form and to question and impugn that act of embodiment. In both these poems, she can explore the tension between the recovery that embodying thought in form permits and also explore the way that the very embodiment recalls the original pain of the loss that made the recovery necessary.

The Paradox of the Isolated Body

The tension and ambiguity about embodiment created by the paradox of loss and recovery in poems like "One Art" and "Five Flights Up" elicits still more fundamental and more frightening questions about the nature of the human body. Just as the central tensions of Bishop's poetic form can be felt in its communicating two opposing messages simultaneously, its combined desire to evade and reveal or to resolve and explode, the central tensions Bishop finds in the human body can be seen in her exploration of the body's paradoxical nature. She investigates the duality of the flesh, both completely isolated and completely connected to all other bodies and the surrounding world; she risks the paradox of her own opposed feelings, the tension of the natural human desire to be both completely alone and also to be loved and to love, to know and to connect. Bishop's exploration of this paradox began in poems like "The Man-Moth," "A Miracle for Breakfast," and "The Fish" in *North & South*. Though she certainly never abandoned the consideration of the body as the medium of connection and the barrier of the self (indeed, it is a theme that runs through all her work), in *Geography III* she comes full circle to the techniques she had used in her first book; she returns to poems that explicitly consider the themes of internalization and perception, the emotional paradox of love and loneliness, solitude and connection. Two poems in particular, "The End of March" and "In the Waiting Room," concentrate on this tension between the isolated human body and the body's connection to all the external world. These poems explore the questions of solitude and connection so that the questions themselves multiply and deepen rather than dwindle or diminish.

The careful details of the first verse paragraph of "The End of March" depict isolation and loneliness, a landscape of disharmony and disconnection:

It was cold and windy, scarcely the day
to take a walk on that long beach.
Everything was withdrawn as far as possible,
indrawn: the tide far out, the ocean shrunken,
seabirds in ones or twos.
The rackety, icy, offshore wind
numbed our faces on one side;
disrupted the formation
of a lone flight of Canada geese;
and blew back the low, inaudible rollers
in upright, steely mist. (*Poems,* 179)

In this opening stanza, Bishop repeats images of singularity and disconnectedness: "seabirds in ones or twos," "numbed our faces on one side," "lone flight of Canada geese." The loneliness of the land-scape undercuts even the togetherness implicit in the first-person plural possessive, "our faces." Because "Everything was withdrawn as far as possible, / indrawn," bodily limits, individual barriers, are reinforced; connection seems unlikely.

However, this lack of connection means that each element re-mains individual; none can be annihilated by being absorbed by the others. Bishop's use of the word "indrawn" to describe this state suggests something more than simple loneliness. "Indrawn" calls to mind Hopkins's ideas about individuality as the mark of divine beneficence, his use of the words "instress" and "inscape" to sug-gest this individualness, a distinctiveness about the nature of each singular detail of the landscape, which can be recognized and com-prehended in the eyes and the mind of the poet. The sound of the stanza itself captures the beauty of this isolation by imitat-ing the sounds of the scene. The repetition of sibilant sounds recalls the sound of the ocean: "the ocean shrunken, / seabirds in ones and twos." In the line that follows, the jarring combination of con-sonants and sibilants imitates the noise of the cold wind howling around a beach: "The rackety, icy, offshore wind / numbed our faces on one side." Even in this first stanza, the isolation of the shrunken ocean, the disrupted flight of geese, and the inaudible rollers is para-doxical, both cold and lonely, and somehow beautiful, and deeply desirable. As Millier notes (1993, 491), and as we see clearly in sto-ries like "In Prison," Bishop had always been drawn to the idea of a solitary retreat, total isolation that would, somehow, allow her to "work," to fix all the messiness of life in relation to others. It is strange but perhaps not surprising that Millier's biography also re-veals a woman whose worst fears included being left alone, aban-doned.

In "The End of March," the paradox of the feared and desired singularity of the landscape creates deep uncertainty, an uncertainty that Bishop's tone and images convey. The second stanza explores this ambiguity; the speaker searches for connection with living be-ings by following the signs of their absence, the tracks of things once there and now gone:

The sky was darker than the water
—*it* was the color of mutton-fat jade.
Along the wet sand, in rubber boots, we followed
a track of big dog-prints (so big
they were more like lion-prints). Then we came on
lengths and lengths, endless, of wet white string,
looping up to the tide-line, down to the water,
over and over. Finally, they did end:
a thick white snarl, man-size, awash,
rising on every wave, a sodden ghost,
falling back, sodden, giving up the ghost. . . .
A kite string?—But no kite.

The kite string and the dog prints are trails that mark absence, trails the speaker follows without ever connecting with the presence that made the trail. The central image of the stanza is the ghostly snarl of kite string. Interestingly, the string does not remind Bishop of a body but of a disembodied ghost, not of the visible world but of an image of the invisible one. In earlier drafts Bishop had played with different lines that would have made the connection between the snarl of kite string and a disembodied human entity still more explicit. In the third draft she writes:

in a thick white snarl, half afloat,
bobbing with each wave,
weirdly rising like a ghost
giving up the ghost. (Vassar Box 30)

In the margin beside this verse, she adds "a drowned ghost" and "ghost of a drowned man." The published version retains the suggestion of death and loss while maintaining the veneer that the object of the description could simply be kite string. The simplicity of the final line of the stanza, "A kite string?—But no kite," embodies both the feeling of loss or absence, even uncertainty, and a strange suggestion of weary freedom, a giving up of something too sodden to carry around, like a ghost "giving up the ghost." Like the phrase "Finally, they did end," the line "A kite string?—But no kite" suggests that the search is ended, that there is no longer any need to search for connection or answers because nothing can be resolved, because ending does not bring with it resolution.

The conflicting tones and the techniques that create opposition in the first two verse paragraphs lead to a climax of revelation in the third verse. In the first section of this verse, the speaker half-teasingly admits to desiring an isolated place in the isolated landscape:

> I wanted to get as far as my proto-dream-house,
> my crypto-dream-house, that crooked box
> set up on pilings, shingled green,
> a sort of artichoke of a house, but greener
> (boiled with bicarbonate of soda?),
> protected from spring tides by a palisade
> of—are they railroad ties?
> (Many things about this place are dubious.)

This description parallels Bishop's description of Edwin Boomer's house in "The Sea & Its Shore," a short story she had written some forty years earlier, in 1934. Boomer (an alternate spelling of Bishop's mother's family name) lives the life that the speaker of "The End of March" desires, walking alone on the deserted beach, collecting meaningless scraps of paper that he keeps and reads, then eventually burns. Boomer's house, in its size and purpose, resembles the speaker's "proto-dream-house":

> This house was very interesting. It was of wood, with a pitched roof, about four by four by six feet, set on pegs stuck in the sand. . . . As a house, it was more like an idea of a house than a real one. It could have stood at either end of a scale of ideas of houses. It could have been a child's perfect playhouse, or an adult's ideal house—since everything that makes most houses nuisances had been done away with.
>
> It was a shelter, but not for living in, for thinking in. It was, to the ordinary house, what the ceremonial thinking cap is to the ordinary hat. (*Prose*, 171–72)

Both Boomer's house in "The Sea & Its Shore" and the dream house in "The End of March" represent a desire for a new kind of absolute isolation that will make incontrovertible the first isolation of the flesh, a second body that will allow the occupants to "do *nothing*," to escape the need for connection, to retire from following trails that seem to promise something and lead only to greater uncertainty.

However, the parenthetical phrase "(Many things about this place are dubious)," like the parenthetical phrases in "One Art" and "Five Flights Up," opens a gap in the simple statement through which the reader sees Bishop's tension with her own expressed desire. Part of what is dubious about the place is the speaker's desire for it, her wish to be isolated rather than risk connection and loss. The remainder of the third verse demonstrates these tensions still more fully. Qualifiers like "*nothing*, / or nothing much" reveal the motion of the speaker's mind as she backs off, evades, rethinks her own assertions:

> I'd like to retire there and do *nothing*,
> or nothing much, forever, in two bare rooms:
> look through binoculars, read boring books,
> old, long, long books, and write down useless notes,
> talk to myself, and, foggy days,
> watch the droplets slipping, heavy with light.
> At night, a *grog à l'américaine*.
> I'd blaze it with a kitchen match
> and lovely diaphanous blue flame
> would waver, doubled in the window.
> There must be a stove; there *is* a chimney,
> askew, but braced with wires,
> and electricity, possibly
> —at least, at the back another wire
> limply leashes the whole affair
> to something off behind the dunes.
> A light to read by—perfect! But—impossible.
> And that day the wind was much too cold
> even to get that far,
> and of course the house was boarded up.

The other person with whom she walks the beach, the other half of the first-person plural, disappears. All of the things the speaker thinks of doing in this palace of isolation are shadows of acts that normally lead to connection. Looking through binoculars is a way of seeing closely without getting close. Reading boring books mimics an act of engagement with another mind without risking actually becoming engaged. Like the "lovely diaphanous blue flame" reflected in the window, the life the speaker imagines is a reflection, a shadow. There is even the suggestion that the "doubled" reflection would be a more perfect doubling than if another person with another glass of grog were there.

Bishop's image of drinking *grog à l'américaine* in the "proto-dream-house" illustrates, on a number of levels, her underlying ambiguity, the simultaneous desire for and dread of this isolation. For Bishop, alcohol itself possessed this frightening duality, and, as an alcoholic, she must have vividly desired and dreaded alcohol's effect. Similarly, the word "grog" has both celebratory qualities and the connotations of weariness, drunkenness, and disorientation. In the same way, identifying the grog as *à l'américaine* not only specifies its ingredients but obliquely calls up the mixed emotions Bishop must have felt about America and her return to America. Although she never specifically deals with her relationship to alcohol in her published work, an unpublished poem called "A Drunkard," which she all but completed just a few years before writing "The End of March," concerns the dichotomy of her disease, the mixture of longing and hatred, of fascination and danger.[2] In a letter to Lowell concerning his blend of translation and interpretation in his "imitations" of Baudelaire and Rimbaud, Bishop's strongest protest is "I feel as though you've spiked it with alcohol" (Kalstone 1989, 206). Her use of a drinking image in "The End of March" spikes the stanza purposefully, connecting the pleasure and danger of alcohol with the pleasure and the danger of the desire for isolation.

As a proto- or crypto-body, then, the dream house provides a more definite and complete isolation than the real body; it is a sort of artichoke, a kind of armor. However, as with all bodies, the only way to imagine the inside is through careful attention to the outside. Bishop's movement in the third stanza from the image of the dancing flame in the window to "There must be a stove; there *is* a chimney" illustrates the motion of the mind backward from the dream life to the practical considerations, food and light, of the living flesh. The line "A light to read by—perfect! But—impossible" accepts and negates at once the dreamed-of isolation. As she had done so brilliantly in the poem "Questions of Travel," in the final lines of the third stanza Bishop creates a sense of the elusive or uncanny by carefully describing and making real a scene, a house, that she then admits to not having seen: "And that day the wind was much too cold / even to get that far, / and of course the house was boarded up." The life of isolation, of beautiful solitude, disconnection, and meaninglessness, has been offered as a possibility and been proven completely impossible.

In the final stanza, retreating from the house and its pull, Bishop explores the possibility of meaning without ever resolving the questions of the isolation of the body that the first three stanzas have raised:

> On the way back our faces froze on the other side.
> The sun came out for just a minute.
> For just a minute, set in their bezels of sand,
> the drab, damp, scattered stones
> were multi-colored,
> and all those high enough threw out long shadows,
> individual shadows, then pulled them in again.
> They could have been teasing the lion sun,
> except that now he was behind them
> —a sun who'd walked the beach the last low tide,
> making those big, majestic paw-prints,
> who perhaps had batted a kite out of the sky to play with.

Returning from the dream of isolation, the first-person plural reappears, as does the uncomfortable reality of the wind and cold. Briefly (the repetition of the phrase "just a minute" emphasizes this brevity), when the sun comes out and shines on the "drab, damp, scattered stones," a moment of integration occurs. Individuality and relation, isolation and connection, happen simultaneously. The relationship between the stones and the sun creates "individual shadows," momentarily thrown out and then drawn in.

Bishop's tone in this stanza seems playful, teasing in its characterization, in the same way that she accuses the stones of teasing the "lion sun." Like the sun, her characterization makes the details of the landscape meaningful, and by positing human meaning she seems to find, if only teasingly and momentarily, a way to synthesize and individuate simultaneously, a way to combine without canceling opposites. By refusing to resolve multiple questions, insisting on the ambiguity of her own emotion, Bishop accomplishes what Hopkins describes in "As Kingfishers Catch Fire"—she creates a landscape of individuality: "Selves—goes itself; myself it speaks and spells, / Crying *What I do is me: for that I came*" (Houghton and Stange 1968, 704). But, for both poets, this individuality can be gathered in one vision, one perspective. For Hopkins that perspective is Christ, "For Christ plays in ten thousand places, / Lovely in limbs and lovely in eyes not his" (704), but for Bishop that perspective is human, the single perspective of the individual human senses apprehending the world, and is thus connected with the human ability to make image and metaphor: "—a sun who'd walked the beach the last low tide, / making those big, majestic paw-prints, / who perhaps had batted a kite out of the sky to play with."

What Bishop said about Hopkins's timing in her February 1934 article for the *Vassar Review* applies equally to her own strategies in combining opposing motions, in parenthetically rephrasing and rethinking, not only in "The End of March" but throughout a lifetime's work. It is extremely interesting that Bishop posits her argument about Hopkins's poetry in physical terms, speaking of poems as though they were bodies in motion, using metaphors of the body to describe the effect of poetic technique: "It is perhaps fanciful to apply the expression *timing* to poetry—race horses, runners, are timed: there is such a thing as the timing of a crew of oarsmen, or a single tennis stroke—it may be a term only suited to physical motions. But as poetry considered in a very simple way is motion too: the releasing, checking, timing, and repeating of the movement of the mind according to ordered systems, it seems fair enough to admit that in some way its discipline involves a method of timing even comparable to that used for literal actions" (Schwartz and Estess 1983, 275). Bishop's timing allows her to depict an emotional state in which she both despises the isolation of the flesh and longs for a deeper and more complete isolation, a second body, an "inscrutable house." In a postcard to John Malcolm Brinnin and Bill Read, the men to whom "The End of March" is dedicated and whose house in Duxbury she and Alice Methfessel stayed in while she wrote the poem, Bishop reports: "My house is GONE! . . . Perhaps the owners saw my poem." After the word "poem" she penned an asterisk and added "I looked at it with new eyes—" (MS 103 F36, Brinnin Papers). I think she means this in two ways; not just that she saw the possibilities of the house, but that she saw the impossibilities of it. She communicated its simultaneous attraction and repulsion. Santos compares her technique in this poem to Alfred Hitchcock's camera angles, always adjusting, correcting the original perception, allowing contradiction and disharmony (1984, 31). In "The End of March," Bishop expresses both the beauty and the danger of the dream of the isolated body.

Bishop carefully establishes the paradox of solitude and relationship that appears in "The End of March" in the first poem of *Geography III*. She deals with the duality between isolation and connection, with the tension between the single human body and the contingent world of people and things, most explicitly and perhaps most strikingly in "In the Waiting Room." As a title for the first poem in the book, "In the Waiting Room" is ominous; it seems to hold the reader in an antechamber or, in Robert Pinsky's term, to detain us inside a "portal" (1983, 50). Like the young Elizabeth, the reader is awaiting meaning, and here may perhaps be given the clues that lead to understanding—especially to understanding the centrality of the human body in the rest of the poems in *Geography III*. The first lines of "In the Waiting Room" are composed of choppy, childlike description, and they move with a kind of step-by-step slowness created by the prevalent pattern of iambic trimeter that is usually falling, a three-beat line often with one unaccented syllable tacked at the end:

> In Worcester, Massachusetts,
> I went with Aunt Consuelo
> to keep her dentist's appointment
> and sat and waited for her
> in the dentist's waiting room.
> It was winter. It got dark
> early. The waiting room

> was full of grown-up people,
> arctics and overcoats,
> lamps and magazines. (*Poems,* 159)

The slowness of these lines brings with it a feeling of rumination, a sense of careful deliberation meant to force meaning from a strange event. Indeed, the occurrence, the odd feeling, at the center of the poem was one that Bishop had tried to write about before, most notably ten years earlier in the short story "The Country Mouse."[3] In that story she identifies the aunt as Aunt Jenny, and though Aunt Consuelo is the name Bishop uses in the first two drafts of "In the Waiting Room," in the third and fourth drafts she conceals or withholds the name of the aunt (really Aunt Florence), writing "Aunt —" (Vassar Box 30). Bishop's choosing Aunt Consuelo, a Spanish or Portuguese name, for an American aunt in a poem that takes place in Worcester, Massachusetts, is strange in itself (Ruark 1991)—perhaps an indication of the losses, or the geography of the losses, that make revisiting this incident necessary, as withholding the name in the earlier drafts may have been an attempt to evade that location.

The problem of location, and the attempt to locate the self, explains why, as Costello says, the child's "inquisitive mind goes toward what is not obviously the self" (1983, 113), or, put more plainly, it explains the importance of the speaker's insistence on the literacy of her younger self:

> My aunt was inside
> what seemed like a long time
> and while I waited I read
> the *National Geographic*
> (I could read) and carefully
> studied the photographs:

Like the parenthetical phrases in other poems in *Geography III* that I have discussed, the parenthetical phrase "(I could read)" demonstrates the mind of the speaker interacting with and in tension with the form of the poem. Language and literacy create connection, and the speaker's insistence that her younger self could read identifies a relationship with the contingent world defined by language and by language's control of time and space.

It is interesting also that the child Elizabeth chooses to read the *National Geographic,* a magazine that is not written for children but which has fascinated many of us as children. If, as Pinsky asserts, we define the self by restoring what we are not (1983, 52), we also and simultaneously define the self by restoring what we are. When we move toward what is "not obviously the self" (Costello 1983, 113), we often find a self we might lose in more ordinary reflections. The photographs the young Elizabeth sees in the *National Geographic* at first appear to be wholly other. Indeed, as Prunty points out, *National Geographic* itself—especially during this period between the world wars, when countries sought to affirm their national boundaries—became a kind of organ for confirming essential presuppositions about the otherness, the "primitive" or "uncivilized" existence, of other races, of faraway nations (1990, 241). On one hand, the child confirms, by examining the photographs, these same limits; not national, but personal boundaries:

> the inside of a volcano,
> black, and full of ashes;
> then it was spilling over
> in rivulets of fire.
> Osa and Martin Johnson
> dressed in riding breeches,
> laced boots, pith helmets.
> A dead man slung on a pole
> —"Long Pig," the caption said.
> Babies with pointed heads
> wound round and round with string;
> black, naked women with necks
> wound round and round with wire
> like the necks of light bulbs.

Each image—the volcano, the cannibals, Osa and Martin Johnson—is shockingly different from anything in the opening description of the Worcester dentist's waiting room. Yet, the child concentrates on, experiences, not just the obvious and overwhelming differences but the simultaneous and opposing feeling of connection. She focuses

on the physical body and on the body's existence in time—things
that make the babies, and the women, and the cannibals, and Osa
and Martin Johnson, the same as her:

> Their breasts were horrifying.
> I read it right straight through.
> I was too shy to stop.
> And then I looked at the cover:
> the yellow margins, the date.

The line "I was too shy to stop" is strange; it forecasts the odd
realization the child is about to have. Already, before she has acutely
experienced the feeling of connection and disconnection, of isolation and interdependence, she feels, in the necessity to keep reading,
a link between her internal world and the external reality—not just
the reality of Worcester, but of Africa, of anywhere. Reading represents a milder version of the strong and complicated feeling of connection she is on the brink of experiencing; reading is both social
and isolated, a way to internalize the other (or at least the thoughts
and voice of the other), a way to make connection, and also a way
to escape the horrible waiting room with the strange grown-ups, a
means of isolation.

The experience of reading, an experience of a simultaneous and
overwhelming sense of connection and isolation, moves, in the lines
that follow, toward a climax of realization about human nature:

> Suddenly, from inside,
> came an *oh!* of pain
> —Aunt Consuelo's voice—
> not very loud or long.
> I wasn't at all surprised;
> even then I knew she was
> a foolish, timid woman.
> I might have been embarrassed,
> but wasn't. What took me
> completely by surprise
> was that it was *me:*
> my voice, in my mouth.

The young Elizabeth has none of the socially expectable reactions to her aunt's cry, neither surprise that an adult would be cowardly nor embarrassment that the coward is her aunt. The first of these reactions could mean a complete sense of otherness: "No one's afraid like I am"—a reaction we might expect of a young child. The second could mean a complete sense of connection—"Everyone thinks I'm a coward because my aunt is"—the adolescent's reaction. Instead, her reaction is a combination of opposing states, both completely connected and completely isolated: to internalize the cry and to become it. The physical connections that the photographs and the readings have suggested become real in the internalized cry of pain. The confusion between voices comes from the connection between bodies. Pinsky has pointed out the lovely ambiguity, the centrality, of the phrase "from inside" (1983, 54), suggesting both the inside of the dentist's office and the inside of the child's body, recalling the miniature cavity in the tooth and the huge cavity of the volcano. "In" and "out," concepts that Bishop has always manipulated and exploded, here become hopelessly, purposefully, and precariously confused. This confusion and connection becomes disorientation, and, at the end of the first stanza, disorientation creates an instant in which language breaks down. Pronouns, normally markers of the barriers between bodies, fail, and even the first-person plural that can unite two beings fails to communicate the sense of simultaneous separateness and connection that the child experiences:

> Without thinking at all
> I was my foolish aunt,
> I—we—were falling, falling,
> our eyes glued to the cover
> of the *National Geographic,*
> February, 1918.

In the second stanza, Bishop flips the coin of the feeling of connection and finds, on the other side, the overwhelming sense of the isolated self. It is not an intellectual connection, because it happens "Without thinking"; instead, it is a more frightening physical, felt connection. To quell the vertigo caused by her growing realization, the child repeats the formula that she knows to distinguish herself from others, and part of this formula is time, dates, the date of her birth, but this is also part of what connects her to the other people in the waiting room, and her aunt, and the women with the "awful hanging breasts." The simultaneous and opposite sense of connection and isolation is a profound experience of the nature of the body, and it causes a split between thinking or saying, the territory of language, and "sensation," the realm where language, where names and pronouns, seem to explode:

> I said to myself: three days
> and you'll be seven years old.
> I was saying it to stop
> the sensation of falling off
> the round, turning world
> into cold, blue-black space.
> But I felt: you are an *I*,
> you are an *Elizabeth*,
> you are one of *them*.
> *Why* should you be one, too?

What is particularly interesting about this passage is not only the constructed split between the thinking and feeling selves but the way that split, like the split between self and not-self, between the aunt's voice and the child's voice, collapses.

The feeling of total isolation and disconnectedness, the danger of "falling off / the round, turning world / into cold, blue-black space," connects inextricably to the feeling that "you are one of *them*" and all of them are individual I's, as lonely and disconnected as you are. In the lines that follow, Bishop holds the profound and ridiculous experience of the human flesh in a very precarious balance. There is no answer to "*Why* should you be one, too?" but all of the questions this one question elicits are sitting across from her amid the magazines, arctics, and overcoats, each inhabiting a body that separates and connects them all:

> I scarcely dared to look
> to see what it was I was.

I gave a sidelong glance
—I couldn't look any higher—
at shadowy gray knees,
trousers and skirts and boots
and different pairs of hands
lying under the lamps.

Amazingly, the child Elizabeth sees in the bodies around her a second doubling, another example of the dichotomy between isolation and connection. The body itself, in its symmetrical structure, its pairs of hands, knees, and feet, re-creates the isolation and connection between bodies; on each side we are the same and not the same. Here is a more profound realization of the same themes Bishop treated comically in "The Gentleman of Shalott." Even a "sidelong glance" reveals to the young Elizabeth that this duality she so profoundly experiences, the paradox of connection and isolation, exists at the absolute center of the body she lives in.

The "sidelong glance," then, does not provide any answers but instead touches off a series of deepening questions about the nature of human existence:

I knew that nothing stranger
had ever happened, that nothing
stranger could ever happen.
Why should I be my aunt,
or me, or anyone?
What similarities—
boots, hands, the family voice
I felt in my throat, or even
the *National Geographic*
and those awful hanging breasts—
held us all together
or made us all just one?
How—I didn't know any
word for it—how "unlikely" . . .
How had I come to be here,
like them, and overhear
a cry of pain that could have
got loud and worse but hadn't?

These questions express the central paradox; it is the similarities that
"held us all together / or made us all just one." What we all have
in common, our common flesh, both separates and joins us. Just as
language, the logical human construct, fails to communicate the
sense of simultaneous and complete isolation and connection that
the child experiences on hearing the cry of pain, so language, it
seems, cannot completely communicate the strangeness of the
child's realization. Therefore, the young Elizabeth begins to repeat
the word "strange" and says, "I didn't know any word for it." However, the word she finds for it, "unlikely," seems to me to capture the
duality of the experience in the same way the word "shan't" in "One
Art" managed to say yes and no at the same time. In earlier drafts
of the poem, Bishop had tried "incredible" for "unlikely," but the
line "How—I didn't know any / word for it—how 'incredible' "
makes perfect sense (Vassar Box 30). "Incredible" comments only
on the contradiction of feelings within the speaker, the speaker's
inability to believe what must be believed, the report of the senses.
"Unlikely," on the other hand, creates levels of contradiction. It is
an ironic word for an experience of a shared sameness. By its emotional flatness it expresses the speaker's feeling of disconnection yet
also communicates an intellectual engagement. The word comments
not just on the speaker but on the situation itself, on the paradox
of the body that seems too impossible and too illogical to be true,
but yet must exist, because all the evidence points toward it. "Unlikely" is a scientist's word, and its appearance in the mouth of a
fainting six year old risks undermining the serious incident with a
comic tone. But this risk in itself reinforces the paradox, the dichotomy, the ever-multiplying questions the poem explores.

Experiencing the paradox of the body affects the physical well-
being of the young Elizabeth, or perhaps the fainting feeling affects
the experience of the paradox of the flesh:

> The waiting room was bright
> and too hot. It was sliding
> beneath a big black wave,
> another, and another.

Strangely, the terms Bishop uses to communicate the most acute physical sensations are impersonal; it is not the child that slides beneath the "big black wave," but the waiting room. The young Elizabeth is disconnected; she is "falling off / the round, turning world / into cold, blue-black space." But, the feeling of disconnection occurs simultaneously with the feeling of most acute physicality. Those of us who have had the experience of fainting can attest to the accuracy of Bishop's description, the feeling of being disconnected from the fainting world and drawn far down or far off inside the cave of the flesh. Feeling faint is the perfect physical state to illuminate the contradictory feelings the young Elizabeth experiences.

Her return to consciousness is also paradoxical:

Then I was back in it.
The War was on. Outside,
in Worcester, Massachusetts,
were night and slush and cold,
and it was still the fifth
of February, 1918.

The word "it" encompasses both sides of the central paradox, and means both her own isolated, physical body, her conscious self, and the world that surrounds the physical body and to which the body connects her, the world where the war is "on" and where "night and slush and cold" can cause discomfort and suffering. The word "in," of course, reaffirms the paradox, calls into question the split between in and out, between the external world and the internal self. It is helpful to note, as Prunty suggests, that the last two stanzas "do not meld, but stand together and apart in a way that characterizes much of Bishop's work" (1990, 242). There can be no melding, no "pure moment of symbiosis" (Costello 1983, 112), because the poem explores the unresolvable, unanswerable paradox of the human body. The world the child sees and experiences turns toward her in similarity and connection as she turns toward it, but both the world and the child also, and simultaneously, turn away in isolation and recognized difference.

Just as in "One Art" and "Five Flights Up" Bishop reveals the paradoxical relationship between speaker and form, reveals her own ambivalence about the act of embodiment in verse, in both "The End of March" and "In the Waiting Room" she examines and attempts to express the confusion of thoughts and feelings, the ambiguity, inherent in embodiment in flesh. The paradox of isolation and connection, the fact of human aloneness and the desire for human interaction, loss and recovery, informs all of these poems. Bishop never permits herself to resolve this rich ambiguity, to let it become the longed-for and comfortable answer, or even a blessedly simple and encompassing question. Instead, she insistently holds the opposing forces in tension so that they release all of the questions, the whole range of questions, that constantly unsettle, disconcert, bewilder, enlarge, and join us all.

"Life and the Memory of It": Creation and Reembodying the Self

The final group of poems from *Geography III* that I will discuss—"Crusoe in England," "Poem," and "The Moose"—combines the strategies and the themes of the other six poems in the book. They examine the relationship between the paradox of loss and recovery and the paradox of isolation and connection, and the relationship between embodiment in the flesh and embodiment in the poetic structure. These three poems explore the experience of human connection that brings loss; they all examine the mechanism of the poem as a device for recovering what is lost by reembodying that life, that self, in new form. And all three face that form's failure to create a permanent, or even, sometimes, sufficient, vehicle for the self, so that the self in the end must constantly be remade, reembodied in new forms that will perhaps improve where others failed, fail where others succeeded. Bishop once again translates her ambivalence about embodiment in flesh into ambivalence about embodiment in poetic form, and her evasions, her richly ambiguous phrases, words, and structures, all preserve that ambivalence and, by saying two things in one utterance, express her uncertainty, her struggle, and her openness to multiplicity.

In Bishop's dramatic monologue "Crusoe in England," the famous character speaks in a way Defoe certainly never imagined, expressing his ambivalence about his life marooned on his lonely island, and still deeper ambivalence about his rescue. From the first verse of the poem, language's ability to capture the human paradoxes of isolation and connection, loss and recovery, is at issue, lies at the heart of the questions, the uncertainties Crusoe explores:

> A new volcano has erupted,
> the papers say, and last week I was reading
> where some ship saw an island being born:
> at first a breath of steam, ten miles away;
> and then a black fleck—basalt, probably—
> rose in the mate's binoculars
> and caught on the horizon like a fly.
> They named it. But my poor old island's still
> un-rediscovered, un-renamable.
> None of the books has ever got it right. (*Poems,* 162)

The phrase "the papers say" in the second line resonates with the simultaneous interest in and bitterness toward such secondhand information—such interest and bitterness for the written word as we might expect from someone who lived on such an island rather than watching it through binoculars. Like the binoculars in "The End of March," these binoculars, and the newspaper Crusoe reads, represent a means of looking closely without really getting close, seeing or knowing without necessarily experiencing.

The action of naming—naming the island, especially—introduces the question of language's ability to control, to solidify, to give human reality to the phenomenological world. The phrase "But my poor old island's still / un-rediscovered, un-renamable" suggests that language has thus far failed to control and solidify Crusoe's island, Crusoe's experience. In fact, this failure is behind both Crusoe's reason for speaking the monologue and Bishop's reason for writing it. In answer to George Starbuck's question "What got the Crusoe poem started?" Bishop said: "I don't know. I reread the book and discovered how really awful *Robinson Crusoe* was, which I hadn't realized. I hadn't read it in a long time. . . . I reread it all one night. And I had forgotten it was so moral. All that Christianity. So I think I wanted to re-see it with all that left out" (1983, 319). Because "None of the books has ever got it right," both Bishop and her character, Crusoe, try again to "get it right," to capture in language the felt experience of reality, an attempt that, like all such attempts, is doomed to failure.

The "Well" that introduces the second verse seems a kind of sigh of resigned acceptance, a reaction to this new attempt to say what really happened, how things really felt:

> Well, I had fifty-two
> miserable, small volcanoes I could climb
> with a few slithery strides—
> volcanoes dead as ash heaps.
> I used to sit on the edge of the highest one
> and count the others standing up,
> naked and leaden, with their heads blown off.
> I'd think that if they were the size
> I thought volcanoes should be, then I had
> become a giant;
> and if I had become a giant,
> I couldn't bear to think what size
> the goats and turtles were,
> or the gulls, or the overlapping rollers
> —a glittering hexagon of rollers
> closing and closing in, but never quite,
> glittering and glittering, though the sky
> was mostly overcast.

Crusoe's musings on the relative size of the volcanoes, the goats, and his body are strange, believably illogical; they zigzag the way the motion of the mind often does as it plays with its own singularity. His musings are exercises in perspective, in how expectations affect perspective, and in the limited power of perspective on the outside world to change an internal reality. If he is a giant, then the size of the contingent world has changed proportionally, but his internal reality, the fixity of his own bodily proportions in his mind, makes the thought of the huge gulls, goats, and rollers unbearable. Like the rollers in the sea that close in but never touch the coast of the island, the play with perspective closes in but never quite touches the mental map of the body's limits.

In the third verse, Crusoe's monologue concentrates on the paradoxical beauty of his island; his remembering the apparent contradiction of glittering rollers, "though the sky / was mostly overcast," seems to prompt fresh remembrance of other strange beauties, of the sensuous experience of the island:

> My island seemed to be
> a sort of cloud-dump. All the hemisphere's
> left-over clouds arrived and hung
> above the craters—their parched throats
> were hot to touch.
> Was that why it rained so much?
> And why sometimes the whole place hissed?
> The turtles lumbered by, high-domed,
> hissing like teakettles.
> (And I'd have given years, or taken a few,
> for any sort of kettle, of course.)
> The folds of lava, running out to sea,
> would hiss. I'd turn. And then they'd prove
> to be more turtles.
> The beaches were all lava, variegated,
> black, red, and white, and gray;
> the marbled colors made a fine display.
> And I had waterspouts. Oh,
> half a dozen at a time, far out,
> they'd come and go, advancing and retreating,
> their heads in cloud, their feet in moving patches
> of scuffed-up white.
> Glass chimneys, flexible, attenuated,
> sacerdotal beings of glass . . . I watched
> the water spiral up in them like smoke.
> Beautiful, yes, but not much company.

Again in the first half of this description, a parenthetical expression cuts through the detail to reveal the action of the mind moving beneath the form. The lines "(And I'd have given years, or taken a few / for any sort of kettle, of course)" seem, at first, tossed off. But on closer reading, these lines indicate the essential ambivalence behind Crusoe's words, his terrifyingly ambiguous feelings about living. The common expression "I'd have given years," with the afterthought "or taken a few," suggests that a quicker death or a more prolonged life are nearly equal punishments, equivalent prices for a kettle.

A prolonged life on the island is presumably a punishment because it is a sentence to a life of isolation. All the sensuous experiences Crusoe describes involve apprehension of the nonhuman world. The beauty of the "flexible, attenuated / sacerdotal beings of glass" is marred by their otherness: "Beautiful, yes, but not much company." Costello suggests that part of Bishop's message involves the acceptability of Crusoe's narcissism and self-pity (1983, 124), his attempt to define himself, as the young Elizabeth attempted in "In the Waiting Room," by what is obviously not the self. However, Crusoe, unlike the young Elizabeth, cannot look sidelong to see other bodies, bodies that look back in different sameness. When Crusoe gives way to self-pity, it revolves around the burden of the isolated self, the home—both bodily and literally:

> I often gave way to self-pity.
> "Do I deserve this? I suppose I must.
> I wouldn't be here otherwise. Was there
> a moment when I actually chose this?
> I don't remember, but there could have been."
> What's wrong about self-pity, anyway?
> With my legs dangling down familiarly
> over a crater's edge, I told myself
> "Pity should begin at home." So the more
> pity I felt, the more I felt at home.

Crusoe's accustomed position, legs dangling down over a crater's edge, represents both a physical and a mental brink: he is poised between two attitudes—humorous self-irony ("the more / pity I felt, the more I felt at home") and serious self-evaluation ("Was there / a moment when I actually chose this?"). While in this verse Crusoe claims to have given way to self-pity, the tone of the verse is much more ambiguous; both he and the poet seem to weigh self-pity and its relative merits. And more than even intellectually considering the merits of self-pity, Crusoe seems to taste its aftertaste, remember the feeling, with self-irony and self-reflexivity. The essential quality of Crusoe at this point in the poem is his isolation. The flood of language (the poem is one of the longest Bishop ever wrote) and the exploration of ambiguous, swirling emotions all happen in the context of Crusoe's remembering a time of absolute isolation from his own kind:

> The sun set in the sea; the same odd sun
> rose from the sea,
> and there was one of it and one of me.
> The island had one kind of everything:
> one tree snail, a bright violet-blue
> with a thin shell, crept over everything,
> over the one variety of tree,
> a sooty, scrub affair.
> Snail shells lay under these in drifts
> and, at a distance,
> you'd swear they were beds of irises.

The momentary and mistaken belief that the snail shells were beds of irises, like the momentary and mistaken belief that the turtles were teakettles, underlines the effect of the old life on the new, the influence of expectation on perception. The world Crusoe has lost is recovered for a moment in the turtles and the snails; the two worlds combine, just as, in the line "and there was one of it and one of me," self-pity and self-irony combine and two basically opposing feelings are communicated in the same utterance.

This ambivalence underlies all of Crusoe's descriptions. In the next few stanzas, building toward the pinnacle of bitterness and isolation, Crusoe indicates not just the pain but also the essential beauty of his forced individuality:

> There was one kind of berry, a dark red.
> I tried it, one by one, and hours apart.
> Sub-acid, and not bad, no ill effects;
> and so I made home-brew. I'd drink
> the awful, fizzy, stinging stuff
> that went straight to my head

and play my home-made flute
(I think it had the weirdest scale on earth)
and, dizzy, whoop and dance among the goats.
Home-made, home-made! But aren't we all?
I felt a deep affection for
the smallest of my island industries.
No, not exactly, since the smallest was
a miserable philosophy.

Although Costello argues that the "miserable philosophy" is that the self must be homemade (1983, 123), this observation seems to capture only half the story, half the tone of the verse. The other half is the celebratory Pan drunk on his homemade brew, playing his homemade flute among the goats. The parenthetical phrase "(I think it had the weirdest scale on earth)" expresses the odd beauty of individuality and perhaps comments on the strange beauty of Bishop's work in general. Like the opening description of "The End of March," the scene is both lonely and lovely. And, like the speaker's desire to drink *grog à l'américaine,* also in "The End of March," Crusoe's home brew is contradictory, both "awful, fizzy, stinging stuff" and the stuff that will allow him to "whoop and dance among the goats."

The miserable philosophy comes not from the celebration of individuality in "Home-made, home-made!" but from the implied isolation that is the other side of that individuality and from the thwarted attempt at long-distance connection, at connecting with the society, the culture, that Crusoe has left behind. Crusoe explains that "the smallest was / a miserable philosophy":

Because I didn't know enough.
Why didn't I know enough of something?
Greek drama or astronomy? The books
I'd read were full of blanks;
the poems—well, I tried
reciting to my iris beds,
"They flash upon that inward eye,
which is the bliss . . . " The bliss of what?
One of the first things that I did
when I got back was look it up.

Of course, the word Crusoe evades, or forgets (from Wordsworth's "I Wandered Lonely as a Cloud"), is "solitude." Although in earlier drafts Bishop had experimented with leaving out the word "bliss," Crusoe's forgetting the word "solitude," especially at this moment when he is striving for some lost connection, comments directly on both the verse that preceded this one, in which he so much enjoyed the solitude that is the other side of the coin of isolation, and this verse, in which solitude is the concept and state most to be evaded.

In the next stanza, Crusoe reveals the depth of his ambivalence toward his isolation. He objects, not just to the sameness of his existence, but to the lack of certainty in this sameness, the preponderance of unanswered questions:

> The island smelled of goat and guano
> The goats were white, so were the gulls,
> and both too tame, or else they thought
> I was a goat, too, or a gull.
> *Baa, baa, baa* and *shriek, shriek, shriek,*
> *baa . . . shriek . . . baa . . .* I still can't shake
> them from my ears; they're hurting now.
> The questioning shrieks, the equivocal replies
> over a ground of hissing rain
> and hissing, ambulating turtles
> got on my nerves.

The play on "gull" at the end of the fourth line of this verse establishes a tone of bitterness so far unequaled in the poem. Unlike the questions the bird and dog seem to ask in "Five Flights Up," the questions the gulls ask, and the sheep's "equivocal replies," do not create even a facade of answer. There is no hope of a huge, ponderous morning that will, at least, resolve the inhuman world, if it cannot resolve human uncertainty, loss and grief.

For Crusoe, the sameness without certainty, the isolation seemingly past hope of connection, grows more desperate:

> When all the gulls flew up at once, they sounded
> like a big tree in a strong wind, its leaves.
> I'd shut my eyes and think about a tree,
> an oak, say, with real shade, somewhere.

I'd heard of cattle getting island-sick.
I thought the goats were.
One billy-goat would stand on the volcano
I'd christened *Mont d'Espoir* or *Mount Despair*
(I'd time enough to play with names),
and bleat and bleat, and sniff the air.
I'd grab his beard and look at him.
His pupils, horizontal, narrowed up
and expressed nothing, or a little malice.
I got so tired of the very colors!
One day I dyed a baby goat bright red
with my red berries, just to see
something a little different.
And then his mother wouldn't recognize him.

The parenthetical "(I'd time enough to play with names)" points up again the importance of language's ability to control, to manage, to forge connection, and it makes a sidelong joke on Adam alone in the garden, naming the creatures around him. Both grabbing the billy goat and looking in his eyes and dyeing the baby goat red represent Crusoe's attempts to forge a connection with the beings around him. Both attempts meet with the same kind of failure; the world he would connect with narrows to exclude him. The billy goat's eyes "narrowed up / and expressed nothing"; the mother goat rejects her baby rather than accepting Crusoe's attempt at change.

Costello sees in these events a signal that the "human order imposed on the landscape never 'takes' as a real presence" (1983, 122). These events also, on a more personal level, mirror the paradoxical reactions of the child looking at the *National Geographic* pictures in "In the Waiting Room" and the speaker's attitude toward the "artichoke" house in "The End of March." Like all of these things, the goats turn toward Crusoe in likeness and away from him in difference; like Crusoe, they are warm-blooded mammals, and he can imagine that they are "island-sick" themselves. In dyeing the baby goat he sets one individual apart from the rest, individuates it, as he is forcibly individuated and set apart from his kind. The connections between the goats and humans become even stronger in the verse paragraph that follows:

Dreams were the worst. Of course I dreamed of food
and love, but they were pleasant rather
than otherwise. But then I'd dream of things
like slitting a baby's throat, mistaking it
for a baby goat. I'd have
nightmares of other islands
stretching away from mine, infinities
of islands, islands spawning islands,
like frogs' eggs turning into polliwogs
of islands, knowing that I had to live
on each and every one, eventually,
for ages, registering their flora,
their fauna, their geography.

Crusoe's dream of slitting the baby's throat, mistaking it for a baby goat, points up the real similarity between Crusoe's isolation on the island and the normal human isolation in the confines of the body, the danger of annihilation inherent in breaking that isolation. It also raises again the question of perception, of how expectation and habit influence perception and how disastrous the failure to see accurately can be. The difficulty and crucial importance of accurate observation, and the paradox of the human body, whose senses represent the only possibility for connection while they simultaneously distort and limit perception of reality—all of this is central to Crusoe's nightmare of infinities of islands that he must live on and learn endlessly, "registering their flora, / their fauna, their geography." Crusoe's nightmare is a nightmare of endlessly repeated isolation searching for connection, loss and recovery that will lead only to further loss. It is a superconcentrated example of the paradoxes of loss and recovery, of isolation and connection, that inform all the poems in *Geography III*, that, indeed, seem to have informed Bishop's life.

However, with the introduction of Friday, the tone and the diction of the poem suddenly shift:

Just when I thought I couldn't stand it
another minute longer, Friday came.
(Accounts of that have everything all wrong.)
Friday was nice.
Friday was nice, and we were friends.

If only he had been a woman!
I wanted to propagate my kind,
and so did he, I think, poor boy.
He'd pet the baby goats sometimes,
and race with them, or carry one around.
—Pretty to watch; he had a pretty body.

After the almost overblown diction of lines like "flexible, attenuated, / sacerdotal beings of glass" and the bitter self-mockery of
"I'd christened *Mont d'Espoir* or *Mount Despair*," the simplicity of
the lines "Friday was nice. / Friday was nice, and we were friends"
is shocking and amazingly effective in accomplishing two opposing things simultaneously, communicating emotional depth by not
trying to. By avoiding, by purposefully evading, language powerful
enough to carry feelings of connection, Bishop expresses her ambivalence about embodying thought in form, as the poem (and
Crusoe himself) has expressed ambivalence about embodiment in
the flesh. However, embodiment in the flesh is the only way to ensure future opportunities for connection, to ensure that isolation
will not be a permanent condition, and thus Crusoe's desire to
propagate his kind becomes a part of the paradox of isolation and
connection. The parenthetical "(Accounts of that have everything
all wrong)" once again reveals the workings of the mind of the
speaker behind the form of the monologue and, paradoxically,
points to language's inability to re-create life experience, the paradox of human emotion, and the necessity that language, that art,
attempt to re-create, to reembody.

This change of tone, simple and beautiful, is followed quickly by
another change, by the only one-line verse in the poem: "And then
one day they came and took us off." The flatness of the line resounds
with paradox—salvation and damnation, recovery and loss. Crusoe
returns to the present, where he tries to sort out the questions
whose answers are still equivocal:[4]

Now I live here, another island,
that doesn't seem like one, but who decides?
My blood was full of them; my brain
bred islands. But that archipelago

has petered out. I'm old.
I'm bored, too, drinking my real tea,
surrounded by uninteresting lumber.

The nightmare of "infinities / of islands, islands spawning islands," the endless repetition of loss and recovery, isolation and connection, becomes finally the dreamed-of life, lost somewhere in the past.

Crusoe seems to find, examining the artifacts of his island existence, that the uncertainties themselves, the paradoxes, the constantly multiplying, shrieking questions, made up whatever meaning he found:

The knife there on the shelf—
it reeked of meaning, like a crucifix.
It lived. How many years did I
beg it, implore it, not to break?
I knew each nick and scratch by heart,
the bluish blade, the broken tip,
the lines of wood-grain on the handle . . .
Now it won't look at me at all.
The living soul has dribbled away.
My eyes rest on it and pass on.

Kalstone (1977, 36) sees in this description Bishop's profound questioning of the faculty of the imagination: What is imagination if it is not directly related to survival? Beyond even the question of imagination, I believe, lies Bishop's attempt to explore the embodiment of meaning in material objects, and what Prunty identifies as the "inscrutable" or "the way time displaces the relations that give us identity" (1990, 243). The necessity to contrive and invent, to impose human meaning on the concrete world, and the Faustian bargain of that imposition, the paradoxes we finally cannot sort out, gather together in Crusoe's knife.

Bishop has always been interested in the necessity to, in the words of Octavio Paz, "make creations from your own ruins," the necessity to invent and contrive, both in poems and in life. In a letter to Robert Lowell dated November 18, 1965, Bishop wrote of her house in Ouro Prêto: "I like Ouro Preto because everything there was made on the spot, by hand, of stone, iron, copper, wood—and

they had to invent a lot—and everything has lasted perfectly well
for almost 300 yrs now.—I used to think this was just sentimental
of me—now I'm beginning to take it more seriously" (Kalstone
1989, 229). She expressed interest in the idea even earlier, writing
of a friend's home in Cuttyhunk Island: "You live all the time in
this Robinson Crusoe atmosphere, making this do for that, and
contriving and inventing" (Vassar Notebook V). However, the final
verse paragraph of "Crusoe in England" concerns how the invented
things can fail to contain the entire, paradoxical, human meaning,
how, instead of being a vehicle for recovery, they themselves can
become, when removed from the environment in which they were
essential, a fresh reminder, like the knife, of the loss:

> The local museum's asked me to
> leave everything to them:
> the flute, the knife, the shrivelled shoes,
> my shedding goatskin trousers
> (moths have got in the fur),
> the parasol that took me such a time
> remembering the way the ribs should go.
> It still will work but, folded up,
> looks like a plucked and skinny fowl.
> How can anyone want such things?
> —And Friday, my dear Friday, died of measles
> seventeen years ago come March.

The final lines of "Crusoe in England" relate the paradox of loss
and recovery to the paradox of isolation and connection, show them
as integral parts of the same human experience. The dash before the
words "And Friday," like the one before "Even losing you" in "One
Art," visually reenacts the verbal pause of a speaker who wants to
evade this familiar loss. The paradox of the dramatic monologue
form itself is that it both momentarily recaptures the uncertainty,
despair, and joy of Crusoe's isolated life and also recaptures the loss
and confusion of his longed-for salvation, his recovery.

I believe Bishop saw this paradox, the paradox of embodiment,
not only in the form of the dramatic monologue but in all poetic
form. The same concerns, the same themes, appear in "Poem," another exploration of the bargain of embodiment. More than a ge-

neric title for a simple statement, the title "Poem" indicates Bishop's attempt to wrestle with what embodying thought and emotion in poetic form means. In "Poem," as in "Large Bad Picture" from *North & South*, Bishop takes as a subject one of her Great-Uncle George's paintings:[5]

> About the size of an old-style dollar bill,
> American or Canadian,
> mostly the same whites, gray greens, and steel grays
> —this little painting (a sketch for a larger one?)
> has never earned any money in its life.
> Useless and free, it has spent seventy years
> as a minor family relic
> handed along collaterally to owners
> who looked at it sometimes, or didn't bother to. (*Poems,* 176)

All the details in this first stanza ostensibly undermine the value of the painting. The colors are drab, uninteresting, like the colors of old money. The parenthetical phrase "(a sketch for a larger one?)" reveals the speaker's uncertainty about even the impetus behind the painting, its claim to independent existence. Bishop's repetition of its monetary worthlessness in the phrase "has never earned any money in its life" and the description "Useless and free" that immediately follows hammers home the "white elephant" quality of the family artifact. Yet, the tone of the sentence that the dash introduces—"this little painting (a sketch for a larger one?) / has never earned any money in its life"—sounds undeniably triumphant. Bishop apparently finds something beautiful about the fact that the painting is "Useless and free," discovers a beauty that does not cancel the painting's worthlessness but comes from it.

The second stanza, like the description in "Large Bad Picture" of her great-uncle's more sizable attempt, depicts the poet's struggle to see clearly and accurately the artifact in front of her. Rephrasings and parenthetical expressions reveal the action of the speaker's mind moving over the form of the small painting:

> It must be Nova Scotia; only there
> does one see gabled wooden houses
> painted that awful shade of brown.

The other houses, the bits that show, are white.
Elm trees, low hills, a thin church steeple
—that gray-blue wisp—or is it? In the foreground
a water meadow with some tiny cows,
two brushstrokes each, but confidently cows;
two miniscule white geese in the blue water,
back-to-back, feeding, and a slanting stick.
Up closer, a wild iris, white and yellow,
fresh-squiggled from the tube.
The air is fresh and cold; cold early spring
clear as gray glass; a half inch of blue sky
below the steel-gray storm clouds.
(They were the artist's specialty.)
A specklike bird is flying to the left.
Or is it a flyspeck looking like a bird?

While in "Large Bad Picture" Bishop concentrated on the painting and how the painter's failed technique prevented connection, here she seems much more interested in the attempt to see than in her great-uncle's failure to reproduce sufficiently what he has seen. Again and again, Bishop breaks the facade of the description to demonstrate her own ways of looking and her own uncertainty: "It must be Nova Scotia," "or is it?" "Up closer," and "(They were the artist's specialty)." Her attempt to see, to see well, draws her into the picture, allows her to make the leap from obvious visual detail to interpreted tactile response: "The air is fresh and cold; cold early spring / clear as gray glass." Whereas in "Large Bad Picture" moving inside the body of the painting meant remaining there until the end of the poem, here the boundaries between in and out, between the artifact and the world, appear more permeable. The speaker and the reader move back and forth between breathing the "cold early spring" air in the painting and breathing the real air beyond it.

This movement, the ability to range between the body of the artifact and the inhabited body of the flesh, brings about the crisis of recognition, the moment of empathy, that takes place in the third stanza:

Heavens, I recognize the place, I know it!
It's behind—I can almost remember the farmer's name.
His barn backed on that meadow. There it is,

titanium white, one dab. The hint of steeple,
filaments of brush-hairs, barely there,
must be the Presbyterian church.
Would that be Miss Gillespie's house?
Those particular geese and cows
are naturally before my time.

The first exclamation—"Heavens!"—marks a moment of connection, a climax of understanding, not just of the painting, but of the farmer whose name she can "almost remember," and of her great-uncle, and of the place. In descriptions like "There it is, / titanium white, one dab," Bishop manages to convey simultaneously the actual scene, the barn, the church, the house, and the techniques of the artifact that both re-create this scene and distance her from it. The final line of the stanza is the strangest of all and demonstrates the motion of the mind of the speaker between the body of the artifact and her own real body. The word "naturally" in the lines "Those particular geese and cows / are naturally before my time" underlines the doubleness, the simultaneous realities of the re-created or reembodied natural world of the painting and the present natural world, the time, of the speaker. It also signals a return to self-possession after the emotional break of "Heavens!"

The fourth stanza opens out Bishop's connection to her great-uncle who painted the scene:

A sketch done in an hour, "in one breath,"
once taken from a trunk and handed over.
*Would you like this? I'll probably never
have room to hang these things again.
Your Uncle George, no, mine, my Uncle George,
he'd be your great-uncle, left them all with Mother
when he went back to England.
You know, he was quite famous, an R.A. . . . .*

The individual and isolated realities of the aunt's memories, of the great-uncle's painting, and of the speaker's poem both connect and fail to connect, remain isolated by time and distance, and come together in a moment of vision.

The final stanza of the poem explores this paradox of isolation and connection and the way this relates to loss and the possibility

for recovery. In draft after draft, Bishop struggled with the final
stanza of "Poem"; on one page there are as many as ten restarts of
the last section. In the published version, she retains that sense of
struggle, that refusal to resolve:

> I never knew him. We both knew this place,
> apparently, this literal small backwater,
> looked at it long enough to memorize it,
> our years apart. How strange. And it's still loved,
> or its memory is (it must have changed a lot).
> Our visions coincided—"visions" is
> too serious a word—our looks, two looks:
> art "copying from life" and life itself,
> life and the memory of it so compressed
> they've turned into each other. Which is which?
> Life and the memory of it cramped,
> dim, on a piece of Bristol board,
> dim, but how live, how touching in detail
> —the little that we get for free,
> the little of our earthly trust. Not much.
> About the size of our abidance
> along with theirs: the munching cows,
> the iris, crisp and shivering, the water
> still standing from spring freshets,
> the yet-to-be-dismantled elms, the geese.

The first line of this stanza proclaims the connection that these
"looks"—knowing and loving, careful enough to memorize small
details—have made possible. The strangeness of the connection that
does not heal or abolish the isolation (both remain "our years
apart") translates into the puzzlement and wonder of Bishop's tone.

"Art 'copying from life' and life itself" are almost indistinguish-
able; both embodiment in form and embodiment in flesh provide
the opportunity for connection and, simultaneously, for a more profound realization of our own isolation. The painting and the poem
describing the painting are both forms that make the absent present,
that give a fresh opportunity for knowing and loving the things that
will pass in time. The admonition "(it must have changed a lot)"
proves crucial to understanding why Bishop titles this "Poem"

rather than "Small Painting," a title she toyed with in the drafts. The painting has rescued from time the transient Nova Scotian landscape by reembodying it in meaningful form, if only for Bishop and if only for a moment; the poem, likewise, has rescued both the painting and the landscape by performing that act of embodiment yet again. However, Bishop concludes that, like the original landscape, the art forms that preserve it are vulnerable to loss.

I see in Bishop's drafts a true struggle with this paradox, this overwhelming uncertainty. In draft after draft she struggles to keep the elms whole; in the first draft she wrote "the elms / never dismantled," in later ones, "four undismantled elms," "the never-to-be-dismantled now elms," and then "the never-to-be-dismantled elms." Finally, she crossed out "never" and wrote over it "yet."

The painting is "Useless and free," and it is a true gift because, just for a moment, it holds the paradoxes of loss and recovery, of connection and isolation, in a pure balance so that accepting one invokes the other and everything moves back and forth between the permeable barriers of these apparent opposites. This balance and movement, the ability to sustain paradox, is the heart of the poems in *Geography III* and finds perhaps its most complete expression in "The Moose."

In 1946, Bishop returned to her childhood home in Nova Scotia after a prolonged absence. After her visit to Great Village, on the trip back to Boston, her bus stopped because a female moose wandered out of the thicket and onto the road. For about twenty years, on and off, Bishop tried to write a poem about this experience (Spires 1978, 129). She never abandoned her original intuition that this incident contained something interesting and provocative. The earliest drafts of the poem are very short, referring to the moose often as the "nightmare moose" (Vassar Box 30). However, the final version, published first in the *New Yorker* in 1972, moves away from adjectives that seem to resolve the meaning of the moose's appearance and toward what the poem calls a "dreamy divagation," an easy wandering that accepts uncertainty and oppositions, even oppositions embodied in the same form, without forcing resolution. One of the typescripts in Vassar's manuscript collection (Draft #40) includes in the margins Bishop's introduction for a performance of

the poem in Boston. She had subtitled the poem "(Back to Boston)
for this occasion—" and explained, "It is a sort of ballad, a simple
record of a bus trip from N. S. [Nova Scotia] to Boston—some time
ago. Some of you may be familiar with the geography of the place—
the names mentioned" (Vassar Box 30). This mention of the geography and names could be literal or metaphorical, and the ambiguity
of the final sentence of Bishop's introduction points to the profound ambiguity of the poem, the way "the geography of the place"
means both the physical landscape and the emotional landscape
through which all travelers pass.

The passionate and fully realized detail of the physical landscape in the opening of the poem creates a sense of slow movement
through both the surrounding countryside and through changing
moods and tones:

> From narrow provinces
> of fish and bread and tea,
> home of the long tides
> where the bay leaves the sea
> twice a day and takes
> the herrings long rides,
>
> where if the river
> enters or retreats
> in a wall of brown foam
> depends on if it meets
> the bay coming in,
> the bay not at home; (*Poems,* 169)

The metrical variation in the short, unevenly rhymed lines, structured in a periodic sentence, gives a dreamy, wandering movement
to the poem's description. Like the poet, and the herrings, the
reader is going for a long ride, and what happens on the ride seems
as uncertain as the river's retreat, seems to depend on other forces
being out or being at home. Bishop highlights the correlation between human circumstances and natural circumstances by quietly
personifying both the river as it "takes / the herrings long rides"
and the bay "coming in, / the bay not at home."

In the stanzas that follow, the speaker notes how perception
changes depending on circumstances, how the landscape changes

according to whether the river enters or retreats. Although this change is not disquieting, the images following this description surround homes and churches, a vision of human attempts at permanence:

> where, silted red,
> facing a red sea,
> and others, veins the flats'
> lavender, rich mud
> in burning rivulets;
>
> on red, gravelly roads,
> down rows of sugar maples,
> past clapboard farmhouses
> and neat, clapboard churches,
> bleached, ridged as clamshells,
> past twin silver birches,
>
> through late afternoon
> a bus journeys west,
> the windshield flashing pink,
> pink glancing off of metal,
> brushing the dented flank
> of blue, beat-up enamel;

Bishop's mention of a "red sea" combines with the earlier "fish and bread" allusion and the "clapboard churches" to establish a quiet pattern of religious images that recalls miraculous events and foreshadows the "miraculous" event about to occur, a miraculous event that is, in the words of her own sestina, "not a miracle" (*Poems*, 18).

The accretion and the movement of the periodic sentence are reminiscent of the opening of Whitman's "When Lilacs Last in the Dooryard Bloom'd"; however, each poet employs the device to a different end. The voice in Bishop's poem is conversational and curious, not solemn or rhetorical. Because Bishop does not end the periodic sentence with the verb phrase "the bus journeys west" but continues past the verb to describe the bus, she gets the "punch" of the periodic sentence, the power that comes from withholding and then finally relinquishing the verb, and yet she undercuts or refashions that "punch" by refocusing the energy into the continued description. Like the bus or the river, the description gathers power but moves along.

In the opening section of the poem, Bishop described the bus as though it were a kind of animal, even using the word "flank" for its side. In the stanza that follows, the bus seems to have a will and an entity:

> down hollows, up rises,
> and waits, patient, while
> a lone traveller gives
> kisses and embraces
> to seven relatives
> and a collie supervises.

However, as the bus starts again, the mood of the speaker and of the poem seems to change subtly; the speaker is disconnected from the world she views. She moves outside the strange world that she looks in on but is not a part of. The world Bishop describes in passionate detail seems to slide past the bus window, to be visible for just a moment at a time, well beyond the other senses.

Having said good-bye, happily, to the elms and the farms and the churches, the traveler joins the other travelers, moves into the new, odd, gliding world of the bus. However, this moment has been held off, delayed by her looking back, and her looking out:

> Goodbye to the elms,
> to the farm, to the dog.
> The bus starts. The light
> grows richer; the fog,
> shifting, salty, thin,
> comes closing in.
>
> Its cold, round crystals
> form and slide and settle
> in the white hens' feathers,
> in gray glazed cabbages,
> on the cabbage roses
> and lupins like apostles;
>
> the sweet peas cling
> to their wet white string

on the whitewashed fences;
bumblebees creep
inside the foxgloves,
and evening commences.

The "cling/string" rhyme in the couplet that begins this ninth
stanza beautifully imitates the action it describes, the rhymes clinging to each other like the sweet peas cling to the string, and also
illustrates and emphasizes, like the "fences/commences" rhyme, the
tendency toward self-contained visual images in this middle section
of the poem. The sentences here get progressively shorter and the
rhyme becomes more obvious, often providing a boundary between
the world of the bus and the world beyond the bus.

Although, in the stanzas that follow, Bishop quietly alludes to
the anxiety this sense of disconnection and movement could cause,
the overall tone of the middle section is consoling. The boundary
between the bus and the world beyond the bus provides the traveler
with perspective, a reasonable distance from which many ordinary
things gain beauty, precisely because they are distant and can be
seen only briefly:

One stop at Bass River.
Then the Economies—
Lower, Middle, Upper;
Five Islands, Five Houses,
where a woman shakes a tablecloth
out after supper.

A pale flickering. Gone.
The Tantramar marshes
and the smell of salt hay.
An iron bridge trembles
and a loose plank rattles
but doesn't give way.

On the left, a red light
swims through the dark:
a ship's port lantern.
Two rubber boots show,
illuminated, solemn.
A dog gives one bark.

The iron bridge trembling and the loose plank that threatens and rattles but "doesn't give way" may represent the threat that underlies and energizes, but never overtakes, the mood of the speaker, the threatening feeling of dissolution, disconnection. Indeed, part of what the poem illustrates in this middle section is the beauty made possible by the constant threat of brevity, the way our motion through time and space causes us to invest the contingent world of people and things with pathos and beauty. These lines communicate a deep sense of ambivalence, a desire for and understanding of disconnection and a simultaneous attempt to connect with and describe the passing world. The numbers in the twelfth stanza— the "two rubber boots," the dog's "one bark"—sound like an attempt to hold on to external, human order, like the young Elizabeth in "In the Waiting Room" repeating numbers to herself— "three days / and you'll be seven years old"—to keep from "falling off / the round, turning world / into cold, blue-black space" (*Poems*, 160).

In the thirteenth stanza, a new passenger enters the bus and the poem shifts gears. Where before the contingent world of people and things was beyond the bus, and inside the bus was the strange, other world, the world of the isolated self, now the bus moves through the strange, other world outside carrying within it the human world of people and things. This shift is forecast and initiated by the "freckled, elderly" woman's arrival and her pronouncement, "Yes, sir, / all the way to Boston":

> A woman climbs in
> with two market bags,
> brisk, freckled, elderly.
> "A grand night. Yes, sir,
> all the way to Boston."
> She regards us amicably.
>
> Moonlight as we enter
> the New Brunswick woods,
> hairy, scratchy, splintery;
> moonlight and mist

caught in them like lamb's wool
on bushes in a pasture.

The passengers lie back.
Snores. Some long sighs.
A dreamy divagation
begins in the night,
a gentle, auditory,
slow hallucination. . . .

The elderly woman seems to round out the passengers, to make
them a group, as her pronouncement reinforces the distance to their
destination. Beyond this group, the natural world that before was
soft and lovely ("sweet peas cling / to their wet white string" and
"bumblebees creep / inside the foxgloves") has become harsher,
more threatening, "hairy, scratchy, splintery." The passengers settle
down into one mood, create together the "dreamy divagation" that
joins them and separates them from the harsh, other world beyond
the bus, a world of unpeopled nature. The punctuation, the long
vowels, the soft "sh" and "l" consonant sounds, and the "divaga-
tion/hallucination" rhyme slow down these lines and differentiate
their mood from the earlier mood of chopped lines like "Goodbye
to the elms, / to the farm, to the dog."

Now the bus has changed, has gone from being the strange animal that passes by outside houses to becoming, because of its human cargo, a kind of house itself:

In the creakings and noises,
an old conversation
—not concerning us,
but recognizable, somewhere,
back in the bus:
Grandparents' voices

uninterruptedly
talking, in Eternity:
names being mentioned,
things cleared up finally;
what he said, what she said,
who got pensioned;

The "creakings and noises" mimic the settling sounds of some old house. Again, the rhyme reinforces the boundary between the outside world and the world inside the bus, connects "us" and "bus," the grandparents' "voices" and the bus's "noises." The rhymed "uninterruptedly," "Eternity," and "finally" pervade the seventeenth stanza with a sense of permanence and finality and a strange sense of consolation, the relief of having "things cleared up finally."

The eighteenth stanza makes it evident that this sense of permanence derives from the ultimate finality of losses and deaths, of tragedies borne and lived through. This is the most colloquial stanza of the poem, omitting all rhyme or other "poetics" to give a convincing sense of overheard conversation:

> deaths, deaths and sicknesses;
> the year he remarried;
> the year (something) happened.
> She died in childbirth.
> That was the son lost
> when the schooner foundered.

> He took to drink. Yes.
> She went to the bad.
> When Amos began to pray
> even in the store and
> finally the family had
> to put him away.

The overwhelming theme of the grandparents' conversation is a litany of life figured as a string of irrecoverable losses, the son dead and the schooner foundered. Even the ceremonies of life they mention are completely mixed with loss and death: he *re*marries; she dies in childbirth. But the tone of these stanzas remains dreamy, accepting, even consoling. It is interesting that, in the nineteenth stanza, the first "Yes," the first verbal indication of acceptance, is couched between the mention of alcoholism—the cryptic "She went to the bad"—and the admission of loss through insanity, both reminiscent of losses that so haunted Bishop's life and particularly her childhood and her memories of Nova Scotia.

The stanza that follows, which I quoted in my introduction to this chapter, suggests the source of the consolation, implies that acceptance comes from the ability to hold and not resolve opposites, to accept, as Prunty suggests, whichever face of the paradox presents itself—connection or loss, life or death—knowing that accepting one necessarily invokes the other (1990, 245):

> "Yes . . . " that peculiar
> affirmative. "Yes . . . "
> A sharp, indrawn breath,
> half groan, half acceptance,
> that means "Life's like that.
> We know *it* (also death)."

This stanza provides a key to both "The Moose" and to *Geography III.* The way the rhyme pairs "death" and "breath," the way knowing life immediately implies the parenthetical "(also death)," suggests the way Bishop accepts, without resolving, the tension of opposition, the way she holds opposites in frightening proximity and struggles with the difficulty of life and death. However, this is not Bishop's voice; it is the grandparents' voices, and while they affirm that knowing life means knowing death, that the two are inextricable, they do not seem to participate in the struggle that the poem and the poet are fighting. The serene acceptance of the grandparents' voices makes this stanza and the following one so consoling, so calm, but these stanzas also suggest a kind of weariness with the struggle, a weariness the speaker has felt but is unwilling still to give in to.

The grandparents' voices seem to lull the speaker into a state in which the struggle could almost end, in which the opposites could unite, all the questions could be "cleared up," finally be resolved, the losses counted and consoled:

> Talking the way they talked
> in the old featherbed,
> peacefully, on and on,
> dim lamplight in the hall,

down in the kitchen, the dog
tucked in her shawl.

Now, it's all right now
even to fall asleep
just as on all those nights.
—Suddenly the bus driver
stops with a jolt,
turns off his lights.

The voices of the grandparents invoke the image of a safe home,
the lamplight, "the dog tucked in her shawl," a home in which acceptance is "all right."

However, just at the moment of peace, at the moment of drifting
off to sleep, a moment that perhaps implies that longer sleep of
death, the "other" world interrupts. The bus stops. The bus that
seemed so much an isolated house, like the artichoke house in "The
End of March," admits a connection with the harsh world beyond
its moving walls:

A moose has come out of
the impenetrable wood
and stands there, looms, rather,
in the middle of the road.
It approaches; it sniffs at
the bus's hot hood.

Towering antlerless,
high as a church,
homely as a house
(or, safe as houses).
A man's voice assures us
"Perfectly harmless. . . . "

The emissary of this inscrutable "other" world, the "impenetrable
wood," turns out to be harmless and gentle—"homely," "antlerless"—as unexpected as the boat hook that lifts Miss Breen's skirt in
"Arrival at Santos," but it is immediately subsumed into the speaker's
human perspective: "high as a church / homely as a house." These
lines, and especially the line that follows, "(or, safe as houses)," recall
the earlier description of the Nova Scotian countryside through

which the traveler has passed, and connect the outer, inscrutable wood through which the traveler is passing to the inner, human world of the bus. The moose itself, strangely, becomes another "inscrutable house." Again, Bishop explores the way the boundaries between in and out, between opposites, can be crossed, can shift. She explores boundaries permeable enough to allow connection, but mysterious, otherworldly.

The stanzas that follow examine the emotions related to the connection, the gratification that comes from careful attention, from curiosity:

> Some of the passengers
> exclaim in whispers,
> childishly, softly,
> "Sure are big creatures."
> "It's awful plain."
> "Look! It's a she!"
>
> Taking her time,
> she looks the bus over,
> grand, otherworldly.
> Why, why do we feel
> (we all feel) this sweet
> sensation of joy?

The moose and the passengers on the bus engage in the same actions: they stop; they look. In this way, the moose, like Crusoe's goats, turns toward the passengers in likeness, in creatureliness, seems to share the same habit of curiosity, seems even to be "a she." But the moose also turns away from the passengers in difference, is "otherworldly," is an "it."

The moose's presence represents a connection with the inscrutable world of the "impenetrable wood" and also forges a new connection among the passengers. The feeling of joy at seeing the moose is universal, "(we all feel) this sweet / sensation of joy." However, in the last stanzas, the moment of connection and joy necessarily turns to a moment of loss, of moving on and disconnection:

> "Curious creatures,"
> says our quiet driver,

rolling his *r*'s.
"Look at that, would you."
Then he shifts gears.
For a moment longer,

by craning backward,
the moose can be seen
on the moonlit macadam;
then there's a dim
smell of moose, an acrid
smell of gasoline.

The driver's "Curious creatures" slants to describe both the passengers and the moose, to connect them for a final moment before he shifts gears and they turn away from each other into their differences. The rhyming words in the final stanza convey the mixed emotion of this departure. The rhymes, like the passengers, crane backward toward the moose. Instead of creating an isolated world within the bus, or an isolated visual image, as rhyming words have done elsewhere in the poem, here they connect the two things, the moose and the bus, that are physically drawing apart. The rhymes "seen/ gasoline" and "macadam/dim" embody the tension of the opposite worlds that have connected and are now pulling away. The poem both recovers the connection and reenacts the moment of losing it. It is this paradox of embodiment in poetic form, the amazing way a poem acts like a body in its ability to both facilitate connection and also to cause loss, that Bishop explores and experiments with most often in *Geography III*. The end of "The Moose" holds, for a moment, a pure balance between connection and loss, isolation and relation.

The poems of *Geography III* seek to recover and yet comprehend and communicate that any act of recovery implies a new opportunity for loss. These are some of the finest poems in the English language precisely because they are willing to risk the loss inherent in embodiment in the flesh and in the word.

AFTERWORD

WHEN ELIZABETH BISHOP died in October of 1979, she left us four published books, a cache of uncollected and unpublished work, and a wealth of wonderful stories, both the ones she wrote and the ones her friends remembered about her. Perhaps more importantly, though, she left us the inheritance of a vision and a spirit that searched and explored more deeply than others, a vision that never shied away from the ever-multiplying questions merely because they did not and could never have answers. Many of the questions Bishop explores in her poems are questions of embodiment. Over and over again, she uses metaphors of the body to examine the paradoxical relationship between the human body and the self that inhabits it, and the relationship between the individual and the surrounding world of people and things. Bishop often creates, and then draws energy and power from, tension between the poetic form she has chosen and the idea or theme she embodies in that form. Because Bishop's four published books span her lifetime, they give us the unique ability to observe and examine the progress of her astonishing vision as she moves from experimenting with the language's ability to express how we know, in *North & South,* toward achieving a tense balance between recovery and loss in the poetic form in *Geography III.* In each of the four chapters of this book, I have demonstrated that Bishop's poems continuously hold in tense opposition at least two sides of her profound ambivalence about embodiment. Her poems are in constant battle with the paradox of bodily existence, the existence that isolates and individuates us and also links us inseparably; they image the body as both the imperfect vehicle that distorts perception, limits imagination, and causes loss, and also the beautiful, only means to connection with others and the surrounding, lively world.

NOTES

Introduction

1. Citations from Bishop's *Complete Poems* and *Collected Prose* will be indicated by *Poems* and *Prose,* respectively, and page number.

2. For more commentary on Bishop's perception of her mother's mental illness, see Kalstone (1989, 25) and Harrison (1993, 133).

3. For an interesting comparison of Frost and Bishop, see Shetley (1993).

Chapter 1: *North & South*

1. See Harrison's (1993) discussion of Bishop's use of Great Village material in these early attempts at a novel. Particularly of interest here is Bishop's choice of a boy persona.

2. For more on Bishop and Moore's friendship and its effect on both women's literary careers, see Kalstone (1989) and Goldensohn (1992).

3. This structure reminds me of "the bubble in the spirit level" in Bishop's late poem "Sonnet"; the similarities invite interesting comparison.

4. By "other" I do not wish to invoke the Derridean "other," a philosophical and psychological concept, but "other" in the sense of the actual world of people and things that are not the self.

5. Of course, the application of lesbian theories of gender space could open these observations out in a different but nevertheless interesting direction from my more concentrated and practical discussion.

Chapter 2: *A Cold Spring*

1. I find Bishop's reactions to fellow poets, especially as expressed in her letters and interviews, intriguing. Although she can be almost vitriolic, especially in her comments about the "Confessional" poets (see Schwartz and Estess 1983), she nevertheless consistently praises Lowell's work and seems to move, as he does, toward more open self-expression. Though she makes disparaging comments about Jarrell's work, having encountered it, she seems afterward to write poems that demonstrate that Jarrell's work has, in fact, had an impact on her own. I theorize that Bishop's sense of separateness from the literary milieu, her insistence, in letter after letter, that she knows few of her contemporaries and has little opportunity for "literary" discussion, was somehow crucial to her creative process. Although she knew many writers in both America and Brazil,

the idea of influence seems to have been difficult for her, and she repeatedly constructs a vision of herself as separate, isolated, and generally disliking the work of her contemporaries.

2. Goldensohn (1992) seems to communicate this implicit assumption that Bishop should have "come out" and declared her sexual identity. For a good discussion of the dangers of that declaration in Bishop's time, see Harrison's (1993) discussion of "The Shampoo."

3. See Millier (1993) for more complete information.

4. For more information, see Stange's note for "Spring" in Houghton and Stange (1968).

5. Although Bishop lived through the war, she writes about it, as she writes about all great pain, indirectly. Both here and in her earlier poem "Roosters," war underlies all the images and action of the poem. I am reminded of Richard Wilbur's poem "Lilacs," which also seems to be about spring flowers but on closer inspection is concerned with the Vietnam War.

Chapter 3: *Questions of Travel*

1. Millier quotes Bishop's book review of W. D. Hudson's *Green Mansions* in Walnut Hill's literary magazine *Blue Pencil:* "I was filled with the longing to leave for South America immediately and search for those forgotten bird people" (1993, 36).

2. Lota de Macedo Soares, an extraordinary woman in her own right, came from a well-established Portuguese family. Deeply involved in Brazilian politics and cultural life, she acclimated Bishop to Brazil and opened doors in Bishop's adopted country that might otherwise have been permanently closed. Elizabeth Hardwick, Robert Lowell's critic and second wife, describes Macedo Soares in a letter:

> witty indeed, civilized—and yet different from the women I had known. She had wonderful, glistening, dark eyes and wore glistening dark-rimmed glasses. You felt, or I felt, in her the legacy or curse of the Spanish-Portuguese women of the upper classes. . . . Her English was fluent fractured and utterly compelling. . . . L. was very intense indeed, emotional, also a bit insecure as we say, loyal, devoted and smart and lesbian and Brazilian and shy, masterful in some ways, but helpless also. She adored Elizabeth and in the most attractive way, in this case somewhat fearfully, possessively, and yet modestly and without any tendency to oppress.
>
> The two were a *combinazione* very striking. Lota would drive a car with great zest and speed and Elizabeth couldn't or didn't drive. Lota was helpless in the kitchen and about the household, which Elizabeth indeed was not. Lota was watchful in the matter of Elizabeth's drinking and the sober period had lasted many years and did not last out the summer, when at the end there was a brief, I think, regression or defiance or just plain inclination. (Kalstone 1989, 150–51)

3. See note 1 in chapter 2.

4. See note 1 in chapter 2.

5. See Harrison's (1993) discussion of "Miracle for Breakfast" for more information on Bishop's views of the form.

6. See Millier's (1993) account of Bishop's Wellfleet play in which she uses many of the same images she uses in "Sestina," including the almanac, the kettle, and the grandmother in the kitchen. It is apparent from the biography that these images haunted Bishop for years before she captured them in this form.

Chapter 4: *Geography III*

1. For an excellent assessment of the upheaval in Bishop's Brazilian life after Macedo Soares's death see Kalstone (1989, 235). I have reproduced the relevant parts of Bishop's February 27, 1970, letter to Lowell about leaving Ouro Prêto.

> Well, you are right to worry about me, only please DON'T!—I am pretty worried about myself. I have somehow got into the worst situation I have ever had to cope with and I can't see the way out. If I could trust anybody in this town, I'd close up the house and leave, or leave a maid or two in it—but that would mean coming back again, sooner or later, and although it would be a tremendous relief to get away—I don't want to do that. I am trying to sell the house, as I think I wrote you—have had several nibbles but nothing at all certain yet. I am trying just to get everything in working order, go through all the books, papers, letters, and so on—(about 3,000 or more books here) so that I can leave if the chance comes. But it may take months or years; meanwhile it is too damned lonely and disagreeable and I have not been able to work. Just the last two weeks I've done a little, but very little—there are endless, endless interruptions, noise, confusion, thefts (you wouldn't believe how much has been stolen and a lot of it somehow right under my eyes . . .), trips to Belo Horizonte for building materials, firing, re-hiring, re-firing. It's a terrible tale of woe. (Giroux 1994, 515)

2. Lines from the unpublished poem "A Drunkard":

> I picked up a woman's long black cotton
> stocking. Curiosity. My mother said sharply
> Put that down! I remember clearly, clearly—
> But since that day, that reprimand
> that night that day that reprimand—
> I have suffered from abnormal thirst—
> I swear it's true and by the age
> of twenty or twenty-one I had begun
> to drink, and drink—I can't get enough
> and, as you might have noticed,

I'm half-drunk now . . .
And all I'm telling you might be a lie. (Vassar Box 32)

3. From "A Country Mouse":

After New Year's, Aunt Jenny had to go to the dentist, and asked me to go with her. She left me in the waiting room, and gave me a copy of the *National Geographic* to look at. It was still getting dark early, and the room had grown very dark. There was a big yellow lamp in one corner, a table with magazines, and an overhead chandelier of sorts. There were others waiting, two men and a plump middle-aged lady, all bundled up. I looked at the magazine cover—I could read most of the words—shiny, glazed, yellow and white. The black letters said: February 1918. A feeling of absolute and utter desolation came over me. I felt . . . *myself.* In a few days it would be my seventh birthday. I felt *I, I, I,* and looked at the three strangers in panic. I was *one* of them too, inside my scabby body and wheezing lungs. "You're in for it now," something said. How had I got tricked into such a false position? I would be like that woman opposite who smiled at me so falsely every once in a while. The awful sensation passed, then it came back again. "You are you," something said. "How strange you are, inside looking out. You are not Beppo, or the chestnut tree, or Emma, you are you and you are going to be *you* forever." It was like coasting downhill, this thought, only much worse, and it quickly smashed into a tree. *Why* was I a human being? (*Prose*, 32–33).

4. The alternate titles Bishop considered for "Crusoe in England" are interesting in themselves and give some idea of the importance of isolation and connection: "Last Days of Crusoe," "Crusoe at Home," "Crusoe in Hell," "Back Home," and "At Home" (Vassar Box 30).

5. From Starbuck's (1983, 314) interview with Bishop:

In my first book there is a little poem called "Large Bad Picture"; that picture was by the same great-uncle, painted when he was about 14 years old. They were a very poor family in Nova Scotia, and he went to sea as a cabin boy. Then he painted three or four big paintings, memories of the far North, Belle Isle, etc. I loved them. They're not very good as paintings. An aunt owned several of them. I tried to get her to sell them to me, but she never would. The Great-Uncle George went to England and he did become a fairly well-known "traditional" painter.

WORKS CITED

Unpublished Sources

Elizabeth Bishop Collection. Vassar College Library. Poughkeepsie, N.Y.
John Malcolm Brinnin Papers. MS 103, Series F. University of Delaware. Newark, Del.
Gibbons Ruark. Spring 1991. Lecture notes on Elizabeth Bishop.

Published Sources

Ashbery, John. 1983. The Complete Poems. In *Elizabeth Bishop and Her Art,* edited by Lloyd Schwartz and Sybil Estess, 201–6. Ann Arbor: University of Michigan Press.

Barthes, Roland. 1974. *S/Z.* Translated by Richard Miller. New York: Hill and Wang.

Bergson, Henri. 1956. *Laughter.* Edited and translated by Wylie Sypher. New York: Doubleday.

Bidart, Frank. 1983. On Elizabeth Bishop: Introduction to a Reading at Wellesley College 1976. In *Elizabeth Bishop and Her Art,* edited by Lloyd Schwartz and Sybil Estess, 214–15. Ann Arbor: University of Michigan Press.

Bishop, Elizabeth. 1979. *The Complete Poems, 1927–1979.* New York: Farrar, Straus, Giroux.

———. 1980. *The Collected Prose.* New York: Farrar, Straus, Giroux.

Bogan, Louise. 1983. On *North & South.* In *Elizabeth Bishop and Her Art,* edited by Lloyd Schwartz and Sybil Estess, 182–83. Ann Arbor: University of Michigan Press.

Brooks, Peter. 1993. *Body Work: Objects of Desire in Modern Narrative.* Cambridge: Harvard University Press.

Brown, Ashley. 1966. Interview with Elizabeth Bishop. *Shenandoah* 17, no. 2 (Winter): 3–19.

Costello, Bonnie. 1983. The Impersonal and Interrogative in the Poetry of Elizabeth Bishop. In *Elizabeth Bishop and Her Art,* edited by Lloyd Schwartz and Sybil Estess, 109–32. Ann Arbor: University of Michigan Press.

——. 1991. *Elizabeth Bishop: Questions of Mastery.* Cambridge: Harvard University Press.

Croll, M. W. 1929. The Baroque Style in Prose. In *Studies in English Philology,* edited by Kemp Malone and Martin B. Ruud, 437–43. Minneapolis: University of Minnesota Press.

Cucullu, Lois. 1988. Trompe l'Oeill: Elizabeth Bishop's Radical "I." *Texas Studies in Literature and Language* 30, no. 2:246–71.

De Lauretis, Teresa. 1989. The Violence of Rhetoric: Considerations on Representation and Gender. In *The Violence of Representation,* edited by Nancy Armstrong and Leonard Tennenhouse, 239–56. New York: Routledge.

Di Cesare, Mario A., ed. 1978. *George Herbert and the Seventeenth-Century Poets.* New York: Norton.

Diehl, Joanne Feit. 1985. At Home with Loss: Elizabeth Bishop and the American Sublime. In *Coming to Light: American Women Poets in the Twentieth Century,* edited by Dianne Wood Middlebrook and Marilyn Yalone, 123–37. Ann Arbor: University of Michigan Press.

Donoghue, Denis. 1984. *Connoisseurs of Chaos.* New York: Columbia University Press.

Doreski, C. K. 1993. *Elizabeth Bishop: The Restraints of Language.* New York: Oxford University Press.

Estess, Sybil P. 1983. Description and Imagination in Elizabeth Bishop's "The Map." In *Elizabeth Bishop and Her Art,* edited by Lloyd Schwartz and Sybil Estess, 219–22. Ann Arbor: University of Michigan Press.

Frankenburg, Lloyd. 1949. Elizabeth Bishop. In *Pleasure Dome: On Reading Modern Poetry,* 328–31. Boston: Houghton Mifflin.

Giroux, Robert, ed. 1994. *Elizabeth Bishop: One Art.* New York: Farrar, Straus, Giroux.

Goldensohn, Lorris. 1992. *Elizabeth Bishop: The Biography of a Poetry.* New York: Columbia University Press.

Gould, Jean. 1984. Elizabeth Bishop. In *Modern American Women Poets,* 51–74. New York: Dodd, Mead.

Gunn, Thom. 1990. Review of *Becoming a Poet: Elizabeth Bishop with Marianne Moore and Robert Lowell,* by David Kalstone. *Times Literary Supplement,* July 27–August 2, 791–92.

Harrison, Victoria. 1993. *Elizabeth Bishop's Poetics of Intimacy.* New York: Cambridge University Press.

Houghton, Walter E., and G. Robert Stange, eds. 1968. *Victorian Poetry and Poetics.* Boston: Houghton Mifflin.

Jarrell, Randall. 1983. On *North & South.* In *Elizabeth Bishop and Her*

Art, edited by Lloyd Schwartz and Sybil Estess, 180–81. Ann Arbor: University of Michigan Press.

Kalstone, David. 1977. Elizabeth Bishop. In *Five Temperaments,* 12–40. New York: Oxford University Press.

———. 1985. Trial Balances: Elizabeth Bishop and Marianne Moore. In *Coming to Light: American Women Poets in the Twentieth Century,* edited by Dianne Wood Middlebrook and Marilyn Yalone, 105–23. Ann Arbor: University of Michigan Press.

———. 1989. *Becoming a Poet: Elizabeth Bishop with Marianne Moore and Robert Lowell.* London: Hogarth.

Kama Sutra of Vatsyayana. 1962. Translated by Sir Richard F. Burton. New York: Dorset Press.

Kaminsky, Amy K. 1993. Sylvia Molloy's Lesbian Cartographies: Body, Text, and Geography. In *Reading the Body Politic: Feminist Criticism and Latin American Women Writers.* London: University of Minnesota Press.

Laurens, Penelope. 1983. Old Correspondence: Prosodic Transformations in Elizabeth Bishop. In *Elizabeth Bishop and Her Art,* edited by Lloyd Schwartz and Sybil Estess, 75–95. Ann Arbor: University of Michigan Press.

Lowell, Robert. 1976. *Selected Poems.* New York: Farrar, Strauss, Giroux.

MacMahon, Candace W. 1980. *Elizabeth Bishop: A Bibliography, 1927–1979.* Charlottesville: University of Virginia Press.

Mazzaro, Jerome. 1980. The Poetics of Impediment: Elizabeth Bishop. In *Postmodern American Poetry,* 166–98. Chicago: University of Illinois Press.

McNeil, Helen. 1987. Elizabeth Bishop. In *Voices and Visions: The Poet in America,* edited by Helen Vendler, 394–425. New York: Random House.

McPherson, Sandra. 1984. "The Armadillo": A Commentary. *Field* 31 (Fall): 10–12.

Merrill, James. 1983. Elizabeth Bishop, 1911–1979. In *Elizabeth Bishop and Her Art,* edited by Lloyd Schwartz and Sybil Estess, 259–62. Ann Arbor: University of Michigan Press.

Millay, Edna St. Vincent. 1951. *Collected Lyrics.* New York: Harper and Row.

Millier, Brett C. 1993. *Elizabeth Bishop: Life and the Memory of It.* Berkeley: University of California Press.

Moore, Marianne. 1983. Archaichally New. In *Elizabeth Bishop and Her Art,* edited by Lloyd Schwartz and Sybil Estess, 177–79. Ann Arbor: University of Michigan Press.

————. 1986. *Complete Poems.* New York: Macmillan.

Motion, Andrew. 1985. *Elizabeth Bishop.* London: The British Academy.

Nemerov, Howard. 1955. The Poems of Elizabeth Bishop. *Poetry* 87, no. 3 (December): 179–82.

Ostriker, Alicia. 1986. *Stealing the Language.* Boston: Beacon Press.

Page, Barbara. 1981–82. Shifting Islands: Elizabeth Bishop's Manuscripts. *Shenandoah* 33, no. 1:51–62.

Parker, Robert Dale. 1988. *The Unbeliever: The Poetry of Elizabeth Bishop.* Chicago: University of Illinois Press.

Pinsky, Robert. 1983. The Idiom of a Self: Elizabeth Bishop and William Wordsworth. In *Elizabeth Bishop and Her Art,* edited by Lloyd Schwartz and Sybil Estess, 49–60. Ann Arbor: University of Michigan Press.

Prunty, Wyatt. 1990. *Fallen from the Symboled World: Precedents for the New Formalism.* New York: Oxford University Press.

Santos, Sherod. 1984. The End of March. *Field* 31 (Fall): 29–32.

Schwartz, Lloyd. 1983. One Art: The Poetry of Elizabeth Bishop. In *Elizabeth Bishop and Her Art,* edited by Lloyd Schwartz and Sybil Estess, 133–53. Ann Arbor: University of Michigan Press.

Schwartz, Lloyd, and Sybil Estess. 1983. *Elizabeth Bishop and Her Art.* Ann Arbor: University of Michigan Press.

Shetley, Vernon. 1993. *After the Death of Poetry.* London: Duke University Press.

Spires, Elizabeth. 1978. Elizabeth Bishop. In *Writers at Work: The Paris Review Interviews Sixth Series,* edited by George Plimpton, 123–49. New York: Viking Press.

————. 1979. An Afternoon with Elizabeth Bishop. *Vassar Quarterly* (Winter): 7–8.

————. 1984. Questions of Knowledge. *Field* (Fall): 20–23.

Starbuck, George. 1983. "The Work!": A Conversation with Elizabeth Bishop. In *Elizabeth Bishop and Her Art,* edited by Lloyd Schwartz and Sybil Estess, 312–30. Ann Arbor: University of Michigan Press.

Stevenson, Anne. 1966. *Elizabeth Bishop.* New York: Twayne Publishers.

Travisano, Thomas. 1988. *Elizabeth Bishop: Her Artistic Development.* Charlottesville: University of Virginia Press.

Vendler, Helen. 1980. Elizabeth Bishop. In *Part of Nature, Part of Us,* 97–110. Cambridge: Harvard University Press.

Voices and Visions. 1987. The Annenberg/CPB Project. South Carolina Educational TV Network.

Williams, Oscar. 1983. North but South. In *Elizabeth Bishop and Her*

Art, edited by Lloyd Schwartz and Sybil Estess, 184–85. Ann
Arbor: University of Michigan Press.

Williamson, Alan. 1983. *A Cold Spring:* The Poet of Feeling. In *Elizabeth Bishop and Her Art,* edited by Lloyd Schwartz and Sybil Estess,
96–109. Ann Arbor: University of Michigan Press.

INDEX

"Argument," 75, 87–90
"Armadillo, The," 6, 151, 156–62
"Arrival at Santos," 129, 130–37, 228
Ashbery, John, 20, 75
"At the Fishhouses," 115–22
Authoritative tone, 5–6, 133–34

Barthes, Roland, 4
Bible, 102–10
"Bight, The," 110–15
Bishop, Elizabeth: alcoholism, 9, 170, 190; attitude toward publishing, 16, 18–19; Brazil years, 123–24, 170–71, 172, 190, 235 (n. 1); childhood, 6–11, 124; creative process of, 1–2, 15, 63; education of: Vassar, 11, 18; Walnut Hill School, 10–11; effect of father's death, 7; effect of mother's mental breakdowns, 8, 127–29; feminism, 15–16; illnesses, 4, 9, 123, 170; life in Great Village, 8, 10, 11, 71, 219; love of music, 10, 11, 18; prose, 125–29; sexuality, 4, 74, 75, 76, 90–91, 234 (n. 2); travels, 1–2, 11–12, 29, 71, 102, 123
Bishop, Gertrude Bulmer (mother), 7
Bishop, William Thomas (father), 7
Black humor, 76
Bordon, Fanny, 19
"Brazil, January 1, 1502," 6, 130, 131, 136–43, 151
Brooks, Peter, 4
Bryn Mawr College: Lucy Martin Donnelly Fellowship, 123

Change: ambivalence about, 74
"Chemin de Fer," 48, 62
"Cirque d'Hiver," 22, 27–29
"Colder the Air, The," 22–25
"Cold Spring, A," 96–101, 110
Cold War, 96
Complete Poems: A Cold Spring, 71–122; North & South, 18–70. See also individual poems
"Con Spirito," 11
Conversation, 80–81
Costello, Bonnie: Elizabeth Bishop: Questions of Mastery, 16, 34, 43, 142, 194, 195
"Country Mouse, A," 236 (n. 3)
"Country Mouse, A," (short story), 194
Crane, Louise, 29, 71
"Crusoe in England," 202–14, 236 (n. 4)
Cucullu, Lois, 17
Cultural suppression, 4

Death and grief, 152–56, 171–80
Diehl, Joanne, 13, 14
Domestication, 13, 36
Donoghue, Denis, 13, 16, 46, 128, 147, 160
Doreski, C. K.: Elizabeth Bishop: The Restraints of Language, 17
"Drunkard, A" (unpublished), 235–36 (n. 1)

Embodiment: ambivalence about, 5, 122, 151, 160, 161, 169, 172, 173, 180, 202
"End of March, The," 185–93, 202

Escaping the Self (Malkoff), 39
Estess, Sybil, 36, 38, 39

Feminists: views of Bishop's work, 3–4, 15–17, 75
"First Death in Nova Scotia," 9, 126
"Fish, The," 5, 20, 56, 66–70
"Five Flights Up," 180–84
Form: in "Questions of Travel," 143–51
"Four Poems," 80–87
Frankenburg, Lloyd, 33
"From the Country to the City," 22, 25–27

"Gentleman of Shalott, The," 32, 44–48
Geography III, 170–230. *See also* individual poems
"Gwendolyn" (short story), 126

Harrison, Victoria: *Elizabeth Bishop's Poetics of Intimacy*, 17, 91
Hopkins, Gerald Manley, 192; "Spring," 95–96; "Wreck of the Deutschland," 179
Houghton Mifflin Award (1945), 21

"Imaginary Iceberg, The," 32, 39–44, 56, 77
In, use of the preposition, 46
Influence studies, 13–14
"In Prison," 46
In the Village (prose), 8, 9–10, 126, 127–29
"In the Waiting Room," 3, 193–202

Jarrell, Randall, 5–6, 47, 71, 73, 233 (n. 1)

Kalstone, David, 126–27, 129, 213
Kaminsky, Amy, 4

"Large Bad Picture," 6, 32, 48–53, 56, 236 (n. 5)
Laurens, Penelope, 49

Lauretis, Teresa de, 3–4
"Little Exercise," 48
Love poems, 75–94
Lowell, Robert, 1–2, 71–73, 125–27, 140, 160–61, 233 (n. 1)

Malkoff, Karl: *Escaping the Self*, 39
"Man-Moth, The," 56, 57–63, 64–65, 70
"Map, The," 32–39, 44, 47
Mazzaro, Jerome, 16
McCarthy, Mary, 11
McNeil, Helen, 35
Merrill, James, 1, 38
Millay, Edna St. Vincent: "Hyacinth," 79
Miller, Margaret, 29, 30
Millier, Brett, 12, 15
"Miracle for Breakfast, A," 56, 63–65
Modernists: influence on Bishop, 17, 18–20
"Monument, The," 6, 48, 53–56, 167
Moore, Marianne, 21, 170; poetic differences with Bishop, 19–21; reviews of Bishop's work, 21; at Vassar, 7–8, 11, 19–21
"Moose, The," 173, 202, 219–30
Motion, Andrew, 16

Neustadt International Prize, 11

"O Breath," 84–86
"One Art," 5, 6, 173–80
Opposites, use of, 147
"Over 2,000 Illustrations and a Complete Concordance," 102–10

Page, Barbara, 150
Parenthetical phrase, use of, 6, 172–81
Parker, Robert Dale, 3, 14
Paz, Octavio, 93
Perception, human, 32–56; and choice, 37, 38; imagination, 39–

40; limits of, 36, 37; of maps and land, 32–39
Personification, 22–32, 181–84; of landscape, 99–100; of the mechanical, 77; of objects, 25–29; of space, 25–27, 87–88; of Spring, 99–100; of time, 87–88; of winter, 22–25
Physical description: technique of, 5
Pinsky, Robert, 14, 39, 57, 144, 193, 195, 197
"Poem," 172, 202, 214–19
Pound, Ezra: in the asylum, 162–69
"Primer Class," 8
Prose, 11, 12, 127–29
Prunty, Wyatt, 16

"Quai d'Orléans," 29–32
Questions of Travel, 123–69. *See also* individual poems
"Questions of Travel," 5, 6, 130, 143–51

"Rain Towards Morning," 81–82
Repetition: use of, 135–36
Ruark, Gibbons, 6

"Sandpiper, The," 11
"Sea & Its Shore, The," (short story), 188–89
"Seascape," 48
"Sestina," 151, 152–56
Sexuality. *See* Bishop, sexuality
Shakespeare: "Sonnet 29," 84
"Shampoo, The," 5, 75, 90–94
Shepherdson, Maude (aunt), 9–10
Short stories: "A Country Mouse," 194; "Gwendolyn," 9, 126; "The Sea & Its Shore," 188–89

Snodgrass, W. D., 73, 125, 233 (n. 1)
Soares, Lota de Macedo, 94, 123, 234 (n. 2); nervous breakdown, 170; suicide, 171
Stevenson, Anne, 6, 8, 15, 43, 48, 95, 97

Tears, 62–63, 152–56
Tennyson, Alfred: "Lady of Shalott," 44–45
Time, 79, 82, 124, 162–64, 167
Traveling, 102–10, 130–51
Travisano, Thomas, 14, 37, 59, 93, 102, 136, 178
"Twelfth Night," 78
"12 O'Clock News," 172

U.S.A. School of Writing, The, 11
"U.S.A. School of Writing, The" (essay), 50

Valdes, Gregorio, 49–50
Van Duyn, Mona, 16
"Varick Street," 75, 76–79, 89
Vassar Quarterly, 18
Vendler, Helen, 36
"Visit to St. Elizabeth's," 151, 162–69
"Voices and Visions," 11

War, 94–101, 160–61, 234 (n. 5)
Westminster Magazine, 18
"While Someone Telephones," 82–84
Whitman, Walt: comparison to, 14
Wilbur, Richard: *Walking to Sleep*, 35
Williamson, Alan, 90, 95
Wordsworth: comparison to, 14

ABOUT THE AUTHOR

Anne Colwell is an assistant professor of English at the University of Delaware-Southern Campus. She received her master's and her Ph.D. from the University of Delaware.

Weaver